HIP HOP HERESIES

POSTMILLENNIAL POP

General Editors: Karen Tongson and Henry Jenkins

Puro Arte: Filipinos on the Stages of Empire
Lucy Mae San Pablo Burns

Spreadable Media: Creating Value and Meaning in a Networked Culture
Henry Jenkins, Sam Ford, and Joshua Green

Media Franchising: Creative License and Collaboration in the Culture Industries
Derek Johnson

Your Ad Here: The Cool Sell of Guerrilla Marketing
Michael Serazio

Looking for Leroy: Illegible Black Masculinities
Mark Anthony Neal

From Bombay to Bollywood: The Making of a Global Media Industry
Aswin Punathambekar

A Race So Different: Performance and Law in Asian America
Joshua Takano Chambers-Letson

Surveillance Cinema
Catherine Zimmer

Modernity's Ear: Listening to Race and Gender in World Music
Roshanak Kheshti

The New Mutants: Superheroes and the Radical Imagination of American Comics
Ramzi Fawaz

Restricted Access: Media, Disability, and the Politics of Participation
Elizabeth Ellcessor

The Sonic Color Line: Race and the Cultural Politics of Listening
Jennifer Lynn Stoever

Diversión: Play and Popular Culture in Cuban America
Albert Sergio Laguna

Antisocial Media: Anxious Labor in the Digital Economy
Greg Goldberg

Open TV: Innovation beyond Hollywood and the Rise of Web Television
Aymar Jean Christian

More Than Meets the Eye: Special Effects and the Fantastic Transmedia Franchise
Bob Rehak

Playing to the Crowd: Musicians, Audiences, and the Intimate Work of Connection
Nancy K. Baym

Old Futures: Speculative Fiction and Queer Possibility
Alexis Lothian

Anti-Fandom: Dislike and Hate in the Digital Age
Edited by Melissa A. Click

Social Media Entertainment: The New Industry at the Intersection of Hollywood and Silicon Valley
Stuart Cunningham and David Craig

Video Games Have Always Been Queer
Bonnie Ruberg

The Power of Sports: Media and Spectacle in American Culture
Michael Serazio

The Dark Fantastic: Race and the Imagination from Harry Potter to the Hunger Games
Ebony Elizabeth Thomas

The Race Card: From Gaming Technologies to Model Minorities
Tara Fickle

Open World Empire: Race, Erotics, and the Global Rise of Video Games
Christopher B. Patterson

The Content of Our Caricature: African American Comic Art and Political Belonging
Rebecca Wanzo

Stories of the Self: Life Writing after the Book
Anna Poletti

The Dark Fantastic: Race and the Imagination from Harry Potter to the Hunger Games
Ebony Elizabeth Thomas

Hip Hop Heresies: Queer Aesthetics in New York City
Shanté Paradigm Smalls

Hip Hop Heresies

Queer Aesthetics in New York City

Shanté Paradigm Smalls

NEW YORK UNIVERSITY PRESS
New York

NEW YORK UNIVERSITY PRESS
New York
www.nyupress.org

© 2022 by Shanté Paradigm Smalls
All rights reserved

References to Internet websites (URLs) were accurate at the time of writing. Neither the author nor New York University Press is responsible for URLs that may have expired or changed since the manuscript was prepared.

Library of Congress Cataloging-in-Publication Data
Names: Smalls, Shanté Paradigm, author.
Title: Hip hop heresies : queer aesthetics in New York City / Shante Paradigm Smalls.
Description: New York : New York University Press, [2022] | Series: Postmillennial pop |
   Includes bibliographical references and index.
Identifiers: LCCN 2021047241 | ISBN 9781479808199 (hardback ; alk. paper) |
   ISBN 9781479808205 (paperback ; alk. paper) | ISBN 9781479808182 (ebook) |
   ISBN 9781479808212 (ebook other)
Subjects: LCSH: Aesthetics, Black. | Gay culture—New York (State)—New York—History. |
   Hip-hop—New York (State)—New York—History. | African American arts—New York
   (State)—New York—History.
Classification: LCC BH301.B53 S63 2022 | DDC 111/.8508996073—dc23/eng/20211115
LC record available at https://lccn.loc.gov/2021047241

New York University Press books are printed on acid-free paper, and their binding materials are chosen for strength and durability. We strive to use environmentally responsible suppliers and materials to the greatest extent possible in publishing our books.

Manufactured in the United States of America

10 9 8 7 6 5 4 3 2 1

Also available as an ebook

CONTENTS

Introduction: Heretical Desire: New York City's Queer Hip Hop Aesthetics   1

1. Wild Stylin': Martin Wong's Queer Visuality in New York City Graffiti   25

2. Nigga Fu: *The Last Dragon*, Black Masculinity, and Chinese Martial Arts   53

3. "Casebaskets": Listening for the Uncanny in Jean Grae   87

4. Queer Hip Hop, Queer Dissonance   123

Conclusion: Queer Trans Black Aesthetic Futures   151

Acknowledgments   159

Notes   165

Index   191

About the Author   201

Introduction

Heretical Desire: New York City's Queer Hip Hop Aesthetics

Hip Hop Heresies: Queer Aesthetics in New York City brings together Black, queer, and hip hop aesthetics through a study of New York City artists and artistic scenes in multiple media genres from 1975 to the present. I argue they *queerly* articulate gender, racial, and sexual identitarian performances through specifically New York–based aesthetic and artistic practices and cues. These performances could emerge and congeal only in New York because of the city's bodily co-mingling (queer, Black, trans, immigrant, and other people of color) and genre experimentation (hip hop, house music, punk, funk, disco). Although these bodies and genres existed in other locales—Chicago: the birthplace of house music; Philadelphia: the hub of contemporary graffiti; and Los Angeles: a city central to the development of hip hop dance—New York City's nexus of vibrant queer, Black, and hip hop worlds colliding and bonding in dance clubs, housing complexes, schools, roller rinks, art spaces, handball and basketball courts, movie houses, specific neighborhoods, the subway system, and other quotidian, subcultural, and ephemeral sites uniquely positions New York as a place of experimental and original aesthetic collaboration. If other cities had some of these elements, why do I argue that New York is unique among them? There are three main reasons for New York's queer hip hop aesthetics: one is the subway. Though the city is over 302 square miles, it is connected by a relatively affordable and easily navigable subway system.[1] This has allowed for travel, exchange, battles, and inspiration—whether collaboration or theft—across the city's five boroughs.[2] For instance, one can travel from Yankee Stadium in the Bronx to Barclays Center in Brooklyn in 40–45 minutes by train for less than three dollars. The second reason is the dense proximity of bodies and the vast national, cultural, linguistic, ethnic, and racial diversity of New York City's population. Unlike other cities that may have had more homogenous populations or clearly demarcated racial neighborhoods, New York's extensive foot traffic, the subway, the bus system, and other forms of forced proximity made cross-ethnic, cross-racial, and cross-cultural aesthetics possible. Finally, New York's multiple industries and scenes—vibrant institutional art, independent art, and street art scenes; similar levels of music industry, a wide network of music venues, and street musicianship; the fashion industry, publishing, a nascent no-wave film school, roller rinks, parks, and other sites of play and improvisation— made the city a cauldron of artistic ingenuity and collaboration.

Azealia Amanda Banks's delectable track "1991" (2012) pays homage to 1980s and early 1990s Black ball culture and house music.[3] For those with truncated musical memories formed in the second decade of the 21st century, Banks's house music–based rap EP *1991* and its title song may sound idiosyncratic in an increasingly homogenous hip hop soundscape. Though she is a part of the millennial generation, Banks draws on a lengthy hip hop sonic tradition steeped in both disco and later house music, before funk, soul, trap, and R&B samples eclipsed other genres used to make hip hop music. Like late 1980s hip house songs such as the Jungle Brothers' "Girl, I'll House You" (1989) and Queen Latifah's "Come into My House" (1989), Banks's work enmeshes Black aesthetics, queer aesthetics, and hip hop aesthetics sonically and visually. Banks's use of Black vernacular dance styles—hip hop and ball/vogue/house—reflects the gestural range of Black dance repertoires, even if these styles of music and dance are hardly ever marketed together. As a '90s kid, Banks gets the mélange of cultural and material aesthetics—especially the queer ones—that have always been part of hip hop culture's recipe. As Tavia Nyong'o writes on queer hip hop, Banks is "immersed in the idiom of the balls—'work,' 'ki ki,' 'banjee,' 'read.' . . . Drawing on . . . dark precursors, th[is] young fabulist[] take fierceness as a property of black being singular plural."[4]

Though more muted in its discursive proclamation of queerness *qua* queerness, Queen Latifah's (neé Dana Owens) video for "Come into My House" more explicitly connects Afrocentricity, vogue and ball culture, and high-culture forms of indigenous dance, including Chinese opera dance, Indian classical dance, and West African dance. The video positions these disparate dance styles and the hybrid sonic ones (hip hop beats and house music) as sensical complements. The perplexity that greets explicit queer and other "odd" aesthetics in contemporary hip hop culture and production represses those aesthetic creations that were part and parcel of earlier iterations of US hip hop styles in New York City, Los Angeles, San Francisco, Philadelphia, and other places.

These aesthetic "mash-ups," more or less prominent depending on decade and place, illustrate the through line of *Hip Hop Heresies*. I argue that New York City hip hop artists actively engage in the transformative and disruptive power of three aesthetic forms often conceived of as disparate, distinct, and antagonistic: Black aesthetics, queer aesthetics, and hip hop aesthetics. This aesthetic modality—sometimes explicit, at others subtended—contours the "truth" of an "authentic" hip hop body often rendered as exclusively male, non-trans, African American (as opposed to Black), urban, poor, and criminal. The subjects studied in this book—visual artist Martin Wong; emcee/producer/director/singer/writer/visual artist Jean Grae; an Afro-Asian martial arts Hollywood film, *Berry Gordy's The Last Dragon*; and hip hop's queer past—reveal the complex aesthetic influences on and products made by New York City hip hop artists. The presence and contribution of women, queers, Caribbean Blacks, Asians, Latinx (including AfriLatinx), whites, middle- and upper-class people, and other "inauthentic" bodies help to flesh out New York City hip hop's palimpsestic and multilayered musical, art, and performance roster. When New York City hip hop's rich aesthetic and performative life is reduced to an archetype of impoverished Black men, this leaves out contributors who don't fit that demographic bill, of course, but it also minimizes the artistic, aesthetic, and visionary genius of the same "impoverished" Black men. My book serves as a robust rebuttal of flattened blackness, while also signaling the ways queer bodies and aesthetics, Black women, and Chinese popular culture all shaped a particular New York City Black hip hop performance culture. Though New York City hip hop emerged from economically penurious sections of the South Bronx, Queens, Brooklyn, and Manhattan, the Black and brown bodies who generated hip hop art had access to their own talents, imaginations, technology, interpersonal connections, artwork, and influences that were completely enriched, enriching, and magnetizing.

Queer Aesthetics, Black Aesthetics, Hip Hop Aesthetics: New York City's Ground

Queer aesthetics is a generative revisiting of the Eurocentric and troubling category of aesthetics. I use queer aesthetics as a framework rather than queer performance to wrestle with the productive tensions aesthetics introduces when paired with a Black artistic form like hip hop. In *Hip Hop Heresies*, queer aesthetics indexes a propagative slippage between racial, sexual, and gender subject positions that sometimes coheres to already-in-place categories, and at other times yields less stable or less recognizable categories that lack or evade value as imposed by the state or the marketplace. This queer aesthetics, whether it conjoins with Black queer trans bodies, Black non-trans heterosexual men's bodies, Black non-trans women's bodies, Asian American queer men's bodies, or other arrangements, produces visual and sonic Black performing subjects who play with staid notions of bodily fungibility. These mostly Black—sometimes Asian—performing subjects don't seek to disavow the violent realities of an anti-Black environment, nor do they espouse anything utopian in nature. Rather, starting with performing subjects from the 1970s and continuing to the present, these artists and artworks instantiate queer aesthetics as a normative category, a very plainly stated and visually presented "Here I am." That is to say, these hip hop artists and artworks take stock of the worlds they inhabit and through queer aesthetics work, bend, extend, and even break the bounded definitions of blackness, queerness, transness, and Asianness with imagination and wit. In contemporary parlance, some of these performing subjects may be called transgender, non-binary, queer, mixed race, or multiracial, but they all share a quality of experimenting with sonic and visual regimes and forms that create visual and sonic persona at odds with safe and rigid categorizations of race, gender, and sexuality. These experimentations are particularly explosive and dangerous when an artist plays with race, gender, and sexuality simultaneously. These performing subjects and their queer aesthetics offer audiences artworks that produce elongated moments in which the viewer or listener may experience confusion, confoundment, anger, revulsion, a desire to regulate or more likely eviscerate, ignore, violate, or hide these performances and their impacts away.

The use of the queer aesthetic lens with which I discuss these various artists is a heretical move and focuses on artists whom I also consider to be heretical with respect to hip hop's historiographical orthodoxy. Engaging in heresy, from the Greek *haeresis*, means I am taking a position within hip hop's critical history. This project positions itself in relation to the work of South African–born, Brooklyn-based rapper/producer/singer Jean Grae; the visual arts and artistic collaborations of the Lower East Side's Martin Wong; the martial arts–romantic comedy *Berry Gordy's The Last Dragon* (1985); and the diasporic musical scene of lesbian, gay, bisexual, transgender, and queer hip hop artists, which all contest the hegemony of a single Black or hip hop aesthetic and challenge the authorized and accepted hip hop cultural histories by deploying queer aesthetics alongside their Black and hip hop aesthetics.

Addison Gayle Jr., in the introduction of his foundational edited anthology *The Black Aesthetic* (1972), argues that the Black aesthetic is "a corrective . . . a means of helping black people out of the polluted American mainstream and offering logical, reasoned arguments as to why he should not desire to join the ranks of a Norman Mailer or a William Styron."[5] Gayle reasons Black aesthetics are necessary to combat the anti-Black impetus of white American mainstream art and entertainment. For Gayle, aesthetics is not merely for artistic pleasure, but must serve as a way to "de-Americanize" Black people at large.[6] This call for the "de-Americanization" of Black people living in the US comes after the long fight for Black civil rights, including desegregation of schools and other public accommodations and voting rights. Gayle and other Black radicals noted the failure of the Civil Rights Movement to eradicate white supremacy and hegemony. *The Black Aesthetic* emerged in an era of Black Power and Black riots and unrest, including the Attica Prison riot (1971) and the Camden, New Jersey, riots (1972). Hoyt W. Fuller, whose essay "Toward a Black Aesthetic" appears in *The Black Aesthetic*, explicitly calls for Black revolt that is antiestablishment. Fuller posits that a worthy Black aesthetic can be found by looking toward the artists and lumpen proletariat in US Black ghettos: "the young writers of the black ghetto have set out in search of a black aesthetic, a system of isolating and evaluating the artistic works of black people which reflect the special character and imperatives of black experience."[7] This aesthetic is grounded in practices of the people and is avant-garde, exploratory, evolving, and locally situated. It is not difficult to see how the early aesthetic practices that formed hip hop culture arose out of this moment. Early graffiti artists, emcees, DJs, and dancers were children, teenagers, and young adults in the early 1970s and had begun to formulate locally popular street aesthetic cultures that were separate from approved, conservative social movements and often involved criminal or criminalized activities. Though the Black Arts Movement was vital wherever there were Black artists, the emergence of the hip hop cultural movement in New York City coalesced around an ongoing series of improvisational performances in public (the subway, playgrounds, building facades, and streets), clubs and performance venues, informal and formal house parties and block parties, and was intertwined with everyday life activities like school, sports, and conflict between rival crews and gangs. Obviously, hip hop performance both benefitted and suffered from its commercialization, starting with the 1979 hit "Rapper's Delight." But its aesthetic and artistic prowess doesn't commence or cease at its commercial arm. As Jeff Chang reasons, "hip-hop's internal creative force does not rest. In the time that it takes for a group of kids in the neighborhood to go from wide-eyed young'ns to confident teen arbiters of style, slang, swing and swagger to grown-folk moving on and out . . . the culture has turned over again."[8] Indeed, one of hip hop's most compelling features is its commitment to aesthetic reinvention and reinterpretation—even at the risk of dismissing or offending older hip hop stylistic orthodoxies. Like Black visual art and other Black art movements, hip hop exists and thrives inside of its generative, simultaneous tensions: it is a global billion-dollar industry, while concurrently generating many independently and hyperlocally influential examples. Hip hop cultural production is fiercely invested in material and capital accumulation, while also in the service of decolonization, sovereignty, and racial justice movements. Hip hop is middle-aged, turning 49 years old in August 2022, while still being associated with teenagers, youth, and young adults. Because hip hop culture's roots, routes, and organs are Black and enmeshed with blackness, hip hop's aesthetics follow (and diverge from) Black aesthetic modalities. In *Travel & See: Black Diaspora Art Practices since the 1980s* (2016), Kobena Mercer reasons, "blackness travels through routes that were initially opened by trade, commerce, and market-based exchange. . . . [T]hese forces enatail[] the exploitative inequalities determined by capitalism, but they also encounter resistances, subversions, and stoppages in their path."[9] Hip hop aesthetics, especially the queer ones, are oriented toward the innovative, introspective, shocking, fun, and carefree—even the highly regulated, boring, duplicating, conservative market cannot help but be shaken out of its lethargy once in a while by a stunning hip hop song and/or its accompanying imagery.[10] So while it is important to attend to aesthetic form, function, and (un)doing, the very heart of hip hop aesthetic practice centers on perfecting the experimental into (the appearance of) the virtuosic.[11]

Hip hop's aesthetics arose from reconfiguring and reconfigured Black aesthetics that were explicitly "street," local, experimental, fusion, and youth-oriented. Jeff Chang elucidates Harry Allen's position on hip hop aesthetics in his edited anthology, *Total Chaos: The Art and Aesthetics of Hip-Hop*: "[Allen] likens the [hip hop] movement's development to the Big Bang. Its vanishing point is in the Bronx, somewhere around '68. Its 'epoch of inflation' is the six-year period before . . . 1979. Sometime [in] that epoch, Afrika Bambaataa famously articulated the outlines of the hip-hop aesthetic by defining four primary elements . . . : graffiti writing, b-boying/b-girling, DJing, and MCing."[12] This is worth quoting at length as it clarifies three items: (a) hip hop's aesthetics were codified before the commercialization of rap music and hip hop culture; (b) hip hop had an aesthetic roadmap and language by the mid-1970s; and (c) hip hop aesthetics were distinct from—though inclusive of—Black aesthetics. Hip hop aesthetics was grounded in practices and in doings by majority Black and brown youth, decidedly located in disorganized street culture and physical practices rather than national, racial, or ethnocultural ones. Hip hop aesthetics, like Black aesthetics, was threatening to the status quo, if for different reasons. While the Black aesthetic movement called for a revolutionary antiestablishment reclamation of Black life, thought, and art, its progenitors were largely male, established writers—they were their own conservative force. Hip hop aesthetics invited anyone who could do its performances well to join (the limitations patriarchy and queer antagonism imposed notwithstanding), making its outlook and practice space boldly utopian in theory.

New York City is framed and famed as the place where dreams can come true. Like Hollywood, it draws artists who want to "make it." But unlike Los Angeles, Philadelphia, and other sites of early hip hop aesthetics, New York also symbolically functions as the "entry point" for the US, with the Statue of Liberty serving, in theory, as a welcoming figure who faces East to those who would approach her. In US idealism, New York City, especially in the 1970s and 1980s, was a place where a person could reinvent herself through art, commerce, or even various underground economies. New York City is the birthplace, or at least the recognizable origin, of global hip hop culture. Its authenticity narrative functions through an aggressive retelling of Black male youth creating a cultural phenomenon comprised of dance, music, fashion, and visual art in the broken, economically devastated regions of the South Bronx. This narrative, although based in some historical facts, usually negates the complicated and complex relations of New York City cultural exchange. This authenticity narrative obfuscates the cultural exchange between the Bronx and the downtown art scene; the multiple influences on New York City youth, including martial arts films, Broadway, the disco, New Wave, and punk scenes, and the generally porous nature of New York City arts and music culture in the 1980s.[13] Yet the artists themselves and the art form itself undermine a sole authentic narrative. New York City hip hop is particularly effective at parodying and ironizing itself. Whether through films that present alternative masculine presentations, songs that complicate Black male identity, dance that highlights the inherent flexibility and changeability of the body, or a fashion movement that ushers the color pink into hip hop iconography and colortopia, New York City hip hop's own culture produces a substantive and wide-ranging critique of itself.

Indexing Black aesthetics emerging directly from the Black Arts Movement as well as Caribbean DJ and other technological innovation and more generally from the long history of diasporic Black artistic and aesthetic practices makes sense. Hip hop's own aesthetic forms and practices, from lyricism to dance and gestural practices to its dense citationality, are all logical topics when writing about hip hop in New York City from the late 20th through the early 21st century. But what about queer aesthetics? The queer aesthetics in *Hip Hop Heresies* are hyperlocal and hypertemporal—they should not be taken to be for all time and for all places or spaces. In fact, the "queer" here is both sexual and gendered, capturing the spectrum of LGBTQIA+ and other sexual and gendered deviants, but it is also very racialized—almost always Black. That is because the queers in *Hip Hop Heresies* cannot be separated from their queer raciality. For here, in *Hip Hop Heresies*, there is no queer space that is not always already Black. In his discussions of Afro-fabulation and Black temporalities, Tavia Nyong'o asks, "What it might mean for black queer and trans aesthetics . . . to 'stay with the trouble' of post-humanism, rather than beat a tactical retreat to a standard of humanism and its accompanying fantasies of citizenry and sovereignty, which always exclude the refugee, migrant, indigene, and slave?"[14] The posture of my archival subjects and objects is that they play with their de-humaned state, seeking neither to integrate into mainstream liberal ideas of a "good" racialized minority nor to delve into a post-humanist material discourse. Instead, they remain in that interstitial space of being both invisible and hypervisible to state and capitalist interests—there they are able to produce, manage, unravel, explore, and perform bodily modalities that are cathected to performance aesthetics. Their queer aesthetics, as identity or as performance modalities, anchor discussions in the subterranean parlance of Black spaces. Those spaces sometimes come to the attention of white gatekeepers, but most if not all of the subjects and objects I discuss in *Hip Hop Heresies* are for horizontal audiences—other Black, brown, and Asian folks. The queer aesthetics in *Hip Hop Heresies* are experimental: the terrain and their navigations of it are constantly shifting. Queer aesthetics use everything available to them—Hollywood money, galleries and museums, friendship, stereotypes, clumsy humor, smart humor, crowded apartments, sexual favors, crude language, pathos, suicidal ideation, and more. These artists and art objects stay "close to the ground," as it were—almost never achieving blockbuster success, but nonetheless influencing and guiding scores of artists, curators, writers, fans, and other invested parties through their own experiences of aesthetic-meaning and aesthetic-doing.

Between History and Heresy: Hip Hop Foundations and Queer Specters

In "Hip-Hop's Founding Fathers Speaks the Truth," music journalist and historian Nelson George interviews three of hip hop's pioneering artists and cultural architects: DJ Kool Herc (Clive Campbell), Afrika Bambaataa (Kevin Donovan), and Grandmaster Flash (Joseph Saddler).[15]

The essay is an important one, especially as hip hop artists and fans, even long-time ones, forget the social, cultural, political, and economic factors which helped to shape the emergent cultures that would coalesce into what we now call hip hop.[16] However, the remembering of those factors often slides into a memorialization, which occludes the ability to make space for other oral histories that do not readily affirm heterosexist and patriarchal Black masculinity as the main source of hip hop culture and performance. The three pioneers offer various remembrances of and insights into the early days of rapping, graffiti, break-dancing (and popping and locking), and DJing. Each man discusses his views on hip hop's circulation and rise to prominence as a cultural force in New York City in the 1970s and early 1980s. Afrika Bambaataa credits his Zulu Nation collective for bringing disparate street arts cultures (rap, dance, graffiti, and DJing) together. Grandmaster Flash troubles the idea that graffiti and hip hop are synonymous, and DJ Kool Herc is the most generous in discussing how he created a certain iconic DJ sound and where and in what ways these disparate art forms were connected by artist collaborations and friendships.[17] Although George labels this conversation "the truth," it is, in fact, a series of perspectives on a specific moment and place in hip hop cultural history that occurred in various neighborhoods in the South Bronx. These events happened and these three men were instrumental in making them happen and recording them. Over a decade after the essay was published, the legitimacy of the "truth" from "founding father" Afrika Bambaataa was shaken after multiple male members of the Universal Zulu Nation (an organization he founded in the late 1970s) accused him of sexually assaulting them when they were boys.[18] Though the Zulu Nation at first issued a vigorous defense of Bambaataa and a disparaging dismissal of one of the accusers, Ronald Savage, the organization issued an apology via open letter in May 2016 just weeks after their initial statement. One particularly salient portion of the letter reads:

> We call for prioritizing expert-informed education on sexuality, sexual orientation, sexual exploitation, and domestic violence. Additionally, we

call on communities to learn about and address rape culture proactively; we realize that we were guilty of acquiescing to cultural norms that implicitly endanger children and adult members of society everyday and ask our communities to share in our commitment to shifting this paradigm in a more favorable direction.[19]

There is a tangle of complications here: first, the devastating and endemic problem of sexual assault perpetuated by Black men in power against those more vulnerable—from Bambaataa to Bill Cosby to R. Kelly. Although he doesn't speak explicitly to the sexualized violence against children, women, and men by their hip hop "mentors," Jay-Z addresses the predatory aspect of both street life and music business mentors and culture when he says: "An older guy will see a kid and think, '*Man, that kid moves differently from the rest. He's ready for this life.*' They know that if they find the right kid, they can put him under their tutelage and he'll get in fast. . . . If that sounds predatory, it's because recruiting new workers is one of the most predatory aspect of the [drug and music] game."[20] Jay-Z acknowledges that predatory mentorship, including "watching" kids who have "old souls," is a part of both street-level drug dealing culture and music business culture. Hip hop culture and aesthetics is one place where those two businesses explicitly intersect, so it is no surprise that abuses in the form of sexualized assault occur. Second, there is the long-standing homophobic and homo-antagonistic conflation of child sexual assault, rape, and pedophilia as synonymous with homosexual desire. These two factors—protecting patriarchal power and denigrating homosexual or queer desire—make talking about queerness in hip hop culture fraught, but hardly impossible. Indeed, the work I present here contests these long-standing forms of patriarchy through its own complex and divergent means. There is more to hip hop's history in New York City than rehearsing the same narratives—even if the alternatives are largely forgotten. By expanding hip hop culture's historiography, our knowledge and appreciation of who was making these cultural products and where they were being made increases, deepens, and sharpens.

The artists and artwork explored in *Hip Hop Heresies* are heretical in relation to the accepted narrative of hip hop culture and performance as solely Black identitarian in its formation and ideology. Valentine Cunningham observes, "Heretics are traditionally wrong believers, wrong readers . . . people who've chosen the wrong meanings, and formed an erroneous party of hermeneutes."[21] Heretics are "wrong believers" in relation to the established, approved ideological power base or heterodoxical forms. One can think of Christ as a heretic of Judaism, Buddha Shakayamuni as a heretic of Hinduism, and Martin Luther as a heretic of Catholicism. Heretics don't simply wrongly mean or wrongly say, they say anew and create new bodies of learning, knowledge, know-how, and ways of being in and experiencing the world. Likewise, the artists and artistic works under consideration here are doing the work of "queering" hip hop. While some of the objects are straight-identified, like the film *Berry Gordy's The Last Dragon*, others, like Martin Wong, are queer-identified. Jean Grae in her typical manner falls somewhere between or outside those classifications. Nonetheless, I argue the work that they do to rethink and remake narratives of black female psychic subjectivity and sound; Afro-Asian articulations of race, gender, and sexuality; Black masculine performativity, desire, and imagination; and gender, race, sexual, regional, and class binaries are "queer"—disruptive—to heteronormative depictions and articulations of hip hop performance. These artists work with queer aesthetic methodologies to unmoor and eradicate settled public modalities of being in the world. These artists are a part of hip hop's flourishing heterodoxy; simultaneously, some of them, are pillars in hip hop's orthodox narrative and use that position to carve out more flexible, heretical musical, sonic, and visual renderings of hip hop culture and performance from New York City. As Cunningham, following Anne Hudson, points out, "Literacy 'begot heresy.'" To be literate is to become heretical through forming a relation with what is already established—these artists offer their works "as models of selfhood, existence, ways of [making art]."²² They go beyond self by helping to form and reform communities of artistic and cultural heretics, challenging the perceived stability of gender, race, sexuality, nation, region, and the affective attachments that accompany those identity positions. In this way, the hip hop heretic who "queers" hip hop commonsense or hip hop historiography is situated in a way similar to how the Black femme functions in Kara Keeling's reading: alternately as chimera, default line, and invisible figure. Keeling argues:

> Attending to the lines of flight set in motion by (un)successful attempts to contain or circumscribe the black femme within existing epistemological categories provides an opportunity to elucidate the workings of the cinematic and the cinematic process integral to contemporary racism, sexism, and homophobic violence. Follow?²³

Like Keeling's Black femme, my queer heretics offer entry through the fault lines of the structural and systemic hip hop ground. That these queer heretics—some heterosexual, others LGBTQIA+—cover the artistic ground of cinema, visual art, and music is vital. *Hip Hop Heresies* makes an argument for the queer aesthetics of New York *hip hop culture*, not simply its music. In doing so, I ask the reader to think alongside me as I weave through the tangle of changing racial alliances, gender and sexual mores, and artistic and aesthetic choices taken up by New York City hip hop artists from the mid-1970s through the recent past.

It's by no means incontrovertible to argue that these Black, brown, and Asian artists remade New York City hip hop performance through their aesthetic choices. Imani Perry succinctly writes, "Hip hop music is black American music. Even with its hybridity: the consistent contributions from nonblack artists, and the borrowing from cultural forms of other communities, it is nevertheless black American music."²⁴ Perry bases her argument on the evidence of the following: the primary language used in rap is African American Vernacular English; rap's politics are ascribed to Black people, music, and cultural forms; it derives from the Black oral tradition and Black American musical traditions.[25] I agree that Black and Latinx diasporic youth, located in the United States, influenced by multiple sources, articulated and popularized rap music. Perry is talking specifically about rap music, and while rap music is one of hip hop's foundational elements, it's short-sighted to ignore the ways that all hip hop elements intermingle with and shape each other. One could easily argue that hip hop is Caribbean, as many of its early practitioners and innovators were born in the Caribbean or of Caribbean descent.[26] The cultural, political, psychic, fantastic, and social influences that coalesced into rap music and hip hop culture and performance in general must be explored more deeply, as they form a particular kind of Black American musical subjectivity and culture. On one level, Perry and I are arguing the same thing: we both are vexed at the notion that "blackness in the United States is constructed as a kind of pure existence, a purity, to most, of the negative kind, defined by a pure lack of sophistication and complexity and a pure membership in a group of undesirables."[27]

For Perry, the multiracial, multicultural reality of US blackness and US Black music is folded into the notion of the Black American (United States) musical and cultural tradition. I posit something different: that in certain New York City hip hop cultural performances blackness is formed, constructed, represented, and expressed in ways that may not be legibly "Black" and may not, in fact, be rendered by people who are racialized as Black. The queer Black bodies or odd Black bodies that have been jettisoned from more conservative hip hop narratives are welcomed and explored here as central to New York City hip hop's formation. The heretics of *Hip Hop Heresies* relate to blackness as an ongoing artistic, cultural, psychic, material, historical, dialogical project of being and becoming. Blackness is art-making and the artworks created out of blackness, in this case, hip hop cultural productions, are investigations with, against, and through the expanding and fraught position of Black subjectivity in the United States. For some, blackness may include a spectrum of influence; I perceive blackness, itself, as a spectrum. As in physics, the Black body of matter (as opposed to the social-cultural-historical "Black" body) is the best absorber of light and the best emitter of light. We can expand this notion to hip hop culture, noting how Black cultural production and performance as a tool both absorbs the cultural spectrum and emits the cultural spectrum, manifesting a fresh, new hybrid performance space. This is the notion of the heretical in relation to hip hop's formation. The danger, of course, is posed by the long history and ongoing practice of erasing Black genius produced by Black people. This erasure is reworked to award white people and non-Black people of color for "innovating" or even "inventing" cultural and performative forms that Black people crafted and perfected over years or even decades. This book is not invested in a blackness without Black people, but rather wants to underscore the creativity and expansiveness of Black genius that gets devalued in the marketplace, the classroom, the office, and the social scene in order to gentrify and resell a form of "Black" creativity performed by non-Black people.

Hip Hop Heresies: Time and Place

This book focuses on New York–based hip hop cultural production from 1975 to 2015, using queer Chinese American visual artist Martin Wong's 1975 arrival in New York City as its chronological starting point. *Hip Hop Heresies* has a queer temporality as it foregrounds and underscores queer subjects (LGBTQ-identified people) and queer moments (oddities, non-normative, not-quite-right fits). Using both contemporary and historical hip hop cultural productions, *Hip Hop Heresies* explores the way individual artists, films, specific hip hop cultural scenes (such as queer hip hop), and hip hop fans engage in and with performances of gender and sexuality. The book seeks to divest hip hop from a narrative of Black and Latinx male authenticity in favor of deepening the roles of the vibrant and divergent cultural influences on hip hop.[28] *Hip Hop Heresies* explores the Asian influence on early hip hop culture (1975–1985), looking at how Chinese American artists, like Martin Wong, along with the powerful influence of Hong Kong martial arts, coexisted and comingled with Black, AfriLatinx, and hip hop aesthetics in New York City. *Hip Hop Heresies* also explores the Black youth obsession with Chinese martial arts culture and film, and how that preoccupation expressed itself in hip hop culture and production. This divestment demonstrates how a narrative of authenticity stilts the reality of Black and Latinx male and female hip hop cultural production and performance, and how that same narrative flattens the ingenuity and openness of Black and AfriLatinx creativity in early hip hop culture. These performances include, but are not limited to, Chinese martial arts films, graffiti culture, graphic novels and the influence of the avatar, New York City's downtown art scene and artists, and films depicting burgeoning hip hop cultural spaces and scenes. Although these performances of gender, race, and sexuality are not limited to hip hop made in New York City, New York's particular vantage point as the so-called "birthplace" of hip hop culture warrants special attention. In this book, I explore the specificity of place (primarily the five boroughs of New York City, along with Long Island, New Jersey, and Connecticut) that has been overlooked by other narratives (popular and scholarly) about gender, sexuality and place in hip hop culture. In doing so, I trace themes of bodily, sexual, and gender expression, placing them side by side with themes of space and place to show the ways that hip hop cultural production originating in New York City is marked with a particular sophistication, wit, intelligence, irony, and deep thoughtfulness about the ways in which femininity, masculinity, and sexuality manifest in the culture.

Hip Hop Heresies examines explicit moments when heretical New York–based hip hop directly challenges mainstream US and "hip hop" notions about Black femininity and masculinity. For example, in my chapter on Jean Grae, I examine her scathing commentary on the figure of the male "playa" in hip hop culture in "God's Gift,"[29] which exemplifies this type of performance. Grae (born Tsidsi Ibrahim) differentiates "God's Gift" from earlier "feminist" hip hop songs such as Queen Latifah's "U.N.I.T.Y." and Salt-N-Pepa's "Tramp" by addressing the underlying misogyny of heterosexist conquests through the deployment of the exact language, tone, and viciousness of a playa, a role usually reserved for heterosexual men. There are no punches pulled, no pleas for unity, in fact, there is no recognizable "feminine voice" in her song. Grae turns the game on its head—or, in this case, on its ear. The effects of such a sonic boom reverberate beyond the discourse on heterosexual relations and unsettle supposedly stable ideas about racial posturing, gender identification, and sexuality. Grae performs this particular masculine posture with such aplomb that the listener is tasked with parsing out the destructiveness of misogynistic values promoted through hip hop melodies.

Why Queer? Why Hip Hop?

I first began thinking about the relationship between queerness and hip hop during my third year as an undergraduate student at Smith College. Though the relationship divides between approved white mainstream feminist politics and hip hop investment improved and shifted radically during my four years at the Northampton, Massachusetts, a women's small liberal arts college, the rigid separation was very clear in those mid-to-late-1990s halcyon days. I recall with particular clarity the academic year opening barbecue at which there was food, flirting, the nerves of new and returning students, and student DJs spinning music. At one point, DJ Noa D—then a budding college DJ, now a popular NYC-based one—began to spin Jay-Z's "Ain't No Nigga," his deliciously naughty collaboration with Foxy Brown from his debut album *Reasonable Doubt* (1996). "Aint No Nigga," produced by Jay-Z's musical mentor Jaz-O (credited as Big Jaz), was the second single released from the future platinum album. In the song, Jay-Z introduces and establishes the player/pimp/gangsta/hustler persona he would perfect over his next ten or so albums. The song's premise is familiar and simple: Jay-Z, the "nigga" character here, is such a fabulous lover and so materially successful that none of his patriarchal or misogynistic qualities make his paramour falter in her desire for him. As the song's Black woman character proclaims, he may "sleep[] around, but he gives me a lot,"[30] and therefore all is forgiven or at least tolerated. The verse structure of the collaboration is unremarkable: Jay-Z, whose album and song it is, gets two verses to Foxy Brown's one. In his introductory volley, Jay-Z's character proclaims to the woman character that he'll "keep [her] fresher the next bitch, no need / For [her] to ever sweat the next bitch, with speed / I make the best bitch see the exit, indeed / [She] gotta know [she] thoroughly respected, by me." It's an interesting set of verbal and conceptual juxtapositions he sets out: he's going to provide material things for his "bitch," she doesn't have to worry about another woman with whom he may or may not be involved, and he respects her. It's beyond the scope of this project to unpack all the ways "nigga" and "bitch" are deployed in hip hop's music, cultural production, and everyday lexicon, but here they metonyms for a certain type of young, street-sophisticated, urban Black man and his Black woman counterpart. This song both praises infidelity as the "natural" state of a player while concurrently giving space for the woman character to respond haptically and in call-and-response ways during the man's verses—while also having a verse/voice of her own. Foxy Brown's character plays this role straight, as it were, accepting the conditions of this brand of Black heteronormative heterosexuality. At 17 years old, Inga Marchand–as–Foxy Brown–as–the "bitch" in this song articulates the capitalistic exchange of contemporary heterosexual relations between Black men and women in hip hop parlance. She starts with an interrogative: "Remember the days when you was dead broke / But now you style and I raised you / Basically made you into a don / . . . You know the pussy is all that / That's why I get baguettes . . . / So who the player?" Though the power is supposedly weighted toward the "nigga" man in this song, Foxy's verse plays out a familiar but less explored trope among Black women rappers and hip hop/R&B singers—the "ride or die bitch" who is able to help her man make it big and is therefore unconcerned about his dalliances because she knows she is his primary. Furthermore, she benefits materially, socially, and sexually from his elevated status.

If that were all there were to say about the song, I could argue that these types of arrangements seem to manifest what books like *The Ethical Slut: A Practical Guide to Polyamory, Open Relationship, and Other Adventures* (2009) propose. Namely that monogamy isn't the natural state for most people and that there are ethical ways to navigate and negotiate sex or relationships with others when already in a primary relationship. However, in reality, Black men and Black women are rewarded and punished differently for sex and sexuality in a white supremacist patriarchal system. Whereas Black men in hip hop can make a career based in sexual exploits and/or exploitation of women, women who make hip hop music are often limited to a handful of archetypes such as the "ride or die bitch," the conscious queen, and the female or feminine thug. Further, if these women perform sexuality in any overt or enjoyable way, they are often reduced to "sex symbol" status and not taken seriously as artists, even though a patriarchal system simultaneously demands overt sexuality from Black women and other, non-Black women of color so that they may demonstrate their "value." Black women musical performers, in particular, aren't immediately gifted the title of "artist" in mainstream US society or in hip hop cultural.

Tricia Rose's first, gestational work on hip hop in the US took seriously the dynamics of sex, gender, race, economics, and cultural history. Her study *Black Noise: Rap Music and Black Culture in Contemporary America* (1994) ushered in serious critical considerations of hip hop culture's value and production. *Black Noise* examines the relationship between forces of race and sex and the negotiations around them in Black contemporary popular culture. Rose covers five important themes, each of which has become a category of study in hip hop scholarship: the relationship between rap (or hip hop generally) and social position; rap music's origins; technological interventions and orality; lyrical content; and the female voice in hip hop culture (rap music). Perhaps not so strangely, *Black Noise* adheres to the normative logic of heterosexual dynamics within Black hip hop cultural production. Given how groundbreaking it was as an intellectual consideration of hip hop, there was, perhaps, only so much the book could do to push the conservative boundaries of 1980s and 1990s academic thought. Likewise, my work, building on Roses's, thinks through hip hop's aesthetics through the lens of performance studies, Black popular culture, and gender and sexuality. Using these three methods allows me to widen understanding of how New York City hip hop culture was a part of the broader arts culture in NYC—influencing and being influenced by the robust avant-garde art scene in New York City in the 1970s and 1980s.

Both *Black Noise* and Paul Gilroy's *Against Race: Imagining Political Culture Beyond the Color Line* (2001) refuse essentialist notions of blackness and hip hop cultural production. Rose understood that "[r]ap music brings together a tangle of some of the most complex social, cultural, and political issues in contemporary American society."[31] Similarly, Gilroy's *Against Race* deploys rap music and iconography to illustrate the murkiness and muckiness of race, sex, gender, speech, and image. He understands certain rap elements as "the ghetto-centric individualism of the poor [that] appears to have defeated the convenient bioessentialism of the elite."[32] So while hip hop culture is hailed as both the savior and demise of Black cultural standards in popular music, it also contains the very elements that oppose stale and rigid notions of blackness. Yet the very examples that both Rose and Gilroy use occlude a wide variety of hip hop aesthetics, in New York City and beyond, which demonstrate through their form and content an always-already quirky Black sensibility. How does one listen to and view an early hip hop martial arts musical like *The Last Dragon* without attending to the ways that film pulls from an imaginative New York that resists notion of racial, gender, sexual, and aesthetic essentialism? Of course, the kinds of questions I can ask about hip hop cultural production are different in part because there *is* a field of hip hop studies. Additionally, interdisciplinary, transdisciplinary, and nondisciplinary attention to hip hop and hip hop studies allows a move past the borderline moralism about hip hop: we can take a refreshing view of hip hop as aesthetic work that does many things in the world, including offering opportunities to think through how hip hop cultural production in New York City affords us examples of its own aesthetic queerness.

The Heretical Archive

Chapter 1, "Wild Stylin': Martin Wong's Queer Visuality in New York City Graffiti," positions Wong (1946–1999) as a foundational influential figure in New York City's early hip hop culture. As the founder of the Museum of American Graffiti (July 1989–October 1989), Wong established the first permanent (though short-lived) home for hip hop art and ephemera. Framing Wong's art and life as a fulcrum around which the burgeoning hip hop street art cultures and the downtown art scene pivoted, I argue that his informal social, personal, and business artistic networks offered a model for queer artistry and sustainability. Queer aesthetics in this chapter centers on Wong's negotiations of romance, art, friendship, mentorship, and livelihood in relation to burgeoning street cultures, neighborhood violence and loyalties, and his position as an insider-outsider as a queer Chinese American man in Manhattan's Lower East Side Nuyorican (New York Puerto Rican) enclave. This chapter recenters graffiti and visual art in hip hop culture, performance, and aesthetics, arguing both graffiti and hip hop visual art are communal activities that spurred the careers of artists like Wong, Jean-Michel Basquiat, Daze, Crash, Lady Pink, and Charlie and John Ahearn.

Chapter 2, "Nigga Fu: *The Last Dragon*, Black Masculinity, and Chinese Martial Arts," argues that the mainstream Hollywood film *Berry Gordy's The Last Dragon* (dir. Michael Schultz, 1985) exposes a complex set of negotiations of fantasy, desire, masculinity, and power placed upon the figure of the Black martial artist film star. I argue the appearance of Black martial artists in early hip hop film is a continuation of the image of Black male exile who must go "East" to locate his masculinity. The chapter investigates the appearances of "Asia," specifically representations of China in other early hip hop films and music, and reads these appearances alongside other works that consider the uses of Asians and "Asia" in 1980s US popular film. This chapter's queer aesthetics proposes a nuanced look at heterosexual romance in *The Last Dragon* that resists heteronormativity and a complex Black masculinity that emerges from identification with cinematic Chinese martial arts masculinity. I argue this resistance to heteronormative heterosexuality stems from a resistance to Black male hegemony informed by white supremacist notions of masculinity and manhood.

Chapter 3, "'Casebaskets': Listening for the Uncanny in Jean Grae," demonstrates how Brooklyn-based emcee/producer/singer Jean Grae sonically disrupts Black heteronormative expectations in hip hop performance. The chapter thinks through the artistic uses of the uncanny, particularly how Grae works with uncanniness to decenter heteronormative Black masculinity, as well as to navigate abjection and social death. Through a sonic and visual reading of Jean Grae's songs "God's Gift" and "My Story," their respective videos, and the short film *Spittin' 'Til They Shame You*, I construct a theory of Grae's interiority that makes room for Black female artistic interventions in hip hop production. The chapter reads Grae alongside her namesake, Marvel's X-Men superhero character Jean Grey, to explore emcee Grae's sonic, lyrical, and aesthetic "darkness" as a recuperative method of psychic and artistic survival. Jean Grae's queer aesthetics expresses itself through a sonic, visual, and lyrical disruption of "approved" roles for Black female hip hop artists. By taking on an avatar expressly related to the psyche, Grae navigates the psychical, material, artistic, and fantastic elements of hip hop culture and production.

Chapter 4, "Queer Hip Hop, Queer Dissonance," is a historical, ethnographic, and archival chapter that focuses on the history and performances of queer/LGBTQ-identified hip hop DJs, emcees, dancers, and graffiti artists from 1982 to 2005. The chapter focuses on early gay hip hop DJ Man Parrish, as well as on the LGBTQ hip hop festival Peace Out East (2004–2007). I argue these artists and spaces have a particular sonic import and queer aesthetic—queer dissonance—that interrupts linear understandings of race, gender, sexuality, and musical acumen inside hip hop culture. The queer interraciality of queer hip hop is rarely mentioned in discussions of queer-identified rappers. The chapter also examines the paradox of non-black artists performing and venerating Black male authenticity inside of queer hip hop culture and performance.

Finally, the conclusion, "Queer Trans Black Aesthetic Futures," looks elsewhere, to the creation of other worlds. I speculate on the future of hip hop by looking at its present to think through the (re)connections to the popular, the insurgent, and the unexpected queer aesthetics that occur in hip hop art forms. Drawing together the themes of the book, I advocate a form of a hip hop that eschews authenticity in favor of performativity, bricolage, and pastiche.

Hip Hop Heresies: Queer Aesthetics in New York City makes a bold attempt—the first of its kind—to connect blackness and queerness with hip hop culture and studies. The book argues that New York City hip hop artists use queer, Black, and hip hop aesthetics to *queerly*—disruptively, generatively, inauthentically—articulate gender, racial, and sexual identitarian performances through specifically New York City–based aesthetic and artistic practices and cues. I do this work through looking at various hip hop forms: music, film, and visual art. *Hip Hop Heresies* makes space for the performers and performances that are considered odd, "queer," and anomalous. I argue that these performers and performances can show and tell us about the through line of queer Black hip hop aesthetics that arise in specific performative contexts in New York City hip hop cultural production.

1

Wild Stylin'

Martin Wong's Queer Visuality in New York City Graffiti

Hip Hop Heresies is an unconventional hip hop book. Its focus on queerness, aesthetics, and the intermingling of race, gender, and sexuality in New York City foreground my investment in covering unexplored ground in hip hop cultural history. Concurrently, *Hip Hop Heresies* remains true to the convention of citing New York City as the nodal point of hip hop culture's recognizable emergence in the late 20th century, as well as centering Black people as the innovators, orators, inventors, and curators of hip hop's aesthetic and cultural elements. As I synthesize both the conventional and the non-conventional, Martin Wong emerges as a key figure in thinking through the racial co-mingling and the queer aesthetics of hip hop forms, especially graffiti, in 1970s and 1980s New York City. As an artist, a lay art historian, a curator of graffiti art, a gay man, a Chinese American man, and a West Coast transplant, Martin Wong is a far cry from the archetypical architect of hip hop cultural historiography. Nonetheless, Wong is straight up hip hop insofar as he was a practitioner, comrade, and visionary in relation to graffiti art, contemporary art, and the communities of artists and fans who inhabited those two worlds. This chapter positions Martin Wong (1946–1999) as a foundational and influential figure in New York City's early hip hop culture. As the founder of the Museum of American Graffiti (July 1989–October 1989), Wong established the first permanent (though short-lived) home for hip hop visual art and ephemera. Through an investigation of and engagement with Wong's archives at the Downtown Collection at New York University, the Museum of the City of New York, and PPOW Gallery, I frame Wong's art and life as a fulcrum around which the burgeoning hip hop street art cultures and the downtown art scene pivoted. This chapter attends to Wong's informal social, personal, and business artistic networks as exemplary for queer artistry and sustainability within hip hop culture. Queer aesthetics in this chapter centers on Wong's negotiations of romance, art, friendship, mentorship, and livelihood inside burgeoning street cultures, neighborhood violence and loyalties, and his position as an insider-outsider as a queer Chinese American man in Manhattan's Lower East Side Nuyorican (New York Puerto Rican) enclave. This chapter recenters graffiti and visual art in hip hop culture, performance, and aesthetics, arguing that both graffiti and hip hop visual art are communal activities that spurred the careers of artists like Wong, Jean-Michel Basquiat, Daze, Crash, Lady Pink, and Charlie and John Ahearn. It reorients the reader away from a history of lone-wolf success in early hip hop culture and instead focuses on the ways in which mentorship, friendship, and collaboration were vital to making careers. I consider two of Wong's signature pieces, *Attorney Street* (1982–1984) and *Sweet 'Enuff* (1987).

Martin Wong's body of work embodies the racial plurality, queerness, and visual art in New York City's early hip hop production, and offers what I call "queer articulations" of race, gender, and sexuality in music, visual art, and film. This chapter and the next, which focuses on the early hip hop film *Berry Gordy's The Last Dragon* (1985), center performances and representations of Chinese identities and Afro-Asian sensibilities in early hip hop culture. As Helen Heran Jun counsels, this is not to "demonstrate[] a strong teleological investment in multiracial solidarity,"[1] but to show how the presence of Asians and Asian aesthetics in early hip hop culture shaped the complex negotiations of cultural acumen, racial wariness and prejudice, street savvy, and interpersonal relations in various hip hop cultural scenes. I argue that Wong's work and collaborations reveal what Mimi Thi Nguyen and Nguyen Tu call the relationship "between affect and aesthetics,"[2] insofar as how Asian Americans and Asian diasporic cultures were rendered in early hip hop culture.

On Martin Wong's Queer Archive

Martin Victor Wong arrived in New York from San Francisco in 1978. Ed Koch was mayor of the city, which was still attempting to recover from its near-bankruptcy in 1975.[3] It was the New York City dramatized in films such as *The Warriors* (1979) and, two years later, the infamous *Fort Apache, The Bronx* (1981): dangerous, crime-ridden, and desolate. For all of the dire depictions and predictions, cultural historian Tricia Rose notes contemporary hip hop culture coalesced under these tumultuous conditions of economic hardship, broken social policy, and political strife.[4] Similarly, social historian David Walkowitz demarcates the ways in which New York City's liberal and conservative politicians failed to adequately address the complex and growing needs of the city's immigrant and migrant populations of color, as well as the ways middle-class whites and business concerns felt slighted by the focus on the city's working poor and working class.[5] Although New York City suffered in the 1970s and the early 1980s from white flight to the suburbs and the desertion of corporations (resulting in loss of tax revenue), influxes of new migrants and immigrants who needed services for which the city had no revenue, political and financial corruption, countless strikes of city workers and racialized violence, the city was swimming with a wealth of underground music and visual art scenes.[6] New York City's economic struggles and the rise of poverty in communities of color, immigrant, working- and middle-class, and queer communities contrasted sharply with the ways in which people within these communities were able to produce and generate art, even if that art wasn't immediately profitable or valued by appraisers or mainstream economic markets. Martin Wong's art flourished during this time of economic and political uncertainty. Wong produced an incredible amount of work during his life, leaving behind permanent collections at galleries like PPOW, Semaphore, and Exit Art, as well as selling his art to the Metropolitan Museum of Art in New York City and the de Young Museum in San Francisco.

The Martin Wong Papers housed at the Downtown Collection in the Fales Library and Special Collections at New York University's Elmer Holmes Bobst Library is an archive of Wong's correspondence, sketchbooks, photographs, source materials, and other artwork and ephemera. Wong's graffiti art lives at the Museum of the City of New York and the majority of his paintings at the PPOW Gallery. These archives, particularly the Wong Papers, offer insight into Wong's relationship to early hip hop culture, specifically with figures within New York City's graffiti and independent film scenes. For instance, Wong often collaborated with his friend Charlie Ahearn, the director of the first hip hop narrative film, *Wild Style* (1983). The film, a collaboration between Ahearn and Fred "Fab Five Freddy" Braithwaite, chronicled the fictitious lives of real-life local graffiti, rap, and dance crews, and starred practicing graffiti artists, rappers, DJs, break dancers, and promoters, such as Fab Five Freddy, Lee Quiñones, Lady Pink, Lisa Lee, Patti Astor, Dondi, Busy Bee Starski, Daze, and the Rock Steady Crew.[7] In his archive, I came upon a logo Wong made for *Wild Style* in the graffiti style of the same name. Wild style, the art technique, is an intricate graffiti style incorporating overlapping and interwoven letters, spikes, arrows, and other stylistic methods that make it hard to produce and difficult to decipher—it's considered the most complex of graffiti visual and linguistic techniques.[8] Wong produced a small *Wild Style* logo, a 6-by-3-by-1-inch Styrofoam mock-up, rendered in a simplistic wild style technique. Though Tracy 168 (founder of the Wild Style Crew) designed *Wild Style*'s logo (based on Dondi's famous subway car piece), and Zephyr, Revolt, and Sharp created the mural in the film, Wong was a part of the ongoing style and design riffing produced by Ahearn's film. This piece was a curious find. It makes sense for artists to experiment and improvise on other artist's work, especially when they test out styles that may be incommensurate with their usual preferences. Yet finding this small, significant ephemeral piece startled me into considering where, when, and how Wong intersected with more widely known graffiti art and cultural objects.

Martin Wong, *Wild Style*, n.d. (1980s), 3D Styrofoam logo.

Wong's archive is a recuperative site for forgotten or silenced queer culture as it pertains to early hip hop culture and performance, Asian American history and culture, and graffiti history and culture. Wong's archive also offers an opportunity to apply deconstructive, nonlinear—queered—methodologies in approaching the pliant archive. Diana Taylor notes the historical Western bias in favor of the archive over "the repertoire of embodied practices as an important system of knowing and transmitting knowledge."[9] Like Taylor, my work with Wong's archives thinks through scenarios—a sketch or outline of the plot of a play, giving particulars of the scenes, situations, etc.[10]—not only to subvert the hierarchy of texts and narratives, but to play with dominant hip hop teleological narratology that demands adherence to a rather limited and essentialist view of blackness, hip hop innovation, and interracial collaborations. I read Wong's life, art, and archive as performative in the sense used by J. L. Austin, because they are works and actions that enact or do in the world, particularly in their effects on early hip hop visual arts and graffiti culture.[11] Wong's archive is also a performance site, alive with photos, sketches, built pieces, letters, cards, art work, and the remains of a vibrant life these objects can't quite contain.

Wong, a Chinese American, openly gay, self-taught visual artist, ceramicist, and poet, was a significant figure in both New York City's vibrant downtown art scene—famous for producing Jean-Michel Basquiat, David Wojnarowicz, Kiki Smith, and Andy Warhol—as well as being part of NYC's burgeoning music, visual arts, and dance scene that would coalesce into hip hop culture. He collaborated with hip hop arts pioneers such as Ahearn, graffiti artists Lee Quiñones, Rammellzee, Lady Pink, Daze, and Nuyorican Poet's Café co-founder and writer Miguel Piñero. Anthony Haden-Guest's *True Colors: The Real Life of the Art World* (1996) explores the connections between the downtown art world and the uptown, downtown, and outer-borough graffiti artists who began to mix together in social and artistic spaces. Graffiti artists started showing their work in NYC galleries as early as 1972.[12] Art world interest in graffiti art waned, but a younger generation of artists, curators, and appreciators emerged in the late 1970s and the early 1980s; Wong was part of that newer generation. So where is Martin Wong in hip hop's historiography? More pointedly, how does the presence of an influential gay, Chinese American man in early New York City hip hop culture reframe discussions of appropriation, cultural legitimacy, and Black-Asian conflict inside of hip hop culture, history, and performance? Wong's life and work in the formative years of hip hop culture offers a powerful indication of alternatives to the narratives of a cloistered, Bronx-only hip hop culture, which erases the ways in which Blacks, Latinx, Asians, and whites were working collaboratively, if not in proportionate numbers, to create a new, multivalent arts cultural movement. Wong's archive and his repertoire point to the significance of Asian-Black-Latinx-white collaboration based on the skills and personal relationships of early hip hop artists. There is a plethora of work on contemporary Afro-Asian encounters, Afro-Asian aesthetics, and cultural production related to hip hop culture.[13] Nonetheless, the majority of the discussion relating to Asians in hip hop culture has focused on the emergence of Asian fan markets in later hip hop culture, or, ironically, on the all-Black hip hop group the Wu Tang Clan.[14] Reinserting Wong and his work into the ongoing chronicle of the vibrant, evolving street-art culture at the moment it was emerging to wider audiences reframes possibilities of Asian participation and influence on early hip hop culture. Wong was an everyday presence in the Lower East Side; unlike Bruce Lee, the most influential and reoccurring Asian figure in hip hop culture, Wong was not a fetishized icon that influenced Black and Latinx artists from afar and through mediated representation. Wong influenced artists by buying their art, getting their art shown and purchased, and collaborating with other graffiti artists on works themselves.

However, Wong's explicit connection to blackness and Black people is much more tentative, implicit, and muted than his overt connections to (Afro-)*latinidad* inside of New York City's hip hop landscape. The majority of writing about Wong and his relationship to his Lower East Side neighborhood stresses his connections to "Nuyorico." The strange erasure of blackness inside of New York Puerto Ricanhood persists, even as Wong's own art work indexes the Black, dark brown, and brown bodies and associations that made up his own aesthetic and personal life. Queer and Latinx studies scholar Roy Pérez writes about "Wong's own queer sense of latinidad and what [he] call[s Wong's] poetics of racial proximity";[15] this attunes those interested in Wong's work and collaborations to works lesser-known than his grand collaboration with Piñero and graffiti artist Pino, *Attorney Street (Handball Court with Autobiographical Poem by Piñero)*, which I discuss toward the end of this chapter. Pérez traverses a rocky terrain as he subtly spells out the stakes of Wong's queer aesthetic modality inside a hypermasculinist proto–hip hop scene. Pérez postulates, "A theory of proximity is more nearly a way to make something out of the aporia created in the Latino archive by the bifurcation of race and sexuality into separate histories, and attend to the gaps and contradictions where queerness seems to be the missing conjunction but where its denotive confirmation is either ignored, inaccessible, or unspeakable."[16] Pérez points here to the strain placed on aesthetic work to represent a confluence of complicated and juicy relations. Further, as aesthetic work makes its way into an official *latinidad* archive (historical, canonized, or in an actual repository), the tendency to erase that which is queer—homosexual, gay, bisexual—must be repressed to "straighten" out the images of a particular Latinx identity. That same resolving, is of course, at work in hip hop historiography, and hip hop studies, as well as Black history and studies more generally. But the lacuna that strikes me upon reading Pérez and others vis-à-vis queerness-in-*latinidad* is the erasure of blackness from that equation. Wong lived in New York City where Black Latinos thrived; it is strange that the particular racialness of Latinx identity falls out so readily when talking about Wong, *latinidad*, and Nuyorico.

Raquel Z. Rivera, a cultural sociologist and Latinx studies scholar, has worked diligently to reposition "New York Ricans" firmly in "the urban Afro-diasporic context, which is crucial in the appropriation of the 'tools of the master' for many Latino writers, especially those from New York."[17] Rivera continues, bonding various Afro-descended Americans through hip hop, poetry, music, and shared aesthetics tastes: "This rootedness of Nuyorican artistic expression within an urban Afro-diasporic context . . . frequently goes unacknowledged. Anglo/Latino and master/subaltern dichotomies are . . . privileged in discussions in U.S.-based Puerto Rican creative expression, and the tensions and connections between African Americans and Puerto Ricans are neglected."[18] To Rivera's point and bringing Pérez back into the discussion, Martin Wong's relationship isn't simply with Nuyorico, but also with *Black* and *Afro*-Nuyorico via personal relationships, artistic connections to hip hop, and Wong's own aesthetic and visual representations of dark-skinned Latinx and Black folks. This visual blackness is vital in discussing Wong's subtle and overt erotic, platonic, and creative investments in the Lower East Side, Nuyorico, and hip hop visual culture. From his more famous figurative works like *Penitentiary Fox* (1988) to his lesser-known works like *Sharp and Dottie* (1984), the figures Wong depicted were always medium-to-dark-brown-skinned people, often with kinky and curly hair—undeniably marking his canvases with blackness that was also Latinx. The visually racially specific figure embodiments are important in Wong's acknowledgment of the specificity of *latinidad* in New York—it was Black and brown.

Martin Wong Paints Queerly

In "Dropping Out: Martin Wong and the American Counterculture," Antonia Sergio Bessa situates Wong inside of a broader countercultural movement of the late 1960s and the early 1970s, as well as firmly placing him in the hedonistic and hypersexual world of New York City in the 1970s and 1980s. Nineteen-seventies New York was a place where "many gay clubs ... emulated dungeons, prisons, and torture chambers" in homage to the European-influenced leather culture.[19] Bessa is one of the few art historians writing about Wong who bothers to contextualize the formal queer aesthetic aspects of his paintings, ranging from recognizable queer subjects such as the late actress and drag queen Divine (*Divine*, 1979) to his street scenes of Lower East Side skateboarders and firemen (*Sweet 'Enuff*, 1988) to his more famous and obvious homage to gay male desire in the form of a giant brick phallus (*Mi Vida Loca*, 1991), Wong's aesthetic focus and musings weren't simply about urban decay, Loisaida (the Lower East Side), or Afro-*latinidad*. Rather, his paintings indexed a complex and complicated set of desires, concerns, and needs related to life in New York City, especially the Lower East Side and the East Village neighborhoods, which he explored through his poetic paintings. This way of seeing and depicting his love for New York is the essence of his queer visuality: chaotic, interpersonal, quotidian, kitschy, idiosyncratic, indulgent, and tinged with secrecy and desire.

In *Sweet 'Enuff* (1988, oil on canvas and muslin),[20] Wong envisions a fantastical Lower East Side scene through some of his most idiomatic visual tropes: firemen figures, AfriLatinx men, meticulously drawn bricks, visual sign language, and astronomical renderings. Like many of Wong's paintings, *Sweet 'Enuff* employs multiple framings: here derelict buildings, brick walls, and barbed wire fences, as well as a split-screen canvas, create multiple enclosures and modes of framing the work's subjects. Bessa emphasizes that Wong's use of enclosure and compartments reflected a preoccupation with carcerality, noting that within Wong's "architectural repertoire . . . [his] objects of desire are kept at a safe distance for his own enjoyment."[21] Lest Wong be rendered as some stereotypical homosexual creep inside a queer-antagonistic logic, his visual musings on the carceral, in terms of both formal prisons and jails and the carceral-in-the-city, demonstrate an attunement to the state management of Black and brown lives. Wong interjects the erotic, the intimate, the quiet, and the interrelational into some of these scenes, especially as the painting itself contains two side-by-side scenes placed together to make one image. The left side of the painting is one of stillness, perhaps mourning. In the foreground, a young man with dark brown skin and a Caesar-style (close-shaven) haircut hunches over a large boombox, his eyes closed and his arms resting over and on the large silent radio as if it is a companion he holds in solace. His well-defined, muscular arms are relaxed and his white tank top is gritty or dirty—matching the color of the decrepit apartment building behind him. A flash of gold chain—the punctum[22] of this part of the painting—pops as it lays gently on the back his neck. Nearby, two dark-brown-skinned men dressed in black-and-yellow firefighting gear stand behind him to our left. They are relaxed, hands tucked in pockets, not noticeably covered in soot or other evidence of fighting a live fire. They look past him in the opposite direction to something we viewers cannot see. The brick wall behind them slants from above the horizon to below it, shifting our gaze back

Martin Wong, *Sweet 'Enuff*, 1988, oil on canvas and muslin. Fine Arts Museums of San Francisco.

to the mourning man. From the decay of the ragged-topped buildings, a pristinely black night sky shines and, in the upper-middle sky, ornate sign language substitutes for celestial phenomena. Wong pulls us into this quiet scene, attuning the viewer to urban decay, melancholy and mourning, the aftermath of tragedy, and the loneliness that is possible in a large, densely populated metropolis.

The right side of the painting is bursting with a silent vitality and possibility: three young dark-skinned men fly through the air on their skateboards over a barbed-wire fence. As in the accompanying image to the left, none of the figures are fully visible. The bare-chested central figure leaps over the barbed-wire fence, performing a crail grab.[23] His face is one of both concentration and exhilaration as he escapes the confines of his surroundings toward an unknown destination. Following his gaze, the viewer's eyes are drawn back to the mourning figure on the right side of the painting. Separated by both the line down the center of the painting and geography, the central skateboarding figure very well might be making his way to comfort his friend/neighbor/lover/relative or he might be completely unaware of the mourning man's condition. The painting directs and entices our view without forcing us to concede or conform to one visual or interpretive perspective. The painting emits a timbre of gentle and solemn masculinity that indexes potential violence, but also interior forms of vulnerability. Darius Bost contemplates Black masculine vulnerability and how "artists . . . creatively and transgressively articulate vulnerability through various modes of expression."[24] Wong's work certainly addresses myriad forms and postures of Black and brown masculinity, including love, loss, desire, happiness, play, anger, and other modes of being. His paintings demonstrate that cultural expression can "explor[e] the intertwined relationship between various forms performances of Black masculinity and quotidian and spectacular forms of vulnerability."[25] Martin Wong's *Sweet 'Enuff* offers viewers a way of contemplating the temporal simultaneity of vulnerable Black masculinities—states of mourning and softness, states of play and contemplation, states of witnessing and aid. His own desire is painted throughout *Sweet 'Enuff*, comingling the whimsical and ethereal with the gritty, hidden, and palpable forms of Black and brown masculine vulnerability alongside Wong's sexual and romantic desire for Black and brown men.

A word of caution. I attempt here to articulate Wong's visual desire as mapped onto many of his paintings and interpersonal relationships. These expressions are not, however, metonyms for radical or progressive politics, lest we mistake sexual or erotic desire for political investments. Instead, I am teasing out some of Wong's social, aesthetic, and interpersonal investments, which certainly have implications for his politics. In many ways, I am following the cautions of Jared Sexton around the rush toward multiracial coalitions based on shared space, affinities, sexual desire, and activities. Sexton writes that we need "a sympathetic meditation on the need for more adequate models of racial analysis and strategies of multiracial alliance-building in and beyond the US context . . . [which do not] gloss over the discrepant histories, minimize inequalities born of divergent structural positions, and disavow the historical centrality and uniqueness of anti-blackness."[26] Sexton's analysis—specifically discussing post-LA riot race relations between Blacks and Koreans—challenges scholars and cultural critics to form coalitions that can bear and hold differing valuation, rather than succumbing to the logics of white supremacy masked as liberalism, which insists on flattening the historical, political, and social differences between racial groups in the US and beyond. My work highlights Wong's contributions and desires without insisting this erase his Asianness and the relative privilege that social location afforded him in both the nascent hip hop art scenes and downtown NYC's art scene.

Hip Hop, the Museum of American Graffiti, and the Downtown Arts Scene

Like his contemporary and fellow downtown artists associated with early hip hop culture, Jean-Michel Basquiat, Keith Haring, and Debbie Harry, Wong moved in circles that did not yet distinguish between the different art forms being produced in New York City's downtown neighborhoods of Soho, the West Village, the East Village, and the Lower East Side.[27] In the early to mid-1980s, the East Village was a "funky spiritual clubhouse to hip-hop crossovers" like Wong, Futura, and Haring; Soho was the bohemian haven of artistic success—Wong was able to occupy both spaces.[28] The "graffiti/neo-Expressionist and neo-Conceptual movements"[29] that flourished in the East Village and the Lower East Side provided a natural connection for graffiti artists traveling from uptown, the Bronx, or the other outer boroughs.

Martin Wong was both a creator and collector of graffiti, as well as a friend and mentor to many contemporary graffiti writers, including Daze, Crash, Lady Pink, Zephyr, and LA2. Wong donated much of his substantial graffiti collection to the Museum of the City of New York[30] and a portion of his estate is housed at the PPOW Gallery in lower Manhattan.[31] But first, Wong opened the now-defunct Museum of American Graffiti.[32] The Museum of American Graffiti was originally located at 6 Bond Street in the Noho (north of Houston Street) section of Manhattan; the grand opening was held on Saturday, April 8, 1989. The initial 50 pieces were from Wong's personal collection and included the work of graffiti artists Lazar, Sharp, Lady Pink, Wicked Greg, Seen, Mico, Futura, and many others, ranged from around 1970 to 1989. A story in *Art in America* underscored the interraciality of the museum's endeavor, noting, "A Chinese-American artist [Wong] with backing from Japanese collectors has established a new showplace for the largely African-American and Hispanic-American art form called graffiti art."[33] The article also mentions that Peter Broda, the co-curator, was Hawaiian of Japanese Ukrainian descent. The museum, its curators, and its supporters engaged in the murky area of racial contestation through their work within the experimental form of hip hop graffiti. Omi and Winant argue that "concepts of race were always politically contested" in relation to racial formation in the mid- to late 20th century. Racial formation in other locales—underground or independent street arts scenes—offer further articulations of racial formations and racial contestations. These sites may also teem with mistrust, misinformation, and anti-otherness. The key difference is that the racial projects that occurred in early New York City hip hop culture allowed for an outcome that wasn't predetermined by unbending political ideology and maneuvering. Omi and Winant describe racial projects as *"simultaneously an interpretation, representation, or explanation of racial dynamics, and an effort to reorganize and redistribute resources along particular racial lines"*[34] (original emphasis). I would argue the "racial" project that was the Museum of American Graffiti revealed something about the supremacy of the graffiti artist's skills over his or her racial grouping—here, the most skilled were primarily Black and Latinx men and a sprinkling of women. The museum was a racial project insofar as it indexed race by way of graffiti virtuosity—a freak, now-defunct aberration that provided a legitimate space for the outlawed practice of graffiti, while mussing up the easy, lazy racial categorization of artistic practices.[35] This is not to say that experiences of race and racialization don't matter, rather it is to index the ways 1970s and 1980s New York City graffiti artists seemingly refused the policing of race (and class, though not gender and sexuality) in their aesthetic and artistic pursuits. This is a strikingly different representation from the hip hop historiographies that have tried to recalibrate the white supremacist market histories by rendering early hip hop production through more contemporary racial logics. Looking back to the 1970s and 1980s with a contemporary eye renders that past quite queer. That Martin Wong, gay and Chinese and from San Francisco, became the de facto graffiti art historian due to his personal and professional relationships with graffiti artists of all five boroughs should speak to the aesthetic richness of hip hop art and its ability to do something anew with racial categorization. It might make sense to be suspicious of my claim that in the 1970s and 1980s race mattered differently in hip hop cultural production—I argue that skepticism is misplaced. Of course, Wong is not white, but his status as non-Black and non-heterosexual conspire to displace him from hip hop aesthetic history. In writing about Wong, I'm constantly reexamining what is at stake for me as a researcher, for hip hop studies as a broader field, and for the status of Black artists and thinkers often erased from the very forms we created and sustained. Pointing to Wong's importance in my work is not an effort to *replace* Black early hip hop artists and aesthetes, but rather to *connect* Wong to those people and communities as a friend, a mentor, and a member of a vibrant hip hop visual arts community. As graffiti and feminist performance studies scholar Jessica Nydia Pabón-Colón argues, "graffiti subculture celebrates social deviance and encourages participants to resist conventional ideas about 'growing up.'"[36] Graffiti's subcultural deviance-as-praxis collides with graffiti subcultural and hip hop cultural historicizing and memorializing practices. Remembering the subversive and free conventions related to hip hop graffiti connect it with practices related to Black and queer aesthetic modalities—furtiveness, community, rebellion, and repurposing—and that sometimes these aesthetic practices—hip hop, queer, and Black—coalesce into artwork and art spaces.

Opening Night at the Museum of American Graffiti

The opening night of the Museum of American Graffiti (MAG) on Saturday, April 8, 1989, was made keenly poignant by the Metropolitan

Transportation Authority's (MTA) recent removal of all subway car graffiti. Graffiti was now recognized as a public art practice, a public menace for the MTA, and studio art worthy of its own museum space.[37] This was a true reception. Wong's museum had letterhead, invitations, a telephone number, and a fax number. Located on the top floor of 6 Bond Street and funded by the shops and restaurants there and nearby, the museum's opener was meant to showcase around 50 pieces from its permanent collection (sourced from Wong's personal collection) and celebrate the artists who had made them. The pieces ranged from one of Barbra 162's designs (ca. 1970) to works made in just the past year. Graffiti and studios artists, as well as friends and family, showed up to celebrate the amazing artwork on display at MAG. Many of the artists, including Kies, Spider, Phase II, and Christopher "Daze" Ellis signed copies of their work. The photos in the Martin Wong Papers from that opening night are all candid, amateur shots, capturing the celebratory mundane of that important night in hip hop graffiti art history. In one photo, Kies and Wong—who is dressed resplendently in his infamous authentic firefighter's coat—sign and draw in sketchbooks for fans. The two stand on opposite sides of an ornate wooden desk and are flanked by other artists and attendees. Behind them, the walls and the floors near the museum's walls are covered in artwork. The museum reminds one of the interior of Wong's apartment, which was filled to the brim with artwork, canvases, supplies, and ephemera. Lee Quiñones's iconic *Howard the Duck* (1988) oil painting is above and behind Wong as he hunches over the table to write in a sketchbook. Lee's painting—a stunning 25-by-30-foot mural—depicts the eponymous Howard the Duck from Marvel Comics and the spectacularly abysmal live-action film adaptation (1986). In the painting, Howard, situated in the far right third of the painting, is pants-less and wearing a blue dinner jacket and a yellow-and-white polka-dot tie. He stands on a gray metal trash can that is tucked into a dark corner of an alleyway. His gloved hands hold the round garbage can top as a shield against the force of Quiñones's name, LEE—painted boldly and taking up nearly two-thirds of the painting. In the photograph, a brown child patron looks toward Quiñones's painting while standing below the "Lee" portion of the painting and faces the photographer, who is setting this whole scene. Though it was impossible to know at the time, Wong's choices in 1989 foreshadowed the longevity and importance of the art he had collected. Wong was an unusual curator, or perhaps I should write "curator." The Museum of American Graffiti was a simple affair with an aspirational name; it was first and foremost a community space for Black and brown artists, their families, and their friends. However, the short life of the museum turns my attention toward the possible tensions that could arise when Asian American and Asian European curators and funders create a museum space for mostly Black and Latinx artists. It's impossible not to think about the power differentials related to access, the actual geography of the MAG (pre-gentrification Soho, but still very much a white artists' location), and other issues of alienation and belonging that arise around institutionalization. Oddly, none of the three books written about Martin Wong's contribution to New York City graffiti and art world give any substantive attention to the Museum of American Graffiti.[38] In a short essay that discusses the museum in relation to Wong's prolific career as a graffiti art collector, Sean Corcoran, curator of prints and photographs at the Museum of the City of New York, makes these terse remarks: "Wong opened his Museum of American Graffiti April 8, 1989, on the top floor of a townhouse at 6 Bond Street in Manhattan. The inaugural exhibition was a salon-style hanging of cherished works from Wong's personal collection. The opening garnered attention from national press ranging from *USA Today* to *Art in America*. The Museum's second installation, a solo exhibition of Daze's work, opened June 2. Due to real estate conflicts, the Museum closed its doors after less than six months."[39] But what of the museum's import to hip hop graffiti and to hip hop historiography more generally? Corcoran illuminates Wong's centrality in revitalizing interest in graffiti across multiple art industries, including film, art studios, and galleries.[40] The essay reveals the importance of the museum to writers as they "came from all over to see Wong and sell him their work."[41] Though Corcoran's essay doesn't offer a more carefully considered analysis of the Black and brown progenitors of hip hop cultural production, it deeply foregrounds the unacknowledged significance of mentorship, sponsorship, or benefactors in hip hop arts. Though Corcoran doesn't explicit name it, most fundamentally, the fact that hip hop *was* art made by Black and brown "urban" youth and young adults who were far outside of the established norms of the art world, the museum world, and contemporary practices of art history curation is key in rethinking who and what make up commercial art worlds. And while the Museum of American Graffiti was short-lived, Wong donated approximately 300 graffiti works to the Museum of the City of New York (MCNY).[42] Reflecting on Wong's prescience during the MCNY *City as Canvas* exhibit (2014),[43] both Sharp (Aaron Goodstone) and Daze (Chris Ellis) noted Wong's expansive vision. Daze muses that Wong wanted to "become the Albert Barnes of Graffiti," referring to the celebrated collector of postimpressionist and early modernist artwork.[44] Sharp concurs that "[i]t's a great moment for Martin Wong because it's a commemoration of his vision. . . . No one thought what we did had any longevity, but Martin loved street culture."[45] Indeed! Sharp, Daze, and other Wong-era graffiti artists, like Lady Pink, continue to have flourishing careers as public muralists, graphic artists, graffiti experts, and studio artists—mixing street art with fine-art media such as sculpture, oil and acrylic painting, and graffiti-on-canvas.[46]

Tensions between graffiti writers showing in art world spaces and showing in open public spaces such as train yards, warehouses, street walls, and subway cars are often articulated as mutually exclusive and differently valued options. Joe Austin remarks on ways graffiti writers in 1960s and 1970s New York City spoke not "from some isolated or specially confined elite space such as an art gallery or museum," but from the highly circulating public space of the subway car.[47] Rather than thinking through the gallery space/subway car dyad as a hierarchy of authenticity, it may be more useful to construct both spaces as sites of public showing aimed at various and possibly overlapping audiences. Both the art gallery and the subway and their representational synonyms enunciate differing mobilities. There's the social and economic mobility made possible by being exposed to larger art world collectors, curators, and audiences and then the mobility of graffiti artists' artwork in and on MTA subway trains, which exposed them to the world and the authorities that would police the writers. As a response to the policing of public graffiti (associating it with criminality, youth of color, newly arrived immigrants, poverty, and urban decay), Wong's and others' focus on private-public spaces like the gallery, the museum, and the archive was a way to subvert moral panic. Though the middle and working classes were in a battle over public space, the elite and the working class made temporary alliances in galleries, cinemas, and other public and private artistic venues.

Collaboration in Martin Wong's World

As other hip hop scholarship has shown, early hip hop culture and the collaborations that came out of it were informal, as they hadn't coalesced under the banner of hip hop.[48] But these informal relations continue to bear aesthetic fruit, as MCNY's *City as Canvas* exhibit demonstrates. Multiple examples of these early hip hop aesthetic collaborations are explored in Charlie Ahearn's *Artist Portrait Videos* (1988), of which Wong's work and life is a part. Ahearn interviewed Wong at his Lower East Side home, showing the audience the apartment densely packed with Wong's own artwork, works in progress, and the work of other artists. *Artist Portrait Videos* begins with two young Black teens rapping and beatboxing on Walton Avenue in the Bronx in 1984. The content of their impromptu music-making is a call for participants to model for the molds that Rigberto Torres and John Ahearn are making of neighbors, friends, and strangers. Finally, Victor, a young Latino boy perhaps 10 or 12 years old, volunteers and steps away from the crowd that has gathered at the impromptu concert and art show. Victor is beautiful: his skin is nut-brown, he's shirtless in deference to the summer heat, his small, slightly muscled chest and skinny arms possess a tentative confidence.

Torres and J. Ahearn, right on the street, cover him in a plaster mold in front of a rapt Black and Latinx audience. They pour the liquid plaster over Victor's body; he's laid on his back on a wooden table, arms crossed over his chest, eyes closed. The crowd takes a collective deep inhalation as the plaster covers first his waist, then chest and arms, neck, and finally mouth, nose, eyes and head. The result is a mold of young Victor, which Torres and Ahearn paint into a startling likeness. Victor then presents the bust to his mother, who cries at receiving such an unexpected gift. Torres and Ahearn craft an additional bust for themselves. This narrative highlights some of early hip hop culture's porousness and intertextuality: rapping, beatboxing, visual art, and sculpture are all happening on the same street corner in the Bronx.

Later in *Artist Portrait Videos*, Ahearn turns his camera to Wong's work.[49] We're taken through a series of Wong's days and interactions: at a Chinese New Year celebration in New York City's Chinatown; showing us his iconic art filled with intricate brick work and images of firefighters;[50] exterior shots of his apartment building in the Lower East Side. Eventually we see Wong painting with both hands and speculating on the genealogy of graffiti artists ("A lot of graffiti artists, their fathers used to be hippies"). This is an unexpected connection, one on which Wong does not further elaborate in the video. What does he mean by hippie? Perhaps Wong was alluding to the ways that some of these artists had fathers who were antiestablishment revolutionaries, many of them inspired by Maoist principles.[51] For example, Ponce, Puerto Rico-born Lee Quiñones, star of *Wild Style* and the hip hop documentary *Style Wars* (1983), was a revolutionary graffiti artist, not only making public art, but reflecting on its significance and effects: "My sense of art was to create art without a reference point to art history, because this was art history in the making. A true art movement never goes by the script, instead it flips the script, faithfully reinventing itself."[52] Though Wong places the countercultural hat on the artists and their paternal lineage, he too was forging atypical paths as an artist and collector in the subcultures of hip hop graffiti art and the downtown art scene. Wong's own subject position as queer and Chinese inside of the worlds of the mostly Black and brown (and publicly straight) hip hop graffiti scene and the mostly white experimental art scene could have left him alienated inside of both art/performance scenes. Instead, Wong saved much of early New York hip hop graffiti art, recognizing its aesthetic, historic, and cultural value. Wong negotiated multiple juxtaposing identities in those early hip hop days: a gay man, a Chinese American, a San Franciscan, a Lower East Side resident, a person living with HIV, and later, AIDS. Though these subject positions could have rendered him a perpetual outsider, Wong's facility at being an unofficial curator of NYC hip hop graffiti aided him in building and sustaining relationships with a wide variety of Black and brown graffiti artists.

This opens up the realm of what I call "informed speculation." Looking across Wong's art and life, his main connections were with other artists, art venues, poets, social deviants, and those on the edges of society. Like New York City itself at the time, Wong embraced "[t]he degeneracy, deviance, and decay" that produced "a bastion for alternative lifestyles, unorthodoxy, and creative ferment"[53] in Wong's personal and professional lives. Like his paintings, Wong was deeply invested in the personal and life's quotidian moments rather than overt movements or social and cultural politics. That's not to say Wong had no politics—obviously as an artist and collector he reveled in coalition, relationality, neighborhood relations, and the connections between artists and writers that transgress borders of race, sexuality, class, and geography. But even those closest to him, and many who write about him, are publicly silent about his queerness, his romantic life, and the position of the homosexual within the hip hop graffiti scene of the 1970s and 1980s. Wong, though certainly not closeted, was clandestine, and I think this served him well. There's nothing I could find of him being part of NYC Asian queer groups like GAPIMNY[54] or even using services at Gay Men's Health Crisis (GMHC)—though, as someone living with HIV and eventually AIDS, he most certainly did make use of services offered at places like GMHC and the now-shuttered Saint Vincent's Hospital AIDS Ward, which was located at the intersection of 7th Avenue, Greenwich Avenue, and 12th Street in Manhattan's West Village neighborhood.[55]

I'd like to close this chapter with both a visual analysis of and some speculation about one of Wong's most famous paintings, *Attorney Street (Handball Court with Autobiographical Poem by Piñero)*. I offer a reading of the painting, but also of the collaboration between Wong, artist and writer Miguel "Mikey" Piñero, and graffiti artist Pito.

In Ahearn's *Artist Portrait Videos*, Wong discusses the unusual paths and influences of various graffiti artists, which leads him to reflect on how he met Miguel "Mikey" Piñero at the Lower East Side performance space ABC No Rio.[56] Wong recounts how the curators at ABC thought it would be great to have a "real criminal do a poem" for their exhibit *Crime Show*, as Piñero had spent time in prison.[57] Wong and Piñero struck up a friendship and Piñero often bunked with Wong when his own apartment on East 3rd Street got "too wild." One day, Wong recalls, Piñero brought four young men over to hang out at his place; one of these young men, Pito (aka Little Ivan), Piñero introduced as his son, even though he didn't have any biological children. Pito was a young, talented graffiti artist who had created an elaborate graffiti piece on a handball court on Attorney Street in Manhattan's Lower East Side. The three of them, Wong, Piñero, and Pito, decided to collaborate on a piece: a painting, poem, and graffiti work that became known as *Attorney Street (Handball Court with Autobiographical Poem by Piñero)*.[58] Wong noted that this was his first neighborhood scene and also his first sale (made to New York's Metropolitan Museum of Art), but it also represented a collaboration that brought together poetry, painting, and graffiti, demonstrating how fluid the bounds of art and hip hop really were and how expansive art-making inside of hip hop culture could be.

Attorney Street

Attorney Street is significant in terms of early hip hop culture and Afro-Asian/Asian-Latinx cultural production. *Attorney Street* is hip hop: it's collaborative, remixed, and reenvisioned (from Pito's earlier graffiti), and its focus is the "'hood"—in this case a handball court in New York's economically depressed Lower East Side: it's lyrical, visual, tactile, and even sonic (Wong's painting of words spelled in American Sign Language). Paintings, and visual art generally, don't often come up when discussing hip hop's genealogy and legacy, but that's short-sighted of those of us who value hip hop culture, performance, and history. Tricia Rose discusses rap music video and production as an opening in "a previously nonexistent creative arena for black visual artists."[59] On one level, that's true—Black visual artists didn't have as much access to certain forms of legitimized commercial visual art. On the other hand, beside the exceptional mainstream success of painter and visual artist Jean-Michel Basquiat,[60] there was the incredibly fertile (and illegal) hip hop graffiti movement that offered opportunities to make art publicly (although not without consequence and contestation from the authorities).[61]

Wong's *Attorney Street* situates Pito's graffito image at its center. The graffito is rendered in the iconic New York City "wild style,"[62] making it hard to decipher through its colorful brilliance. The painting, with its elements of architecture, sign language, poetry, and trompe l'oeil, is a series of frames and framing, narrow openings and fecund, overflowing enclosures—much like the neighborhood and city where it was produced. The interlocking geometries of Pito's art on the handball court's bottom half contrasts with the bare, grayish-white top half. The entire painting reflects this dichotomy of bareness/bareness and fullness/creativity of generating art in space. The black-and-red graffito is framed by smaller tags of other artists' names and messages. Two straight yellow lines that go up the vertical sides of the handball wall further encase it. Of course, the handball wall itself offers the canvas for the graffiti art. In the same perspectival line, Wong placed intricately painted hand signs (sign language) just below Pito's graffito. The sign language serves as a frame to the graffito, but also literally points toward it, directing one's eyes to what's directly above the abandoned brick buildings and the metal fencing that surrounds the handball wall: Miguel Piñero's "Autobiographical Poem."[63]

On one level, one could be dragged down by the desolation of the scene Wong paints—the empty handball court, the seemingly abandoned building just behind it. On other levels, the painting teems with life: the graffito itself evidences vibrant and vital creativity. The sign language not only speaks to us anew, the hands that speak it bring a quality of aliveness and human agency to the piece. Piñero's ethereal, dark words atop the painting underscore Wong's world making and remaking in his paintings. Dan Cameron explains that Wong's paintings in the 1983–1999 period "become a portrait of the artist in the unending process of analyzing and interpreting his environment, searching for points of access and identification that are resonant with his own experience."[64] Wong's work did expose a concern, a preoccupation, and a love for his neighborhood and surrounding neighborhoods. The Attorney Street in *Attorney Street* becomes a location of possibility and artistic ingenuity, which was the ethos of early hip hop: create something spectacular with and out of the mundane. The two outermost frames of the painting encapsulate Wong and his work; the top of the inner frame, made out of his painstakingly rendered brick motif, makes *Attorney Street* his and Piñero's. It reads from left to right: "Autobiographical Poem by Miguel Piñero • Attorney Street Handball Court 1982 • Rendered in paint by Martin Wong." The outer frame, the literal wood pieces that contain the painting, has hand signals carved into it on top. On the bottom, Martin Wong composed a short, whimsical street-poem/rap: "It's the real deal Neal / I'm going to rock your world / Make your planets twirl / Ain't no wack attack."

I have chosen to discuss *Attorney Street* because of the collaborative nature of the painting, as well as its intertextuality. Though Wong is well known for his figurative work, *Attorney Street* places him directly in hip hop's lexicon of visual artists. Though collaboration is itself not solely a "queer" method, the overlapping elements of erotic friendship between Pito, Piñero, and Wong, the continued speculation that Wong and Piñero were lovers, and the Asian-Latinx collaboration in early New York City hip hop graffiti culture make *Attorney Street* the perfect object of analysis. Additionally, discussing and analyzing *Attorney Street* in a book on queer aesthetics in New York City hip hop figuratively brings it out of the museum where it is decontextualized from Wong's hip hop life and work. *Attorney Street* is a queer hip hop work both methodologically and in terms of its content—it is Wong's most significant work in terms of conjoining hip hop aesthetics with queer aesthetics in New York City hip hop culture.

The Metropolitan Museum of Art lists Martin Wong as the sole author of the painting, although Wong himself titled the work *Attorney Street (Handball Court with Autobiographical Poem by Piñero)*, alerting viewers, art reviewers, curators, and collectors to the collaborative provenance of the painting.[65] Though Wong physically painted and conceptualized the work, it was built around Pito's already completed and "neighborhood famous" graffito, coupled with Piñero's poem and the Lower East Side landscape where all three of them lived and loved. It's not unusual for such collaborations to be erased by mainstream institutions—after all, they are the recorded memory institutions of the "master" artists, the overground, the establishment, and capitalist approval. Wong's art was messy, undisciplined, irreverent, collaborative, and hyperlocalized; *Attorney Street (Handball Court with Autobiographical Poem by Piñero)* is the collaborative curio hiding in plain sight. The title is the doorway to deep and sustained collaborations and reminds us as reviewers and appreciators of Wong's art to never forget his investments in creating, collecting, and curating alongside and in concert with others. It's also a reminder that one of hip hop aesthetics' most powerful and salient features is the insistence on collaboration, deconstruction, reimagining, reinterpretation, and group effort to produce artworks, dance moves, songs, videos, films, fashion, trends, and soundscapes.

Clones of Bruce Lee

I sometimes imagine what is must have been like for Martin Wong to pursue artmaking in the Lower East Side (LES) in the 1980s and 1990s.

Certainly, his homosexuality was a source of discomfort for *others* in the graffiti art world, though Wong's artwork demonstrates he was boldly and humorously out as a gay man—see the glorious *Mi Vida Loca (My Crazy Life)* (1991), a monumental painting that depicts a giant brick penis, made even more whimsical by the ornate gold-leaf frame in which it is displayed.[66] It is also clear that Wong was not the ever-alienated Asian in a hostile Black and brown world—he was embraced as a part of the LES graffiti world, as well the downtown NYC art scene. As graffiti artist Sharp makes clear, Wong "got a 'ghetto pass' to the LES. After getting jacked a few times, [he became] recognized as part of the community and people would let him go."[67] Here, Sharp notes that Wong "paid his dues" after initially getting robbed and harassed in the neighborhood. Once it was apparent that Wong was a member of the community, he became a staple. Wong was a confidant, a friend, a collaborator, a mentor, an inspiration, and a safe haven. This gay Chinese American, native San Franciscan made the Lower East Side his own; he forged relationships based on mutual respect with his graffiti artist collaborators and subjects.[68] Wong was in a cadre of artists, many affiliated loosely or closely, who occupied Manhattan's Lower East Side, East Village, Soho, and West Village as spaces of residence or work or both. Martin Wong, interested in the longevity of graffiti art, was both a vociferous collector and a prodigious artist. He, along with the Ahearn brothers, Patti Astor, and Diego Cortez, used his cultural capital as a museum and gallery artist to aid graffiti artists like Daze, Sharp, Dondi, and others to get their work in front on broader art audiences. As Wong's art, life, and collections are revisited through works like *Sweet Oblivion: The Urban Landscape of Martin Wong* (1998); NYU's Asian/Pacific/American Institute exhibit *Downtown Crossing* (2009); the Museum of the City of New York's *City as Canvas: Graffiti Art from the Martin Wong Collection* and the book of the same name (both 2014); and the Bronx Museum of Art's exhibit *Martin Wong: Human Instamatic* (2015–2016) and the resulting publication (2016), as well as increasing interest from scholars and artists in Wong's archives at New York University, PPOW, the Museum of the City of New York, and other venues, his hip hop legacy and his significant contributions to New York City's graffiti culture continues to grow, expand, and flourish. In 2014, nearly 20 years to the date Martin Wong donated his prolific collection to the Museum of the City of New York, the museum produced *City as Canvas* both as an exhibit and a printed volume to irrevocably connect Martin Wong to New York City hip hop graffiti art.

2

Nigga Fu

The Last Dragon, *Black Masculinity, and Chinese Martial Arts*

This chapter locates Black desire inside of the martial arts cinema house, wherein the burgeoning aesthetics of hip hop culture in New York City and the well-established Black and Latinx[1] audiences of Chinese martial arts cinema met in the 1970s and 1980s, making for a queer site for Black masculinity. "Nigga Fu"[2] argues that the modestly budgeted Hollywood film *Berry Gordy's The Last Dragon* (dir. Michael Schultz, 1985), financially successful on its original release and now regarded as a cult classic, narrates a complex, queer set of negotiations relating to fantasy, desire, masculinity, fetish, and power placed upon the figure of the Black martial artist film star. Unlike Martin Wong, who was somewhat of an anomaly in Black and Latinx arts communities, the Black martial artist, paradoxically, is located comfortably inside of African-diasporic aesthetics.[3] I argue that the appearance of Black martial artists in early hip hop film is a continuation of the Black male exile who must go "East" to locate his masculinity.[4] I propose a nuanced look at the heterosexual love story in *The Last Dragon*, which manages to resist heteronormativity and give us a complex Black masculinity that emerges from identification with Chinese martial arts masculinity.

Eating Popcorn with Chopsticks: Revisionary Black Masculinity in *Berry Gordy's The Last Dragon*

Berry Gordy's The Last Dragon performs a disruption of racist Hollywood depictions of Black men through the use of satire, stereotype, kitsch, camp, and fantasy. The film depicts its unconventional hero,

Leroy Green, a young Black martial arts master, as an endearingly odd embodiment of Orientalist stereotypes. For instance, in one scene Green watches Bruce Lee's film *Enter the Dragon* in a midtown Manhattan movie theater, while wearing traditional Chinese male clothing (Cantonese: *cheongsam*) and a straw hat as he eats popcorn with chopsticks. This mise-en-scène is heavily coded in Western Orientalism and also in Black fantasies of and desire for the grandeur of Chinese culture.[5] White society is absent in the film and both the Black hero and Black villain of the film are invested in parodic and limited versions of Chinese and Japanese cultural forms, respectively. The film relieves us of the inevitability of a Black-white racial binary by reframing this particular world as Black-yellow. As M. T. Kato argues in discussing the globalization of martial arts popular culture, "The popular cultural revolution . . . offers a space in which autonomous subjectivity alternative to the dominant mode can be constructed."[6] *The Last Dragon*, a box office success,[7] functions as a fantastical space wherein Black (director Michael Schultz) and mixed-race (screenwriter Louis Venosta) authors and the audience engage in a complex, entertaining, and problematic relationship with Chinese and Japanese martial arts popular culture placed in a New York City context. The movie theatre functioned as another site of early hip hop aesthetics, especially in the 1970s and 1980s, as martial arts, Blaxploitation, and hip hop films all attracted hip hop youth.[8] In her review of Kimberly Monteyne's *Hip Hop on Film: Performance Culture, Urban Space, and Genre Transformation in the 1980s*, Rennette McCargo underscores Monteyne's emphasis on the ways the hip hop films communicated "[u]nderground messages of societal woes from Latino and African American performers. . . . [Consequently,] film producers featured Latino and African American street performers alongside performers who were considered a part of a more disciplined art form."[9] Though Monteyne does not include *Berry Gordy's The Last Dragon* in her study of hip hop film musicals, her description of such films and the way they have been reviled in broader hip hop and hip hop film history speaks directly to the explicit queer aesthetics in *The Last Dragon*. She argues, "The very first hip hop film musicals . . . have generally been considered poorly made works . . . regarded as disposable and unremarkable cinematic effort[s]." Monteyne goes on to describe the critiques from notable hip hop and film critics—and academics—as dismissive largely due to what she maintains is the "heterogeneous and rather unruly nature of these early productions."[10] Because these films eschewed standard narrative tropes of "authentic" hip hop film—the Black gangster, the meditation on particular neighborhoods, and a sort of race loyalty—their import is muted or ignored. *The Last Dragon* shares many of the qualities of these "inauthentic" or "frivolous" hip hop films: it centers racial heterogeneity through metaphorical and embodied miscegenated characters (Leroy Green, Laura Charles, the Yi Brothers); gangsterism is a gag; and the film mashes up film genres (musical, comedy, satire, martial arts film, coming-of-age story, love story, urban dramedy) with gleeful wildness. Louis Venosta, *The Last Dragon*'s screenwriter, told me he wanted the film to reflect what he experienced growing up in 1970s New York City and that he had incredible ambitions for the work. For Venosta, the film obviously referenced and cited Blaxploitation and Hong Kong martial arts films, but he also wanted to do something different and tell a story about a Black Harlem family.[11] Venosta recounts seeing Bruce Lee's famous film *Enter the Dragon* on 42nd Street Times Square, noting that young people would wear martial arts regalia to watch the film. He dreamt of making the film a Broadway musical with the martial arts fighting standing in for dance sequences. Venosta originally envisioned this genre-crossing film as a more straightforward urban coming-of-age story with either actor Mario Van Peebles or martial artist Billy Banks playing Leroy Green, but Taimak's portrayal adds an unexpected queer element. Taimak's portrayal of Green is key to my reading of this film as a queer hip hop object. Taimak's Leroy is meek, naïve, a virgin, and the opposite of the worldly Black men in both hip hop and Blaxploitation films. This unexpected casting, with Prince protégée Vanity as the love interest, makes for much more nuanced and complex Black cinematic masculinity than either Van Peebles or Banks is known for. The employment of Michael Schultz as director makes sense as his cinematic relationship to Motown started a decade previously with his helming of *Cooley High*—a coming-of-age dramedy whose soundtrack featured Motown hits of the 1960s. Schultz's extensive directorial experience telling the stories of young Black men in urban settings in feature films that were heavily musical (*Cooley High*, *Car Wash*, *Krush Groove*) allowed him to bring a cinematic expertise to match Venosta's vision. Schultz's own canny ability to negotiate multiple generic devises enabled him to keep *The Last Dragon* from becoming too incoherent or unfocused under the film's tremendous narrative ambitions to be a love story, a martial arts hero's journey, and a coming-of-age story. Yet that same wonky narrative ambitiousness provides compelling material related to *The Last Dragon*'s queerness. Below, I explore how Leroy Green, the film's protagonist, embodies Black masculinity in a way that queers hip hop, urban, and Black film expectations and traditions.

The Last Dragon narrates the journey of a young Black Harlem martial arts practitioner, Leroy Green (Taimak Guarriello), who has reached the end of his training with his teacher (Thomas Ikeda). Leroy must venture into the wider world (other parts of Manhattan) to attain his last stage of actualization—the Glow (the culmination of the pupil's "dragon" training). During his search, Leroy finds a love interest in a local club celebrity, Laura Charles (Vanity), and encounters two raffishly, comically wicked bad guys—a bullying martial arts tough guy–for-hire named Sho'Nuff, the Shogun of Harlem (Julius J. Carry III), and Eddie Arkadian (Christopher Murney), an impish arcade czar. The feel-good narrative ends with Leroy defeating the bad guys, winning the heart of the successful, worldly woman, and cementing his reputation as a local hero. Although *The Last Dragon* ends in a typical, formulaic heterosexual romance, the film resists heteronormativity. Instead it provides us with a queerly virginal hero who is able to navigate martial arts masculinity and Orientalist feminization in order to offer a new model of Black masculinity that contradicts and contrasts with that of hip hop film protagonists. Leroy is immersed in the imaginary martial worlds of places like Hong Kong or Foshan, even though his material world is defined by Harlem hip hop dance, slang, and fashion. Leroy's embodiment as an odd—queer—figure, a Black man obsessed with martial arts culture, materializes the experience of Black and brown youth at the time. The twist is that his lack of worldliness and sexual prowess, rather than his martial arts obsession, is what queers his Black masculine performance.

The opening scene of *The Last Dragon* unfolds like many films from Shaw Studios and Golden Harvest, the two preeminent Hong Kong martial arts film studios in the 1970s and early 1980s. Like the opening sequence of the Hong Kong print of its genealogical, aesthetic, and nominative forebear *Enter the Dragon* (1973), *The Last Dragon* commences with a musical martial arts montage.[12] The viewer is treated to Leroy Green—a young, sweating, brown-skinned, wavy-haired, muscular man—practicing his martial arts forms. There are three quick shots of him—frontal, profile, and back to a frontal shot. It reads as a riff on a mug shot. Rather than ending on the profile shot, the camera reorients the viewer, interrupting the overdetermined idea of the young muscular Black man as a criminal. Leroy begins with a bow before cycling through punching and kicking poses, flips, and pectoral flexes. His topless torso is awash with perspiration. It's clear from his precise, fluid movements that he's no novice. Leroy performs a final front kick—his right thigh touching his chest and his foot coming above his head. During his routine, we're privy to shots of his white kung fu pants clinging to his firm, round posterior. The camera jump cuts from more flowing movements to Leroy flexing his chest and arm muscles. He's in a contemporary industrial interior setting, complete with plywood floors and brick walls.

The viewer's expectations of a martial arts training sequence are interrupted by the prolonged, delightful display of the Black male physique moving in rhythm with the musical accompaniment. Leroy's punches are thrown to music, his forearm flexes are on the downbeat, and he sometimes gestures in cosmetic ways that have no discernible practice or fighting efficacy. This display of the body and of martial arts is aligned with grace, beauty, flexibility, improvisation, and femininity, as well as with power, force, precision, mastery, and masculinity. In the 20 seconds between Leroy Green bowing to his absent *sifu*, or master, and doing a spinning back jump kick, it's almost impossible to read this as only a martial arts story. As the opening credits appear and the title song, "The Last Dragon," by Dwight David, begins, Leroy's movements become increasingly recognizable, though not less fluid, as fighting moves: he kicks, he punches, he lets out an audible yell, he performs manly push-ups. One might imagine a bit of relief coming from a typical martial arts film viewer seeing this for the first time: "Ahh, phew! This *is* about martial arts. I was scared there for a minute." Scared of what, one might ask? That the film would fail to reaffirm the masculinized artistry of martial arts and the Black martial arts body, as well as that body's violent potential. The fear/relief dyad frames the way Leroy is characterized throughout the film as non-macho and as possessing untrustworthy or alien masculinity. Leroy is a Black Orientalist construction. As Asian American and African American studies scholar Helen Heran Jun argues, "black Orientalism encompasses a range of black imaginings of Asia that are in fact negotiations with the limits, failure, and disappointments of black citizenship."[13] Ironically, Leroy confounds US racial categories and logic precisely because his characterization as a Black-Chinese hybrid places him outside of strict Manichean categories of racial taste, behavior, and aesthetics. Leroy is racialized as a Black man inside of a Black family, yet his performance of blackness is wholly informed by Chinese martial arts film and culture. Chinese popular culture is the genealogy of his particular blackness—an Afro-Asian hybrid masculinity. In the preceding chapter on Martin Wong, I explored how the visual artist expressed the connections between Black and Asian masculinities in his paintings of Black and brown men of Manhattan's Lower East Side and East Village neighborhoods; here, Leroy Green's character internalizes and embodies an exaggerated and naïve vision of a Black Asian man. Leilani Nishime's work on multiracial Asianness is useful for thinking through Leroy's racial characterization in *The Last Dragon*. In one set of arguments,

Nishime rethinks the political and material possibilities and limitations of visibility politics as they apply to race.[14] Nishime argues, "We can not . . . learn or wish away the visuality of race. To literally not see agreed-upon markers of racial difference would mean that one did not learn to see the world in a socially meaningful way."[15] Leroy's self-image and self-stylization is not contingent on already established categories of racialization; in fact, he more closely aligns with another of Nishime's insights in which she follows Michele Elam's work on Black-white mixed-race representations in media in asserting "[a]esthetic forms can indicate the everyday and emergent expressions of cultural meaning before they coalesce into empirically measurable phenomena."[16] At the level of martial arts aesthetics and *The Last Dragon*'s own pastiche aesthetics mixing funk, disco, hip hop, martial arts, and New York City 1980s fashion, Leroy's Afro-Asian presentation is a rational experiment in the context of 1980s New York City.

The film consistently plays with and reminds the audience of its multiple aesthetic and generic legacies. For instance, the aforementioned opening scene also highlights the intersection and comingling of Blaxploitation and martial arts film cultures. African American studies scholar and historian Sundiata Keita Cha-Jua, following David Desser, notes that Chinese martial arts films, like Blaxploitation films, were popular with Black audiences as they "were the only films [shown in the US] with nonwhite heroes and heroines . . . and they featured 'an underdog of color,' often fighting against the colonist enemies, white culture, or the Japanese."[17] Another factor in their popularity among Black audiences is that Blaxploitation and martial arts films were shown in the same theaters,[18] often as double features. Whereas Cha-Jua performs a Pan-Africanist and Black nationalist reading of the intermingling of Black-Asian cultures, in this chapter I show how Leroy Green offers an alternative model for Black racial formation, queer heterosexual Black masculinity, and a hybrid cultural identity. He and the film serve as an example of the popularity of Chinese martial arts films in US Black communities.

The Last Dragon seems to elude either Pan-Africanism or Black internationalism, which some scholars have argued underpinned Black audience interest in Chinese martial arts films.[19] The film is a comedic urban kung fu musical that was able to capitalize on the US kung fu craze of the 1970s and early 1980s. Film historian David Desser notes, "Warner Brothers realized with particular clarity that the Blaxploitation audience and the emerging martial arts audience were rather consonant."[20] Although the success of famed Blaxploitation films like *Superfly* (1972) and *Foxy Brown* (1974) and Hong Kong martial arts films like *Fists of Fury* (1971) and *Five Deadly Venoms* (1978) had waned in box office performance by the early and mid-1980s, the two genres maintained established and emergent fan bases through replay on local television stations ("Drive In Theatre") and in specialty movie houses located in the Chinatowns of large cities.[21] Unlike the virile cinematic demonstrations of dark-skinned Black masculinity on display in many such films, Leroy Green (and the actor, Taimak, who plays him) wears his racial mixedness in the body as well as on the body. Taimak, an acting neophyte, brings a tentativeness that sometimes makes him appear stiff and out of place next to more experienced actors; this sometimes detracts from a scene. At other times, Taimak's newness to acting adds a fresh-faced quality to Leroy's character and makes Leroy's cluelessness more palatable. It is in fact, director Michael Schultz's proficiency at comedy that significantly shapes *The Last Dragon* and its camp aesthetics, particularly his ability to depict outrageous characters like Sho'Nuff and Eddie Arkadian alongside more "straight" characters like Laura Charles and Leroy Green.

The obvious Hollywood contemporary to *The Last Dragon* is *The Karate Kid* (1984). In that film, Daniel (Ralph Macchio), a dark-skinned Italian, working-class, New Jersey transplant to California, finds himself an outsider in his new, more affluent white Anglo community. Although white, Daniel, like Leroy Green, does not fit into the localized idealization of racialized masculinity. It is through Daniel's martial arts training and prowess that his "foreign" white masculinity is recontextualized as powerful and recognizable. Leroy makes a similar journey in *The Last Dragon*.

Leroy Green (Taimak) enjoying some popcorn at the movie theater. *Berry Gordy's The Last Dragon* (dir. Michael Schultz, 1985; Motown Productions, TriStar Pictures).

Though *The Last Dragon* was part of a wider trend of martial arts fetish in Hollywood films including early hip hop films, it differed from films like *Breakin'* (1984) and *Beat Street* (1984), which were only peppered with visual cues of a martial arts and hip hop arts relationship. *The Last Dragon* centers the martial arts and martial arts identity of the protagonist in a multiracial New York City context. It also differed from an independent Black martial arts film centered in New York City's Lower East Side, *The Deadly Art of Survival* (1978), by featuring a protagonist who demonstrates counternormative forms of Black masculinity, rather than the more normative modes of Black masculinity of 1970s Blaxploitation films.

The Last Dragon's politics are localized even as certain characters and relationships may hint at macro-allegories such as enduring East Asian conflict (Leroy/Sho'nuff), US interventionism (Eddie Arkadian), and diasporic racial identities (Yi Brothers). There are myriad vectors that shift when place, space, and context are reframed. Leroy Green offers alternatives to hegemonic heterosexual patriarchal masculinity, inflexible and rigid ideas of Black masculinity, and demasculinized and Orientalist notions of Asian masculinity. Concurrently, he is able to embody a masculinity that embraces and celebrates qualities that have been traditionally socialized as feminine. Leroy, who "fails" at a particular form of idealized Black masculinity, concurrently "succeeds" in forging an alternative Black masculinity that takes its aesthetic, philosophical, and social cues from a fantasized Chinese martial arts identity.

The Last Dragon as Intervention

Ed Guerrero's foundational book on Black cinema, *Framing Blackness: The African American Image in Film*, investigates the "dialectical push of Hollywood's cultural construction and domination of the black image and the pull of an insistent black social consciousness and political activism that . . . generated waves of black-focused and independent films into commercial cinema's trajectory."[22] *The Last Dragon* was a "Black" production on many levels: from its producer, Motown's Berry Gordy (who came to the film late in the process but nonetheless placed his name in the title), to its Black director, Michael Schultz; its screenwriter, Louis Venosta, who is mixed race with Black, Native, and white ancestry; to its stars Vanity, Julius Carry III, and Taimak (who is Black and Italian). *The Last Dragon* is a visual narrative about the lives of Black people living in Manhattan in the mid-1980s, but also a Black intervention into the business and industry of cinema. It's by no means perfect: its use of parody, satire, and camp sometimes render the narrative silly or incomprehensible, and it's sometimes just poorly executed. Yet these aesthetic methods also disrupt masculine hegemony and open up the possibilities for an "incoherent" masculinity. Performance studies scholar Tamara Roberts's reading of masculinity-as-performance in Teatro Luna's play *Machos* is illuminating for my read of Leroy's queered Afro-Asian masculinity. Roberts narrates:

> This queering of masculinity . . . comes from the play's resonance with the predominant theatrical venue for cross-gender performance: drag

shows. *Machos* differs from drag by focusing less on heightened, stylized, or kitschy performances of gender and more on its everyday performativity, but there is no doubt it similarly capitalizes on the titillation of cross-dressing. . . . [D]rag is generally performed in LGBTQ venues and often to arouse queer desire. . . . This framework does [not] negate the potential for queer consumption, but it does suggest that the target audience is not a queer one.[23]

The Last Dragon is cinematic, so its conventions like staging, audience, environment, scripting, direction, intimacy, and blocking are all different from theatrical ones. In cinema, the camera (and lighting and score) is the main orienting and framing device, while in theater the physicality of the actors often determines the focus of the viewers' eyes and attention. Still, Roberts's observations on *Machos* invigorates my thinking about the relationship between masculinity, queerness, and race in *The Last Dragon*. While *Machos* queers cisgender-heterosexual Latinx masculinity by disrupting gender-sex norms through gender drag, *The Last Dragon* explores racial drag through camp, kitsch, and stereotype. Here, I'd like to focus on kitsch and camp as they signal a lack of seriousness, value, and masculinity. Kitsch is associated with inauthentic, cheap, gimmicky, low/pop culture, with imitation, gaudy, tasteless "art": think shot glasses from Myrtle Beach, South Carolina, or a T-shirt with President Obama as Che Guevara (something I actually purchased in Beijing). I'm invoking multiple meanings of Black and kitsch: first, there is cinema studies scholar and filmmaker Manthia Diawara's discussion of Donald John Consentiono's neologism "Afrokitsch" or, as Diawara writes it, "afro-kitsch," which he describes as ambivalent and multidirectional.[24] In a terse, pithy essay, Diawara concludes that films like Spike Lee's *Do the Right Thing* (1989), a 1965 Radio Mali performance of Junior Wells and His All-Star Band, US R&B of the 1960s, and political figures like Malcolm X and Angela Davis exemplify Pan-African modalities of the "kitsch of blackness," which he describes as "zones of ambivalence [of] identity formation, sexual politics, and hybridization [as a series of] . . .

postmodern subjects of blackness [that] attempt to prevent [blackness] from falling into the same essentialist trap as whiteness."[25] This bizarre, ahistorical ending, in which US Black art is somehow paralleled with an unspecified whiteness, does not quite derail from Diawara's more cogent points: blackness reorganizes relationships to categories and categorization, including with itself. As Tavia Nyong'o told me when I queried him about the difference between racist kitsch and racial kitsch in his stellar essay, "Racial Kitsch and Black Performance," Nyong'o envisioned racial kitsch as "holding open a space to appropriate racist kitsch."[26] The appropriation and redeployment of racist, as well as misogynist and queer- and trans-antagonistic kitsch, is part of the strategic messiness of Black and queer and hip hop performance. These redeployments do not emerge neatly or without gaps, remainders, and critiqueable claims, yet they provide space and form to modes of being and expressivity which complicate the misshapen violence that racist (and/or misogynist and/or queer/trans-antagonist) claims seek to make. These Black/Afro kitsch performances mark rebellious, unsanctioned blackness that speak or act or appear with interrogative flamboyancy. And though *The Last Dragon* predates "post-blackness" as a hermeneutic and artistic movement, as an art object it takes up the challenge of queering Black images as it redeploys them through kitsch and camp.

The second meaning of Black and kitsch I invoke draws on the work of Derek Conrad Murray, who deliberates on the relationship between kitsch, queerness, post-blackness, and art in "Mickalene Thomas: Afro-Kitsch and the Queering of Blackness." In this essay, Murray works through the tangles of the rise of post-blackness as an artistic modality and form in Black visual arts. Murray argues that Black Gen X and millennial (and presumably Gen Z) artists use their work to "open[] up a needed conversation around post-blackness and its significance in visual culture as an iconoclastic queering of blackness. Post-black discourse questions the ideological parameters and visual rhetorics of blackness as potentially alienated and noninclusive on gender and sexual difference."[27] Murray locates post-blackness temporally and generationally in relation to the post–Civil Rights Movement and post–Black Power Movement era, rather than simply as an expression of post-Black identity. The conflation of "post-Black" with shedding identarian, communal, psychic, political, and relational Black bonds is troubling to Murray. He wonders, "What happens when an African American [or Black] artist no longer sees the critical potential of the black body, or has become disinterested in the political and polemical importance of its imaging?"[28] In many ways, Murray answers his own question by turning to Mickalene Thomas's famous riff on 1970s Blaxploitation imagery in her mixed-media painting *Hotter than July*.[29] Thomas is customarily placed into the category of "post-Black," yet the artist centers Black women—almost exclusively—across her paintings, photography, collages, and mixed media works. Thomas's post-blackness is elastic, queer, kitsch, relational, and firmly oriented toward the historical and present weight and importance of Black imagery. Murray argues that *Hotter than July* reconceptualizes heteronormative sex tropes through a "distinctly [Black] queer-feminist lens." Further, Murray considers this "queering . . . a means of rendering the black body strange: of giving it a signifying potential that allows the possibility for new meanings to be constructed."[30] *The Last Dragon* and Leroy, specifically, is a ripe site to re-view Black masculinity through Black queer-feminist modalities: camp and Black kitsch. Leroy's queered anomalous Black masculine presentation opens up the discourse around Black men and hegemonic masculinity. Akin to Mickalene Thomas's *Hotter than July* painting, one can view Leroy as a redeployment of 1970s Blaxploitation figures in films such as *Dolemite* (1975) or the original *Shaft* (1971). While these films relied on Black heteronormative tropes such as sexual prowess associated with dark-skinned Black masculinity, as well as skilled martial arts and other forms of violence, Leroy represents the anthesis and possibly even a rejection of Black Power–era masculinity. He is "post-Black [Power]" and displays an exaggerated form of martial arts masculinity. Further on in this chapter, I'll discuss Leroy's feminization in relation to Chinese martial arts. Here, I'd offer that in comparison to figures like Dolemite

Mickalene Thomas, *Hotter than July*, 2005, acrylic, rhinestone and enamel on wooden panel. Rubell Museum, Miami.

and Shaft, or even Sho'Nuff, *The Last Dragon*'s Black villain, Leroy fails to live up to Black Power–era and other forms of popular hegemonic Black masculinity. Patricia Hill Collins argues that hegemonic masculinity is "primarily defined as *not* being like women. [This masculinity is] forceful, analytical, responsible, and willing to exert authority."[31] This construction of "real men" is meant to distinguish them both from women and from other men who lack access to approved masculine performances.

Leroy's characterization interrupts the seamless relationship between hero, violence, and masculine hegemony. His soft-spokenness, inscrutability, pacifism, and humility align him with racialized and feminized modes of being according to hegemonic and patriarchal logic. In fact, Leroy Green's uncommon cinematic Black masculine gender affect resonates with Mark Anthony Neal's meditation on another Leroy—Leroy Johnson (Gene Anthony Ray) from the film and television hit *Fame*

(1980, 1982–1987). Although the characters are radically different, sharing only a first name, racial and gender status, and neighborhood (Harlem), their differing but important interventions into popular images of Black masculinity might reframe popular imaginations to include more expansive gender performances rather than favoring and reaffirming hegemonic masculinity, ad infinitum. Neal argues that Ray's Leroy possessed a "radical quality to [his] queerness]." Though neither the character nor the actor who portrayed him was ever confirmed as gay, as both a street tough and a prolific dancer, as hard-bodied yet introspective and world-weary, Leroy Johnson "offered a view of black masculinity that is so seductive . . . because it challenged the pervasive and undecidedly unsophisticated images of pimps and petty criminals . . . that regularly circulated on commercial television in the 1980s."[32] To be clear, Neal is not arguing that Leroy Johnson was a "positive" image; rather, he concludes that Johnson was a complex, nuanced image of Black masculinity. The circulation of images is not the only thing that influences and impacts Black youth (and others) who consume them. These images, both Leroys in this case, grab our attention because they so decisively move away from cardboard images promoted by a white media establishment that reinforces the notions that Black masculinity is either pathologically violent or obsequiously acquiescent to hegemonic (white) masculinity. When one encounters a representation of Black masculinity that wanders off those well-worn and wearying paths, it is worth noticing and contemplating.

Bruce Lee, Bruce Leroy, and the Feminized Hero

One of the ways *The Last Dragon* disrupts dominant images of Black masculinity is by shifting the genealogy of Leroy Green's particular masculine embodiment. Though Leroy inhabits a phenotypically Black body, the prototype for masculinity in this film is Chinese martial arts masculinity as popularized by the figure of Bruce Lee. As Asian American studies scholar Mimi Thi Nguyen observes, Lee "inhabits the film as a spectral mentoring presence"³³ right down to Leroy Green (nicknamed "Bruce" Leroy by his younger brother, Richie, and others in the film) wearing a replica of Lee's famous yellow-and-black jumpsuit from *Game of Death* (1978). Ngyuen argues that Lee's image is used in *The Last Dragon*, sometimes to comedic effect, to underscore Leroy's devotion to and absorption in Lee. In one scene, Laura Charles, Leroy's platonic paramour, "attempts to seduce Leroy with a wall-high video montage of Bruce Lee's films . . . resort[ing] to another male's body as a sexualized spectacle."³⁴ The idea of getting in the mood for love escapes Leroy; instead he is inspired by Lee's use of disguise in his own quest for the fictitious Master Sum Dum Goy. Part of Leroy's characterization as an innocent and sexually pure warrior is an updated version of the Chinese romantic hero from 1950s and 1960s Hong Kong cinema.³⁵ Film theorist Stephen Teo explains, "The tradition of the effete romantic hero had been established in literature and theater. Character roles in Chinese opera and the traditional theatre were divided into *wen* (meaning civil) and *wu* (meaning martial). On the *wen* side was the *shushing* (or scholar), a role with a performing tradition which passed into cinema through opera film and other period films."³⁶ Yet the *wen/wu* division is not always so clear as Teo asserts. Teo's own reading of the *wen* and *wu* demonstrates the overlap and shifting value of idealized masculinity across nation, time, media, and genre.

In "Body, Masculinity, and Representation in Chinese Martial Arts Films," Chinese literary and film scholar Jie Lu argues, "Despite a weak and effeminate body, the *wen* type is no less masculine than the *wu* type. In fact, because elite scholar officials, the embodiment of the *wen* type [in premodern China and its representations], held the reins of political power, the *wen* was more highly regarded than the *wu* type."³⁷ This proliferation of Chinese masculinities gets lost in translation as US action heroes are rarely of the "unheroic" type, unless they are the alter egos of superheroes. Lu notes the transition of esteem from *wen* to *wu* was a Maoist project aimed at combating Orientalist notions of the Chinese as the "sick men of East Asia."³⁸ Bruce Lee as a contemporary *wu*

Chinese martial arts star was the literal and symbolic embodiment of the "proletarian body of Mao's China . . . [and helped] to redefine Chinese masculinity and reconstruct the cultural image of China."[39] The US-born Lee was the poster boy of contemporary Chinese masculinity and emblemized anticolonial masculinity in both China and the US. Lee's characters were often from lower social classes and his type of muscular, powerful, working-class hero also constituted a challenge to Chinese normative masculinity. As noted earlier, a working-class martial arts hero resonated with Black audiences, but a de-eroticized hero presented an affective fission for a US hegemonic audience engaging a Black masculine hero.

Leroy, modeled in part after Bruce Lee, follows a different iteration of a *wu* hero. Though Leroy Green would be in the lineage of the *wu* Chinese hero, he also incorporates aspects of the traditional *wen*. Lu elaborates: "The *wu* hero shows strength and maleness by totally eschewing feminine charms; while the *wen* scholar, always associated with women, demonstrates masculinity by giving up erotic desires in order to fulfill ethical obligations."[40] For most of *The Last Dragon*, Leroy seems to be unaware of Laura Charles's romantic attraction to him. His is not a suppressed heterosexuality but rather an asexuality—or a lack of visible sexual attraction or sexual desire. This seems to distinguish him from the traditional *wu* and *wen* types as he is not *choosing* celibacy or practicing sexual abstinence, he simply does not express any sexual or romantic desire until the film's very end. Leroy's masculinity is also situated in relation to his lack of heterosexual prowess. When placed alongside other cinematic representations of Black heroes in the martial arts, Leroy can be said to still be a boy. Although he is a martial arts master, he fails to pass the test of Black heteronormativity due to his virginal status that is at odds with his martial virility. Patricia Hill Collins reasons, "Boys constitute yet another benchmark used to construct hegemonic masculinity. . . . Boys are quasi women. . . . [U]nlike men who have had sexual intercourse with adult women, primarily by genital penetration, boys remain sexual virgins."[41] Leroy fits other Collinsian markers of boyhood: financial dependence (in the form of living at home), submission to an authority (when he kneels to Sho'Nuff so his student, Johnny, won't be hurt), and a lack of collegial homosocial bonds. As a matter of fact, most of Leroy's interpersonal relations involve other teenagers like himself or his younger sibling, Richie. His social circle consists of his family and teenage and child students. At the same time that Leroy's virginity, fastidiousness, soft-spokenness, and naïveté fail hegemonic Black heteronormativity, these characterizations help to reinscribe enduring and problematic stereotypes of Asian masculinity.

The *wen* scholar and *wu* fighter recognizable in Chinese cinema and stage as two of many proliferating masculinities get collapsed into a stand-in for Asian masculinity in US cinema. How does having that type of masculinity in a Black body disrupt the fantasy of Chinese male effeminacy and Black male bestiality? For one, Leroy's virginal innocence coupled with his martial arts prowess marks him as an enigma in the film and also in the lexicon of Black film heroes. When the villain Sho'nuff, the Shogun of Harlem, and his fighting crew first appears in the movie house where an eclectic, rowdy multiracial crowd is watching *Enter the Dragon*, Leroy is amused and unperturbed by Sho'nuff's showmanship. Leroy, seated in the front row of the theater, enjoys a snack of popcorn (eaten with chopsticks) while Sho'nuff discursively and physically establishes himself as a martial arts fighting force. Leroy is literally unmoved by Sho'nuff's threats and instead responds with amused smirks and Confucian-esque proverbs. Sho'nuff's inspiration for challenging Leroy is prompted by the outrageous tales of Leroy's martial arts prowess such as catching bullets with his teeth. Sho'nuff frames Leroy as "mysterious [and] elusive]" but also reacts to his alleged exploits by properly framing Leroy within a common US Black vernacular lexicon of disbelief by saying, "nigga, please." Sho'nuff is one of the few characters that attends to Leroy's Black Orientalist identity, allowing him both the stereotyped attributes of the "Asian"—elusiveness and mystery—and the more pedestrian characterization of an unremarkable Black man in New York City ("nigga, please"). Sho'nuff also displays a similar penchant for hybridized

Asian-Black masculinity. As his name demonstrates, Sho'nuff favors the Japanese-inspired clothing and affect of a shogun. He mixes shogun and samurai traditional clothing with more contemporary flair—high-top Converse sneakers.

Sho'nuff's appearance and his conflict with Leroy play out as a familiar narrative for viewers of *The Last Dragon* who were also martial arts fans. Japanese forces often represented bitter colonial memories in Chinese martial arts films. Defeating a Japanese foe was a standard plot in many 1970s and 1980s Chinese martial arts films. Sho'nuff's invocation of the familiar, vernacular "nigga" pulls the viewer out of the fantasy Leroy's presentation mandates. As one might expect, Sho'nuff calling Leroy "nigga" fails to regulate Leroy into proper Black masculinity, as Leroy has shaped himself through Chinese martial arts masculine genealogies, making him less susceptible to localized methods of racial and gender shaming. Leroy understands he is Black, yet his relationship to the blackness of his contemporaries is tenuous, at best. Leroy fails to respond to certain Black vernacular calls. Part of his journey throughout the film is learning to pay attention to the Black world around him as much as the fantasy Chinese world of the films he so loves. Leroy, then, gets to rework his relationship to Black masculinity vis-à-vis his conflict with a dark-skinned Black man and a love relationship with a light-skinned Black woman—he "grows into" his blackness through these relations.

What might fasten together Leroy's particular relations, set of desires, emergent heteromasculinity, Black sociality, and Asian martial arts fantasy? Critical anthropologist Jafari S. Allen makes a series of theoretical arguments that illuminate how we might arrive at an answer. Allen makes the case for thinking "Black" in conjunction with "diaspora" when he schematizes "Black/queer/diaspora [as] an organic project of multivalent and multiscalar reclamation, revisioning, and futurity (yes, all at once)."[42] Allen reminds us that Black diaspora incorporates locations, rooting and uprooting, and routes in reference to "conditions of movement and emplacement, and to processes of (dis)identification."[43] Most relevant for my thinking is his assertion—following Jacqueline Nassy

Brown's work—that diaspora is constructed through "relationality . . . [as blackness is] conditioned by particularities of place, in relation to discourses and practices within other places."[44] Leroy's process of negotiating Black masculinity, Black heterosexuality, Asian masculinity, and sexuality inside of the local economy of mid-1980s Manhattan does not appear more or less complex than the processes that other characters engage in, yet we are meant to view him as strange and/or exceptional. I reason that this is, in part, because of the anxieties Leroy's character raises in being relatively divested from a Black masculinity that is rendered through white Eurocentric norms. Leroy does not appropriate Asian martial masculinity in order to dominate, reclaim, or bolster an emasculated Black masculinity. Rather, he is invested in martial arts aesthetics: film, form, genre, conduct, propriety, legacy, and decorum. In this way, Leroy becomes a queer figure, as he—like the Black queer— has found "ways to connect some of what is disconnected, to embody, and re-member."[45] Leroy's project of remembering or reinhabiting and corporealizing Black masculinity evidences the expansive possibilities of Black masculine embodiment. Black masculinity as an embodied, emergent project need not be based on relation to white, patriarchal, or hetero norms. Instead, it can be a project that emerges in and through embodied engagement with aesthetics of Black fantasy, martial arts films, Black communal relations, family ties, and space for creative embodiment. In the next section, I rethink Black masculinity through the figure of Leroy.

Rethinking Black Masculinity

Like other Black youth, Leroy makes "meaning out of the material and imagined resources of the popular world . . . contribut[ing] to the creation of a global popular culture that is geographically boundless."[46] Fanon Che Wilkins is speaking here more broadly of the connection between hip hop youth and the hip hop artists who embraced martial arts philosophies based on Shaw Brothers martial arts films; they merely take another path in an Afro-Asian martial arts sensibility. Leroy's masculinity is asynchronous and extrinsic, but it's not ahistorical. Can his particular type of Afro-Asian masculinity, which reaches beyond admiration for the disciplined martial arts body and embraces a queer spectrum of gender performances, be seen as a revision of the problems of feminization? It is a generative puzzle whether the process of feminization of men can be recuperated as something liberatory and whether feminization can be used as a new way of living and embodying masculinity. In *Scripting the Black Masculine Body*, Ronald L. Jackson II poses this provocation: "What does one do with fictive corporeal representations that eventually become so fixed in the public imagination that they are no longer considered false?"[47] *The Last Dragon* is not a mere inversion of scripted Asian, Asian American, and Black American masculinities so much as it is a pastiche of localized New York City cultural and popular influences. In this fictive cinematic setting, Leroy was not completely unusual, even if his particular expression of a hybrid Chinese-Black masculinity was odd.

Leroy serves to destabilize the fiction of fixed universalist white heterosexual masculinity. Bruce Lee, and Bruce Leroy by extension, advocated for adaptation, flexibility, and hybridity both in martial arts and as a larger moral philosophy.[48] This type of flexibility reflects Leroy's disruption of racialized gender systems. As J. Jack Halberstam reasons, "[racial m]inority masculinities and femininities destabilize binary gender systems in many locations . . . [and] they also have the power to reorganize masculinity itself."[49] Halberstam argues that characters like butch lesbian Cleo in the film *Set It Off* (1996) inhabit the "intersection of stereotyping and counterappropriation."[50] Leroy is similarly situated in the interstitial space between Asian stereotypes and Black ones—a place of possibility. Might we rethink the conundrum in relation to the feminization of "the Asian" in Western epistemology if we frame Leroy as having a form of feminized masculinity or alternate masculinity that is valorized rather than devalued? Leroy is a phenotypically Black male imbued with stereotypes of Asian men, a precarious deployment that never fully shakes off its troubling aspects of reinscribing the desexualized Asian man. Perhaps Leroy opens up a space for a meditation on the play between masculine and feminine performance in martial arts films. He exemplifies how we might contemplate the complexity of Chinese gender presentation in martial arts films.

Jie Lu articulates the complexities of the masculine performance of Li Mu Bai (Chow Yun-fat) in Ang Lee's *Crouching Tiger, Hidden Dragon* (2000). Lu claims *Crouching Tiger, Hidden Dragon* has been "feminized" through Ang Lee's intervention into "the macho tradition of martials arts,"[51] noting that three of the film's five martial arts protagonists are women. This feminization of the traditional macho martial arts film narrative yields complex masculinities and femininities among the film's heroes and villains. Li Mu Bai, for instance, through environmental displacement and the removal of the homosocial bond, is afforded a pensive, exploratory relationship to his masculinity.[52] Lu also observes that the technology of martial arts mastery allows Jen Yu (Ziyi Zhang), daughter of a Manchurian governor, to play with an ambivalent, transgressive, and aspirational gender performance that can be read as "an intrusion into the traditionally masculine territory of violence."[53] Similarly, Leroy Green destabilizes notions of what we think is true about Black men, Asian men, and heroic masculinity. The character embodies an erasure of Asian (American) male bodies from the heroic position, but also deters us from foreclosing "knowledge" about said bodies. Leroy is a racial possibility at play: problematic and generative at the same time.

David Eng reminds us of the concomitant relationship of race and sexuality. Eng, following Lisa Lowe's insistence that racism and (hetero)sexism cannot be comprehended in isolation, posits that racial and sexual fantasies "must be understood as mutually constitutive, as drawing their discursive legibility and social power in relation to one another."[54] The mutually constitutive forces of race and gender narratives concerning Black and Asian masculine legibility and authenticity play out in *The Last Dragon* on the body of Leroy Green. A recurring motif in the film is that Leroy is unrecognizable or incomprehensible. Leroy frustrates other characters precisely because he evades controlling images of Black men and Asian men through his synthesis and application of his idealization of Bruce Lee's type of heroic martial arts masculinity. Leroy never suddenly transforms from awkward nerd to worldly hero, thereby refuting a well-known trope in heroic and martial arts films. Throughout the film he remains wide-eyed, gullible, literal, and earnest. His characterization is refreshing in this context as he performs as rescuer and martial arts combatant without assuming normative modes of masculinity. Even though Leroy seems aberrant in this New York City context, he has achieved martial arts mastery and a type of martial arts masculinity through quite conventional means—he's worked under the tutelage of a recognized martial arts master. In a rigid racial and gender taxonomy, however, Leroy is coded as other—unable or unwilling to present a cohesive Black, Asian, or masculine performance. He navigates an exploratory masculinity and femininity that defeats normative modes of masculine physical violence and power (Sho'nuff) and masculine economic violence and power (Eddie). Leroy's points of "feminization" do not result in a (permanent) lowered status, ostracization, or deviation from heterosexuality. There is no punishment for his gender trespass. Leroy exemplifies a heroic, popular, "feminized" Afro-Asian masculinity, which serves as a template for alternatives to hegemonic masculinity. Yet director Michael Schultz smartly confounds the expectation that most masculine places and spaces are safe for Leroy. If Leroy does not quite fit in with notion of Black masculinity as laid out in the film, neither does he find initial acceptance in Asian spaces outside of his *sifu*'s *kwoon*.[55]

"Black and Yellow, Black and Yellow": Leroy Green and the Yi Brothers

Another example of Leroy's queered hybrid masculinity comes through his two encounters with the Yi Brothers—sometimes called the "Seoul

Brothers" by fans—which serves as a geographic and material conflation of Korea and China, while also working as an aural and auditory pun on "soul brother." In these two cinematic moments, Leroy is unable to pass as Black, even though he "is" Black, while the Yi Brothers inhabit blackness as a racial affect, even though, as men of Chinese descent, they "aren't" Black. The Yi Brothers, Hu (Henry Yuk), Lu (Michael G. Chin), and Du (Frederic Mao),[56] speak jive, effortlessly embody contemporary Black social dances, and inhabit Black aesthetic coolness. Leroy first encounters the Yi Brothers after another romantic "disaster" with his would-be paramour, Laura Charles. After rescuing Laura from villain Eddie Arkadian, Laura and Leroy return to her sumptuous bachelorette pad, where she attempts to seduce Leroy. (She also returns his lost medallion that he still believes once belonged to Bruce Lee.) Though Leroy is quite attracted to Laura, it is clear that he is out of his comfort zone. As they lean in for a kiss, he snaps out of his erotic haze, jumps up, recites a parable about the "cock's crow"(!), and leaves. Laura is bemused and charmed by her effect on Leroy. As she ponders the potential meanings of "cock's crow," repeating the phrase out loud, the song for the next scene begins, serving as a transitional device between their romantic encounter and the masculine display of the Yi Brothers. The pop-R&B song "Suki Yaki Hot Saki Sue," performed by Raw Dog, written by Kerry Ashby Gordy and John West, and produced by Ashby and Benny Medina, brings into stark relief the complexities of racial stereotypes, fantasy, camp, kitsch, and popular expressions of Black Orientalism.

On the first syllable of the song, "suk," the scene shifts from the interior of Laura's house to the exterior of New York City's Chinatown. We're oriented in Chinatown through a quick shot of a replica of a traditional Chinese multistory building (*lou*). Leroy makes his way through Chinatown via Canal Street asking for directions to or information about Master Sum Dum Goy. The scene underscores his difference via apparel: he is the only person in traditional dress as everyone else is contemporarily attired. By contrast, the Yi Brothers are hip, even cutting-edge. Hu, the tallest, wears an embroidered *kufi* (a West African men's cap), Lu wears black leather pants and a mesh see-through black top, and Du, the youngest, wears a sleeveless muscle shirt and sweatpants. Their dress contrasts with Leroy's concealment and restraint as they wear multicolored clothes that accentuate their bodies through fit or style. Their dress communicates their "blackness" while Leroy's demonstrates his foreignness, oddness, or queerness.

"Suki Yaki" moves from an exterior orienting and descriptive function to an interior perfomative scene when, 30 seconds in, we see the Yi Brothers lip-synching and dancing to the song. The three brothers dance in sync while attracting a crowd of Asian, Latino, and Black men and women. They, like Leroy and the city around them, deploy a mix of cultural signifiers and gestures: a black Afro pick, a white fingerless glove (referencing both Michael Jackson and Madonna), moonwalking, and the dancing style of male Motown groups from the 1960s and 1970s. Leroy enters the scene about a minute into the song, and his confusion is apparent. Unlike the other members of the crowd, he is not entertained, happy, or clapping along. He is searching for the master and cannot reconcile the brothers' dancing with the signs "Sum Dum Goy" and "Fortune Cookie" that hang above the building. When they finally end the song and the crowd begins to disperse, Leroy engages them. The Yi Brothers are quick, dismissive, sharply funny, and cutting with their "disses" of Leroy. Du starts off asking, "What yo' look'n fo'?" When Leroy responds that he is looking for the master, the brothers respond:

> HU: Ain't no masters here, dude. Ain' no slaves, either. (*The Yi Brothers laugh and high-five each other.*)
> LEROY: (*stares blankly, then back at signs*) Is this not his fortune cookie factory?
> DU: The master, he uh, doing his wisdom thang. (*The brothers laugh.*)
> LEROY: I seek only the wisdom of the master.
> HU: You want wisdom? You buy fortune cookie.
> DU: Take a hike, cool breeze.
> LEROY: Please, I must see the master. It is very important to me.[57]

At this point, Du becomes visually and verbally agitated with Leroy and denies the would-be acolyte access to the master, saying the illusive figure "doesn't see nobody." Du also insults Leroy's social skills and ability to read social cues by calling him "chump." He then racializes the insult by calling Leroy a "jive coolie," disrespecting Leroy with a mixture of Black vernacular cool and Orientalist, imperialist dismissal.[58]

The scene turns somewhat sinister though not violently so (after all, we know Leroy can handle himself in a fight). The Yi Brothers' insults shift from making fun of Leroy based on his anachronistic presentation and affect, calling him a "square," to specifically calling out his foreignness. The first time Lu intercedes in the conversation he serves as a "translator" between his brothers, the gathered audience, the film audience, and the "non-native" Leroy. Lu offers to "say it so that [Leroy] can understand." He removes Leroy's hat and adopts an exaggerated "Chinese" broken-English lexical pattern:

> LU: You go now. Chop chop. Haul ass out of this place. (*He turns to his brothers.*) Am I saying right, my man?

Leroy is dumbfounded. Unable to respond in the moment, he stares blankly as the Yi Brothers laugh at his misfortune and say goodbye to him in various languages. Lu even neglects to return Leroy's hat.

The scene repositions the legibility of both Black and Asian masculinity. Through its deployment of inverted stereotypes (the Black man as the out-of-place foreigner, the Asian men as the arbiters of effortless cool), our fixed renderings of Black and Asian male representations are upended, temporarily. This modality returns us to Mark Anthony Neal and his discussion of the ways that Leroy Johnson "represented the foundation for a queering of black masculinity in contemporary popular culture."[59] Leroy Johnson, young, handsome, dark-brown-skinned, muscular, and from the hood is "queer" not by his racial affect—he is after all marked by his Bronx-bred, angry Black man, "hood nigga" status—but by his gendered trespass. Leroy Johnson, resplendently muscular, cornrowed, and in possession of a fierce eye roll, is marked as a challenge to or interruption of seamless heterosexual Black masculinity by his commitment to and passion for ballet and modern dance. Though their queer markers differ, both Leroy Green and Leroy Johnson intercede in popular notions of *proper* or *authentic* Black masculinity. Neal argues that this Black male illegibility serves as a "radical rescripting of the accepted performances of a heteronormative black masculinity."[60] Hence, the Yi Brothers could not see Leroy because they could only to him in only two ways: either as a fellow modern Black man who was able to speak their language and look like them—tasks that Leroy failed—or as an unassimilated Chinese foreigner who could never gain access to the master because he was too "square" to be trusted. To the "brothas," Leroy doesn't read as a proper Black male subject; his racial affect and performative identity is at odds with his visible racialized skin color. Leroy's concerns—meeting Master Goy, attaining the Glow, teaching martial arts—differ from those of his contemporaries. His masculinity is atemporal, as well as aracial. He is not defined by intra- or intergroup discourse on Black American masculinity, nor is he defined against it. Rather, Leroy seems to be open to exploration, resisting simple "cures" to systemic racism and claiming to be solely defined by his individual qualities. Concurrently, Leroy remains curious about what he is "missing" vis-à-vis Black popular culture; he is inquisitive about certain aesthetic and affective choices attributed to Black people, but he lacks any sense of shame about how he comports himself. *The Last Dragon* offers us a possibility quite different from the Black masculinity of 1970s Blaxploitation films: skin color or any other phenotypical characteristics doesn't determine racialization in this world. "Race," in the film, seems more related to cultural references and experiences, language and speech patterns—race is a crafted project rather than a historically or socially determined one. But what is the impact of this framing or my reading of it in this way? There are myriad ways this framing could be taken up. Here, I am not arguing that race is simply an illusory construct without attendant historical, material, contemporary, and structural impacts and effects on racialized bodies—particularly those rendered as Black. Rather, *The Last Dragon* operates as a fanfiction[61] and reimagines racial geographies, histories, and implications inside of its world. This type of "what-if" scenario, typical in speculative and science fiction narratives, allows *The Last Dragon* to manipulate racial codes and signifiers, and to animate Black masculinity with the tools of fandom, fantasy, kitsch, and imagination.

Leroy Strikes Back: Leroy vs. the Soul Brothers

When Leroy next encounters the Yi Brothers, he's shed a tad of his naïveté. Sho'nuff has harassed his family, his students, and humiliated Leroy by demanding he "kiss [Sho'nuff's] Converse" in order to protect one of his martial arts students. He's even shared his first kiss (with Laura) while watching a Bruce Lee film. Inspired by Lee's phone technician disguise in *The Chinese Connection* (1972), Leroy returns to the Yi Brothers' storefront posing as a pizza deliveryman. This time he is dressed to the nines in dark shades, a white Borsalino small-brim Havana hat, a form-fitting button-down maroon shirt, and some unflattering (but contemporary) green slacks. Before ringing the bell to the Yi Brothers' business, Leroy practices his Black vernacular greeting, "Hey, my man, what it look like?" in various timbres and cadences, each iteration sounding hilariously stilted and unnatural.

Unlike the previous encounter, Leroy is allowed entry into the Sum Dum Goy fortune cookie factory. His clothing style and his poor adoption of Black vernacular "jive" speech forestall the Yi Brothers' dismissal. But something has changed with the Yi Brothers. They still perform *de rigueur* 1980s New York City urban working-class Black masculinity: they play "craps," they speak jive, they wear stylish and outlandish outfits, and they relentlessly police the boundaries of cool. However, the move inside of the fortune cookie factory conjures up other facets of the Yi Brothers' Black affect and shifts the racial dynamic relationship between the brothers and Leroy. When the brothers discuss Leroy's pizza delivery, they break into Cantonese; as a matter of fact, in this scene they speak Cantonese among one another three times. They seem confused, unsure, and wary of the impact of their decision to allow Leroy into their sanctum. Finally, they lapse into standard English. Rewatching the scene, it may invoke a sense of unease in the viewer. Was this scene undoing the performative possibilities of their Black masculine affect? Leroy isn't similarly made to fit into more recognizable forms of Black masculinity: he never masters "cool," or jive, or any of the contemporary moment's Black affectivity that would allow him to pass as authentic or recognizable. How might one parse the unease that accompanies the Yi Brothers' very last speech acts in the scene, which are unaccented, well-spoken standard English, as it seems that both Black vernacular speech and Cantonese are linguistic covers for a "model minority"?

In *Excitable Speech: A Politics of the Performative*, Judith Butler asks us to think through the performativity of the speech act. Her chapter "Burning Acts, Injurious Speech" takes seriously linguist J. L. Austin's "distin[ctions] between illocutionary and perlocutionary acts of speech, between actions that are performed by virtue of words, and those that are performed as a consequence of words."[62] What are the consequences or impact of the Yi Brothers' shift in speech? The second Yi Brothers scene accentuates the performativity[63] of speech—words, vocal patterns, affects, gesture, accent—to enact an effect; here they are constructing a prophylactic racial subject through citation. "Prophylactic" because this racial performativity can be shed or can cover, at least in the case of the Yi Brothers, depending on the exteriority or interiority of a situation. These racialized speech acts offer safety and protection from anti-Chinese violence, but they expose the elasticity of racialization, even when using the broadest and most clichéd Black stereotypes. A Butlerian performative also brings to bear the reality of power. Butler's "perfomative 'works' to the extent that it *draws on and covers over* the constitutive conventions by which it is mobilized. . . . [N]o term or statement can function performatively without the accumulating and dissimulating historicity of force."[64] The Yi Brothers' trilingualism exhibits the negotiations of safety, assimilation, and desire. They are able to master linguistic and discursive markers that facilitate making a living, while providing them with the protection of Black masculinity's "sophisticated cool" when they relate to other non-state actors. Since the state and its forces (police, court systems, state-appointed lawyers) are absent from the film, it is unclear how the state would view the Yi Brothers' Black affect—perhaps as a curiosity or a joke, most likely not as a threat to state power.

Leroy's encounters with the Yi Brothers demonstrate the film's early-to-mid-1980s imagined New York City, where "race" is shed at will. It's a destabilizing vision couched in comedy. Perhaps the comedy, the absurdity, and the well-worn stereotypes contribute to the film being dismissed as a site of racial investigation, but *The Last Dragon* refashions the dialectics of US racial "truths" that form along the white-Black dyad. George Lipsitz challenges readers to encounter what is "generate[d by] new ways of knowing by concentrating on objects of study that confound conventional modes of inquiry."[65] "Bruce" Leroy Green and the Yi "Soul" Brothers are complicated, rhizomatic instances of the interstices of racial performance. They are not authentic, they are not even necessarily "positive." They offer slippery moments of racial unintelligibility. Though Leroy and Lu, Du, and Hu are in some ways managed by other characters in the film or the film's own writing of them, their ongoing resistance to staid classifications reminds us of the embryonic quality of race in *The Last Dragon*—Black and Asian bodies are constantly reperforming, remaking, undoing, redoing, and exploring racial positions, racial affect, and racial subjectivities.

Fraught Representation: The Question of "Bruce" Leroy Green

In her essay "He Wanted to Be Just Like Bruce Lee: African Americans, Kung Fu Theatre and Cultural Exchange at the Margins," literary scholar Amy Abugo Ongiri explores the pronounced African American interest in Asian kung fu and martial arts culture. Ongiri is especially interested in the ways that African American usage of Asian kitsch commodities differs from white mainstream Hollywood usage. She prods

Black engagement with what she calls "Kung Fu Theatre" (and, more broadly, the "Drive-in Movie") and the cultural exchange that occurred between Black and Latinx audiences and Chinese filmmakers."[66] Ongiri, unlike many others interested in Black-Asian exchange around martial arts culture and film, mentions *The Last Dragon*. Ongiri troubles "the obvious danger in conflating African American interest in kung fu films with a positive possibility for cultural exchange.... *The Last Dragon* ... was replete with outdated stereotypes and oddly scripted 'jokes' around the infatuation of the central African American character, who is called 'Bruce Leroy,' with Asian culture."[67] Ongiri rightly points to the use of stereotype and the Black imagination in relation to Asian and Asian American martial arts masculinity, but we differ in our readings of the usage of these tools. Indeed, the film uses racial stereotypes as sight gags and as sites of critique. The film has running jokes about Leroy's naiveté and non-normative Black masculinity and shocks on a whole host of levels in homage to earlier martial arts, Blaxploitation, and camp films. The film unapologetically adopts racial stereotypes about Black Americans, Asian Americans, and white Americans. It fetishizes the mixed-race body in the form of Leroy, Laura, and even Johnny, Leroy's Asian-white martial arts student. *The Last Dragon* is about Afro-Asian plurality and performativity, not necessarily Afro-Asian unity.[68] *The Last Dragon* exemplifies a more typical Afro-Asian reality—one that relies on ahistorical borrowing and adaption of other national and cultural artifacts and affect. To dismiss the film solely because it uses stereotypes misses what the film does with those stereotypes. The film's multiple moments of critique of Leroy as well as the central fact that Leroy, with his queer and quirky masculinity, *is* the central heroic figure serves to complicate, though certainly not eradicate, racial and gender stereotypes. By casting *The Last Dragon* as solely exploitative of Chinese and Chinese American culture and performance, Ongiri forecloses a reading of the film's considerable Black queer masculine affect, as well as the ways Leroy's and the Yi Brothers' racial performativity and deployment of racial stereotypes destabilize race and racial abjection.[69]

Ongiri's argument flattens the fecundity of the film, which uses racial and ethnic stereotypes smartly and subversively. For instance, Leroy's racial "infatuation" is an embodied one—one that also destabilizes tropes around authentic Black heterosexual masculinity and around effeminized Asian masculinity. Leroy's character and characterization, it seems, presents a different sort of revolutionary: he's racially coded as Chinese, even as his skin color, tone, and familial lineage relations code him as Black. In fact, Leroy Green never verbally self-identifies his race, or class, or gender, or sexuality. This film most definitely shows and doesn't tell, except that other characters *do* tell of his racialization (his brother calling him a "coolie"), as well as his gendered sexuality (calling him a wimp when he refuses to fight, saying he doesn't have sexual moves).

The film shows that young, urban Black men don't have to be confined by popular, state-mandated, or state-mediated notions of Black masculinity. Neither does a Black man have to rely on prescribed whiteness in order to find an alternative to restrictive heteronormative Black masculinity. Leroy is a constructed Black masculine project: his "Chineseness," based on valorization of Bruce Lee's cinematic martial arts masculinity; his *wu* performance, wherein he is asexual but develops and explores his attraction to his paramour, Laura Charles; and his non-normative feminized masculine embodiment contour, extend, and compliment the limitations of racial stereotypes and redirect us to the expansive work that racial performance and racial affect can do.

Further, the film and its characters, especially Leroy and his nemesis, Sho'Nuff, live on in a curious space: hip hop iconography. Though hip hop culture has been taken to task for its hypermasculinity,[70] the affective nonmimetic relationship to Leroy Green in hip hop is telling vis-à-vis his heroic prowess and longevity in a cultural sphere that is purported to reject masculinities like the one Leroy inhabits. Yet hip hop film festivals consider *The Last Dragon* a foundational hip hop film,[71] rappers name themselves Bruce Leroy, and a fan site dedicated to the film has an active Twitter and web presence.[72] Its influence comes from hip hop artists, Black youth, and those into Black pop culture circulating and recirculating the film within and outside of Black cultural spheres. *The Last Dragon* and its erstwhile hero have not toppled patriarchy and did not undo the hold hegemonic masculinity has on Black popular culture, but it has survived and thrived in the most unlikely of places: at the intersection of the homosocial world of hip hop, kung fu, and fantasy. Leroy Green, virginal, awkward, and ill fitted for the "mean streets" of mid-1980s New York City, has been elevated to iconic masculine status. His revolutionary queer and hybrid Black masculinity continues to intercede into masculine hegemony and offer Black boys, men, and masculine people a different and exploratory means of embodiment.

3

"Casebaskets"

Listening for the Uncanny in Jean Grae

In the first two chapters of *Hip Hop Heresies*, I've argued that, though grounded in Black diasporic aesthetic forms and interpersonal relations, New York City hip hop is also a rich site of Asian diasporic cultural production and Afro-Asian imagination. Martin Wong's contribution to the downtown art scene, as well as to New York City's vibrant graffiti and street art culture, made flesh the connection between Asian American visual artists and AfriLatinx hip hop production in New York City. *Berry Gordy's The Last Dragon* and its Afro-Orientalist hero, "Bruce" Leroy Green, served as a cinematic bookend to Wong's real-life influence on New York City graffiti and New York City hip hop culture's salient and powerful performance aesthetics while displaying the Black communal affection for martial arts popular culture through the vehicle of a Hollywood film. *The Last Dragon* attempts to reconfigure an idealized version of mid-1980s Harlem and downtown New York City where Black people and their social life move unmolested through both New York City and various cultural, institutional, racial, and economic worlds with ease and aplomb. In differing ways, both chapters address the relationships between masculinity, queerness, hip hop aesthetics, and race.

If the first two chapters worked through Asian American and Afro-Asian visual culture and forms of queer masculinity in New York City hip hop, this chapter attends to Black womanhood, queerness, and aesthetics inside of New York City hip hop cultural production, specifically through the figure of Brooklyn-based[1] rapper, singer, and producer Jean Grae. In shifting from the visual to the musical, I turn toward Black feminist thought and psychoanalysis as primary methods of analysis.

There are a great many women and girls in hip hop culture and history who deserve critical attention. Many scholars are writing or have written academic works about hip hop feminism;[2] hip hop luminaries such as Lil' Kim and Nicki Minaj;[3] women and the US South;[4] Black women, sex work, and hip hop;[5] and much more. Scholars continue to write and present conference papers on important women hip hop figures such as Rapsody, Megan Thee Stallion, NoName, Cardi B, Missy Elliott, Junglepussy, MC Lyte, Queen Latifah, Saweetie, Salt-N-Pepa, Lauryn Hill, Remy Ma, and many others. Jean Grae as a figure and performer presents unique opportunities to think through physic affect, gender performance, queerness, and Black womanhood. She is socially and historically important not only as a long-standing, independent, successful woman hip hop artist, but also for the vibrant insights she gives us into her character's interior. Though Grae rarely raps or sings about Black womanhood in familiar contemporary US terms, she manages to reinvigorate themes of heterosexual love, depression, competition, alcoholism, and even meditation on abortions through her complex lexicon, flow, and phraseology. I mostly focus on Grae's work through 2008 (the year of her "retirement" and the end of her association with rapper and producer Talib Kweli's Blacksmith Music label), though she continues to make free and paid live and recorded music, including a set of stellar collaborations with husband, Quelle Chris,[6] and releases her work through various social media and media platforms such as Patreon, Instagram, MySpace, and Bandcamp.[7] Post-2008, Grae has also produced visual art and writing.

I encountered Jean Grae by happenstance, or maybe I should qualify it the old hip hop way—at a small live performance featuring other artists. I along with a group of mostly young women and girls gathered in an anonymous New York University dormitory basement for a benefit thrown by DJ Kuttin' Kandi and indie supergroup Anomolies.[8] I attended the fundraising event at the behest of Invincible, a member of the Anomolies crew—I can never thank them[9] enough for introducing me to one of the most fascinating contemporary emcees/producers/

singers/actors/performers in hip hop and beyond. The performance was intimate: Jean Grae had to encourage the crowd to come closer to her as she performed. She talked us through her process, noting she was working on some new material—she was about to release her debut album, *Attack of the Attacking Things* (2002). As such, she had a pile of notebooks filled with scribbled-down and scribbled-out rhymes. I took a deep breath, hoping against hope that I was seeing evidence of a "real" emcee—a craftsperson willingly trying out her new work on a small, unassuming crowd. Of the songs Jean Grae performed that night, I vividly remember "God's Gift" (which I talk about later in this chapter). The song was raw, bordering on bitter in its sardonic commentary on misogynistic attitudes toward Black women. Here was an emcee not only capable of spitting "bars" (good rhymes), but thoughtfully creative in her meditation on Black heterosexual relations. Thus, I was introduced to Jean Grae, and my decades-long investment in her work continues.

This chapter meditates on the Black female psyche in and through hip hop cultural production via the case study of Jean Grae. Though the mere presence of women in hip hop cultural production is significant and worthy of attention, I show here how Jean Grae's gender performances lend us a vocabulary to discuss the queerness of New York hip hop culture and its artistic products.[10] Grae gives us permission to think about the psyche, the mind, and the uncanny, specifically, through her *nom de plume*, her various avatars,[11] and the content of her work. Jean Grae's namesake, Jean Grey of *The Uncanny X-Men* (1963–), is a founding member of the X-Men mutant superhero team and a powerful telepath and telekinetic. Grey, the superhero, is perhaps best known in the comics genre for possessing the Phoenix Force, which turns her into an unstoppable, world-destroying villain. She also frequently dies and is reborn.

The Black Female Psyche in Hip Hop Culture

Much of the writing and exploration of Black women, and women in general, in hip hop culture focuses on their relationship to the culture involving struggles with misogyny, patriarchy, and other forms of oppression.[12] Another type of scholarly work delves into the significant and oft-overlooked contributions of women in hip hop culture—ranging from fashion to musical innovations to production.[13] These contributions by hip hop scholars, journalists, artists, students, and fans are extremely significant and have built a corpus of women's work within hip hop culture. Some, though not all, of these works tend to collapse hip hop culture and performance into an ethnographic or sociological phenomenon, leaving little room for hip hop culture and performance's utility as a representational art form. Hip hop culture and performance has evolved into a global, billion-dollar juggernaut, yet many scholars still discuss it as if it were a small-scale scene in its infancy. Hip hop culture and performance is complex: both global and hyperlocal, a culture that produces performers who are incredibly critical of social injustice, racial and gender inequality, and war, as well as artists who embrace patriarchy, capitalism, and imperialism—at times this might be the same artist. This chapter integrates the examination of systems of oppression, as well as paying attention to the work of female hip hop artists through the example of South African–born, mixed-race, Brooklyn hip hop artist Jean Grae.

Though the rapper Jean Grae's work deserves serious contemplation, her tongue-in-cheek presentations, her exaggerated depictions of violence, her attention to enjoying drinking, cooking, stand-up comedy, and having a good time demand that neither her fans nor her critical interlocutors take her too seriously. Discussions of trauma, misogyny, abortion, drinking problems, fraught relationships, and other challenging topics are often treated with kid gloves. Grae's fearless contemplation of the surplus and detritus of desire invites those who encounter her to do so with a flexible and accommodating mind. To that end, I turn to psychoanalysis, which, as Claudia Tate remarks, "evolves from a set of theoretical propositions that has been most concerned with examining the manifestations of such surpluses in language [and can help] illuminate the workings of desire in [hip hop]."[14]

Using W. E. B. Du Bois's idea of double consciousness and Sigmund Freud's theory of the uncanny, this chapter formulates a theory of Jean Grae's ability to expose, confound, reveal, and delight in psychic contradictions and possibilities. Grae's unique storytelling style, simultaneously intimate and confrontational, lends itself well to the terrain of Freudian and Lacanian theories. This is not a simple attempt to yoke contemporary hip hop culture to psychoanalysis. The purpose of this binding is to highlight the ways that psychoanalysis can be usefully applied to hip hop musical performance, Black femininity, and Black female psychic structures. Applying hip hop to psychoanalytic theory modifies, informs, and revises psychoanalytic theory on identification, desire, and, specifically, Freud's theory of the uncanny. Furthermore, Jean Grae's own name demands a contemplation of the relationship of hip hop performance to both psychoanalysis and the uncanny.

Rapper Jean Grae, born Tsidsi Ibrahim, daughter of South African jazz musicians Sathima Bea Benjamin and Abdullah Ibrahim, settled on her name after a brief career as What? What? She named herself after the Marvel Comics *Uncanny X-Men* character Jean Grey, a young white female telekinetic/telepathic mutant superhero and one of the founders of the X-Men. While the relationship to comic books and psychoanalysis has been explored,[15] that relationship has not extended to hip hop emcees, DJs, and others who utilize superhero avatars as part of their real-life performances, as well as those who make the connection between hip hop and psychoanalysis.[16] According to Geoff Klock, "any given superhero narrative stands in relation to its conflicted, chaotic tradition, and continuity as the ego stands in relation to the unconscious."[17] The *Uncanny X-Men* leads us to a discussion of the Freudian and Lacanian concepts of the uncanny,[18] not only because of its name, but also its content relating to repression (and the return of the repressed), telekinesis, fantasy, dreams, the non-rapport of the sexual relation, desire and sexuality, terror, alienation, and death. Jean Grae's alignment with the *Uncanny X-Men* is a deliberate move that opens the doorway to think through her artistic relationship to the Freudian unconscious and the uncanny.

Black feminist philosopher Hortense Spillers asks, "how might psychoanalytic theories speak about 'race' as a self-consciously assertive reflexivity, and how might 'race' expose the gaps that psychoanalysis theories awaken?"[19] Spillers reminds Black intellectuals of the curious lacuna in the collective refusal to take up psychoanalysis as a theoretical modality to examine Black literature and art, as well as the missed opportunity to delve into the Freudian *imaginary*.[20] Though Du Bois (1868–1963) and Freud (1856–1939) were contemporaries, the former and his theories are *au courant*, while the latter is often considered passé within Black studies. One of the reasons for choosing psychoanalytic theory over autobiography as a methodology for examining Jean Grae as an emblem of the Black female psyche was to make room for fantasy, invention, and absence. Autobiography has a scent of authority to it, while psychoanalysis makes room for the murky, porous nature of memory, identity, desire, and interpretation. Grae's varied and wide discography, as well as her videos, interviews, and other writings, leads one to note that, while her artistic works include autobiographical elements, they can be viewed as utilizing interiority and exteriority to invoke an unorthodox way of seeing and hearing Black female psychic content. This chapter is more interested in Grae's musings on race, gender, culture, and sexuality as sites of identification, or places of emotional and psychic investment, rather than as fixed identities. Race is an uncanny home wherein one lays one's figurative hat. And frankly, no one does the uncanny like Sigmund Freud.

Because psychoanalysis deals with psychic structure, but also the psychic effects of stimulus, its serves as a way to think about how power affects individuals and groups.[21] Starting with Sigmund Freud's theory of the uncanny originally published in 1919, the chapter continues with a discussion of how the uncanny relates to gender, race, sexuality, and Jean Grae's work. This serves as a critical queer, gender, and race critique into the work on the uncanny and likewise makes critical queer and psychoanalytic interventions into the conversations on hip hop and gender, misogyny, homophobia, and hip hop feminism. Next, the chapter explores

W. E. B. Du Bois's work on racial double consciousness in his canonical *The Souls of Black Folks* (1903). Here the chapter thinks through how Freud's idea of the double in his discussion of the uncanny and Du Bois's idea of racial double consciousness generate a possibility of thinking of the racializing process and the racialized subjects as horrific. Both men's theories insufficiently theorize the psychic, psychological, and affective lives of Black women. Jean Grae is a corrective to that deficit.

The Uncanny Jean Grae: X-Men, Freud, and the Uncanny of Race

In the Marvel Comics series *The Uncanny X-Men*, mutant telekinetic/telepath Jean Grey-Summers,[22] a founding member of the X-Men superhero group, dies[23] and is reborn. Her many iterations, as Marvel Girl, Phoenix, Dark Phoenix, and the revived and powerful Jean Grey, leader of the new X-Men group X-Factor, offer important insight into the allusive power of rapper Jean Grae's name. Jean Grae, the emcee, doesn't have telekinetic or telepathic powers, nor has she lain at the bottom of the ocean. The constant reinvention, the renaming, the obvious reference of the Phoenix (the return) are important in her work. Themes of life and death, love, heartbreak, betrayal, psychic breaks, and real pathos are the substance of her work. Grae also has a sharp tongue and a wicked sense of humor and timing, as well as an extraordinary vocabulary.[24] The entire X-Men universe deals with the concept of the mutant "race." The mutants, endowed with powers ranging from the ability to make one's skin steel (Colossus) to the ability to shape-shift (Mystique), are good, evil, and outside of those categorizations. Some mutants favor learning how to control their powers and how to coexist with humanity (Professor Charles Xavier), while others think it is the destiny of the mutants to rule humanity (Magneto).[25] Uttering "mutant race" brings to mind our contemporary and past preoccupations with "the races," divisions of humanity into racialized classifications. The mutants themselves seem to have no concept of "race" as skin color or heritage, though they are hyperaware of their position as "raced" other versus homo sapiens.[26] The *Uncanny X-Men* series is significant to this project precisely because it exemplifies the uses and possibilities of Sigmund Freud's theory of the uncanny, which he presented in a 1919 essay. While Freud never mentions race in this essay, his ideas of homelessness, the horror of proximity, and the doppelgänger generate ways to engage with racialized bodies, or what we might think of as uncanny bodies.

Sigmund Freud's theory of the uncanny is presented in three parts: the first is a semantic, affective, and etymological study of the word *unheimlich*, which can be translated as "uncanny" or as "unhomely." The second part is a reading of E. T. A. Hoffmann's story "The Sandman." In the final portion, Freud attempts to answer the question of what makes something or some experience uncanny. Freud's lengthy linguistic journey culminates in his proclaiming, "this word *Heimlich* is not unambiguous, but belongs to two sets of ideas, which are not mutually contradictory, but very different from each other—the one relating to what is familiar and comfortable, the other to what is concealed and kept hidden."[27] To be clear, I'm interested in the performative ("what can be done with") relationship between Freud's theory of the uncanny and Jean Grae's work. There is ample contemporary work on race, gender, and the speculative that speaks to comics,[28] but I am tarrying with the uncanny.

Freud's definitions of *heimlich* and *unheimlich* are somewhat archaic, although they have retained some of their etymological tendrils. Uncanny and unhomely (or perhaps, unhomed) ring quite differently in contemporary English. Uncanny is the term with which this section will work. The uncanny is a visceral experience of the unconscious—a sudden flash of something tucked away inside of the mind that appears but is absolutely not known. Freud also offers compelling arguments about the double and its "horror"—that is the connection this section explores in relation to the uncanny, the Black female psyche, Jean Grae, and the sight(s) of blackness in the US. Freud explains the double (the doppelgänger) as "the appearance of persons who have to be regarded as identical because they look alike. This relationship is intensified by the spontaneous transmission of mental processes from one of these persons to another—what we would call telepathy—so that the one becomes co-owner of the other's knowledge, emotions and experience."[29] The one who is a look-alike is dangerous because s/he physically resembles another and blurs the lines of individuality, autonomy, and authenticity; there is a threat, as well, in how the doppelgänger shares the affective, cognitive, and psychic life of the other. The horrific possibilities lie in having no psychic or affective privacy and in being subsumed/consumed by the other.

In a short section in her essay "Black, White, and in Color, or Learning How to Paint: Toward an Intramural Protocol of Reading," Hortense Spillers thinks through, with, and around the tangles of the uncanny in Paule Marshall's *Chosen Place, Timeless People*. Spillers rightly foregrounds the relationship between the Freudian uncanny and sight, noting the horror and confusion that accompany shadow, light, and duplication. She describes the uneven but provocative fit, stating:

> Though the Freudian view of the "uncanny" does not indicate this version of the dramatic as a case in point, we could very well place these haunting scenes under its auspices and say that the shadow—a "not me" as the mirror image is not—is so apt an analogy on the living body, so remarkable a trace of its occurrence, that the shadow's sudden projection can take a body out, so to speak, destroy it.[30]

The relationship between Black womanhood and shadow relevant to this chapter is different than the relationship Spillers addresses (Verne shadowing the Black woman), yet her observations are nonetheless impactful regarding Jean Grae and Black womanhood in hip hop. The Black woman inside of hip hop lurks in/as a shadow to Black men, and also to non-Black men (see Eminem, DJ Khaled, Post Malone). She often functions as a sexual prop—an object of desire or derision, or an object lesson—the mother or daughter or relative who sacrifices to ensure success for the Black male protagonist. Rarely is she seen as an independent being—a competitor, say; she is more or less always attached or a shadow to the Black man's main character. But the potential she has, as a shadow, as a projection that can destroy the main body, is provocative. In Jean Grae's work, especially in the song "God's Gift," which I later discuss, she exemplifies the power of the shadow to destroy, interrupt, and distort patriarchal narratives that disembody Black women as simple darkened spaces, or interruptions, or obscurations.

The Double/Consciousness

> Here, then, is the dilemma. . . . What, after all, am I? Am I an American or am I a Negro? Can I be both?[31]

Paul Gilroy discusses W. E. B. Du Bois's formulation of the term "double consciousness" as referring to a triad of "unhappy symbiosis between . . . thinking, being, and seeing."[32] Gilroy continues that double consciousness is "racially particularistic . . . nationalistic in that it derives from the nation state in which the . . . not-yet-citizens find themselves [and] diasporic or hemispheric."[33] As Gilroy points out, Du Bois uses the example of the Black American ex-enslaved person and her[34] encounter with modernity as the nexus of this double consciousness. Exemplary of this is the "social construction and plasticity of black identities,"[35] which is both a strike against eugenic reasoning and a kind of permanent relationship to homelessness. That the Black American at the turn of the 19th century is "an adaptable creature," generates possibilities for engaging in culture and behavior that is not constrictively bound by skin color, ethnicity, history, or nation. Instead, this plasticity affords the Black American opportunities to explore to the realities, psychic effects, and pitfalls of "relocation, displacement, and restlessness."[36] Although Gilroy is speaking about the physical realities of the Black Atlantic and her subjects, these terms and experiences also carry significant psychic power. The modern Black subject always holds this double consciousness, her internal psychic doppelgänger. This presents an opportunity to see where Freud's ideas on the double might offer some insight into the psychic experience of a modern (and postmodern) Black subject.

Both Du Bois's and Freud's relation to the "doubling" of psychic experience—the Duboisian double consciousness of the Black American experience, and the Freudian doppelgänger—help us formulate ideas about the Black female psyche. Du Bois's double consciousness articulates a cognitive, self-aware split that the Black or subaltern subject gradually comes to know: "They do not want me here, even though I belong. But to whom and where do I belong?" In the post-bellum US context, this was both an internal psychic reality for Blacks and an externalized, juridical, material manifestation in law, customs, and violence inflicted by whites. Whereas racial equality has been codified as law, the material and psychic experience of equal rights in relation to race under the law is dubious, at best. Blacks continue to have the experience of both fitting and not fitting into what it means to be the ideal American subject.

Black Women's Double Bind

How do Black women as a group, and the Black woman as a figure, fit into the Duboisian and Freudian ideas of the double? On an overt level, they don't. Let's make a crude break between Duboisian and Freudian theory. If Du Bois's double hinges, at first, on sight and place (the Negro as physical manifestation of difference in white imagination) and the US is both home and not home to the Negro, Freud's idea of the double relies on sight and space, the doppelgänger, the sameness, as a site of proximity's horror. These manifestations of double are exterior, interior, and interpersonal processes. According to Du Bois and Freud, they are highly sexed (man as subject), which obscures the ways in which women's exterior, interior, and interpersonal experiences vis-à-vis the doubling process take place. As Hazel Carby points out, "Gendered structures of thought and feeling permeate our lives and our intellectual work, including *The Souls of Black Folk* and other texts which have been regarded as *founding* texts written by the *founding fathers* of Black US history and culture."³⁷ The same can be said of Freud's work on female psychic structure and sexuality, which placed women in the realm of the hysteric.³⁸ In fact, Freud's "The Uncanny" ends with the assertion that female genitalia are an example of the uncanny (for a neurotic man). If Freud had imagined woman as his subject, would her own genitalia be uncanny? Perhaps, but probably not for the same reasons. If the womb was once home, a place from which the (male) subject emerged, and is now, according to Freud, a place of desire and dread, do women live in and with an ambiguous relationship to their own former "homes"? Freud may have answered yes or no, but the question itself was never asked. If the male is the assumed subject of Freudian (and most classical psychoanalytic thought), that subject is also raced as white. Does Black female psychic experience even register in a Freudian schema? It does resonate particularly in the notion of the "dark continent" that stands in for both female genitalia and the continent of Africa.³⁹ Rather than letting that be the only place to which any proximity of Black female psychic or material experience is relegated, disappeared, assumed, or obscured, we'll take the idea of the dark continent as a place from which we can speak about Black femininity.

Freud had virtually nothing to say about blackness in any of his writing, yet Freud's own position as a racialized subject (white Jewish male in Germany and Austria in the late 19th and early 20th centuries) places him in proximity to Du Bois's social position in the United States as a Negro. The white Jew in Europe, like the Negro in the US, occupied this position of the fraught double, or the fake, and was under constant pressure to prove "his civilized nature" in the face of terrible accusations, legal action, violence, and harassment that debased the racialized bodies of both Blacks and white Jews. This isn't a declaration that Du Bois's and Freud's mutual biographies are all there is to say about their writings. These ways of structuring theory are relevant precisely because they attempt to write certain people into social power and write others out, through omission, denial, and degradation. As Carby argues, *The Souls of Black Folks* "suffers from Du Bois's complete failure to imagine black women as intellectuals and race leaders. The failure to incorporate black women into the sphere of intellectual equality . . . is not merely the result of Du Bois's historical moment. . . . It is a conceptual and political failure of imagination that remains a characteristic of the work of contemporary African American male intellectuals."[40] Even though Du Bois advocated for women's equality and feminism later in his life, as Carby states, "It is a necessary critical task . . . to examine the gendered intellectual practices which structure *The Souls of Black Folks* [as it] imagines a community and organizes its 'framework of consciousness,' its 'soul.'"[41] Du Bois creates this community through "a complex evocation of the concepts of race, nation, and masculinity."[42]

Where, then, is the Black woman in this "souls of black folks" if the soul is structured as solely Black male? Du Bois declares Black that people in the United States have a double consciousness, are aware of how they don't fit, even as they are asked to confirm to social order. This double consciousness is a part of the "soul" of Black folks—Black folks led by and materialized as Victorian Black masculinity.[43] This dovetails nicely with one of Freud's speculations about the power and place of the uncanny: "none of this helps us understand the extraordinary degree of uncanniness that attaches to [the double] . . . the defensive urge that ejects it from the ego as something alien. Its uncanny quality can surely derive only from the fact that the double is a creation that belongs to a primitive phase in our mental development. . . . The double has become an object of terror."[44] As Freud describes in his analysis of Hoffmann's "The Sandman," Olympia, the "living doll," becomes an object of terror for Nathanael, the protagonist, but also replicates the "uncanny" figure of the Sand-Man in Coppelius and Dr. Coppola. One could say that, in Freud's reading of Hoffmann's story, the case of mistaken identity leads to madness and death. That the very presence of those who look alike, or appear *alive*, hold dangerous potential for . . . well, for whom? For the one who wishes to see something that is not there, or for the one who wishes for there to be a something that can be hidden and revealed. If we place Du Bois and Freud together, we encounter the dangerous potential of the double. The Black male double is aware that he does not fit and knows that he is always othered in the social order of US society. Yet we also see the potential of the (white) woman to be replicated as a living doll (e.g., the airbrushed model/actress) that commands more attention over the male gaze than the flesh and blood woman. Female sexuality in the uncanny, in the doubling process, is mechanized. The Black woman in these formations, obviously then, is not even a speck on the horizon. Or perhaps that's exactly what she is: a distorted glimpse of something quite far away—referring back to the discussion of the shadow earlier in this chapter. Yet we know she is close by, close to Black masculinity, close to white femininity, and close to white masculinity. Due to this proximity, we might say she is, in this schema in-between the theories of Du Bois and Freud, a shadow—elongated, temporal, distorted, necessary, fear-inducing at times, unavoidable, inanimate, darker, reliant on light for contrast. This is exactly where I insert Jean Grae. I'd like to think through the ways in which this particular Black female artist articulates desire, femininity, sex, reproduction, rage, and creative prowess in the wake of the overdetermined ways in which Black female creativity has been elided, ignored, and/or pathologized.

"Dumb Bitch, Play Your Position": The Creativity of Refusal in Jean Grae

How does Jean Grae "appear" as a shadow inside of hip hop cultural production? Rather than simply play out and along with the inevitable psychic scenes Du Bois and Freud (and their adherents) set up, Grae's interjects into this set of structural scenes disruptions of time and place. By lyrically, sonically, and tonally inhabiting Black masculinity in her song "God's Gift," Grae reorients the listener to focus on the casual and chronic misogynoir Black men and boys aim at Black women and girls inside of the hip hop milieu. Her Black feminist futurity deploys temporal and sonic disruptions of the past and present to ask listeners the question: well, what are you going do about this dynamic? Black feminist futurity is, as Tina Campt enumerates, a "tense of anteriority, a tense of relationship to an idea of possibility that is neither innocent nor naïve. Nor is it necessarily heroic or intentional. . . . [I]t is devious and exacting. . . . It is frequently quiet and opportunistic, dogged and disruptive."[45] Campt's descriptions of the tense of Black feminist futurity's "quiet soundings" exemplifies the work that Grae's music often does. Her subtlety is often lost on audiences looking for big declarations with neon arrows pointing the way. I would argue Grae's writing—whether hip hop or R&B lyrics, her blog, recipes, tweets, or other posts across social media—deploys the hallmarks of a thinking wordsmith: slyness, allusion, parody, subtlety, deflection, curiosity, and complexity. These are hallmarks of both Black feminist and Black queer aesthetics, ones that are often overlooked, stolen, or buried.

Jean Grae has an uncanny ability to deconstruct heteronormative heterosexual relationships, applying the language, cadence, inflection, and tonality of some of her male counterparts. Grae's aim, it seems, is to go beyond naming acts misogynist, or even delineating the effects of misogyny. She goes to the heart of the matter by sonically offering up the innards of patriarchy to her listeners. What makes her work beyond mimetic is her convincing and comfortable habitation in the world of patriarchal masculine speech. In fact, her mastery of such speech is key to the effects of "God's Gift."[46] Jean Grae is one of precious few rappers/emcees, female or male, who addresses the complexities of gender performance, Black sexuality, transgressing gender norms, and the nuances of Black male female heterosexual relationships.

Jean Grae, rapper, singer, producer, and rap fan favorite, is a curious figure in hip hop culture.[47] Grae is a prolific and talented contemporary artist. She's released nine full-length albums, ten EPs, and a handful of mixtapes since 2002. She's also recorded countless guest appearances on the albums of other independent-label stars (The Herbaliser, The Roots, Masta Ace, Mr. Len, Talib Kweli, Mr. Lif, Rapsody, and Cannibal Ox) and firmly stayed at the center of hip hop's independent-label golden elite. She is not yet well known beyond the circles of dedicated hip hop and music critics, as well as some hip hop scholars, fans, and artists. She is a favorite emcee of many rap artists, including Talib Kweli, Jay-Z, and Black Thought of The Roots. Grae is a gritty rhymer, emphasizing thick, dense lyrical mastery and emotional power over complex tracks, which are often produced by North Carolina whiz 9th Wonder.[48] Grae addresses sex, trauma, abortion, cheating, tragedy, fantasy, complicated friendships, rivalries, and heartbreak without being unnecessarily shocking or outrageous, yet her very real and provocative directness is, in fact, quite shocking to hear. One example is "The Illest" (2001, re-issued 2004),[49] from DJ/producer/emcee Immortal Technique's debut album, also featuring independent emcee Pumpkinhead (another version of the song features major label rapper Canibus and rap star Lil Wayne). The song's premise is to show how, through his or her lyrical skills, each rapper is the illest, or the best with metaphors, similes, imagery, and evocative wordplay. Many rappers use the opportunity of a freestyle track to go all out and "spit" lyrics without a filter, and one hears "bitch," "homo," and "nigga" frequently. Grae is no exception, employing the staple words of independent rap music with deftness and acumen. Yet there is a key difference in her delivery. When she's rapping about her skill in this song, she proclaims: "[My] rhyme documents [are] infamous like the Bill of Rights. Illa-tight, havin' niggas open like the thrill of dykes."[50] One might think Grae is yet another hip hop artist utilizing homosexuality as a joke or insult. Here, lesbianism or female bisexuality might be taken as a "thrill" for Black heterosexual men. Grae is deploying thickly layered similes, comparing her writing to an incomparable document like the United States' Bill of Rights. She moves on to describe her rhymes as being "tight" in a positive sense—as in "air-tight," incorruptible. Tight also has a sexual connotation, that the tightness of various orifices is often seen as pleasurable and desirable for sexual partners. The combination of the "illa" along with the "tight" might also signify an extraordinary rhyming ability—so tight that it makes one feel ill; that it's dizzying in its effect; ill, taking on all of the connotations of the word as deployed in both hip hop culture and in standard English: weird, strange, excellent, bizarre, unhealthy, diseased. In short, it stands out in some way, whether for good or ill. Grae also alludes to the ways in which men are swayed by their fantasies of queer female sexuality. For someone to be "open" is for him or her to be receptive. A great deal of pornography is dedicated to "lesbians" (aka straight women getting paid to fuck each other) pleasuring each other for the benefit of heterosexual men. However, here there's no pay off, no money shot, it's just the thrill of the idea of dykes. While the men are open and distracted by their straight male fantasy, Grae slips in to lyrically crush the mic and master the space with her lyrical and imagistic complexity.

The song's entire efficacy rests upon each artist demonstrating why she or he is "the illest"—the best. In this particular song, the lyrics, delivery, intonation, and mastery of language are foregrounded, while the music itself seems little more than supportive scaffolding on which the artists play. The musical structure is quite *largo*, slow. A sparse drum machine opens the song, soon accompanied by a tinny, unflattering synthesizer. The soundscape evokes a sense of the barren, a poverty of sounds, which leaves room for the emcees to fill it in with their aural and sonic power. The skeletal music allows the emcees to build sonic worlds through their words. The effects of Grae's words, which are thickly woven metaphors and similes, range from violent births ("a rebel born from verbal holocaust") to quick wit and intellect ("swift as stealth assassins / snipe you from balcony shots"), as well as connecting her particular verbal skills to a long line of "authentic" iconic hip hop cultural performances and practices ("*Wild Style*, my mouth bomb the train up / I spit Krylon in five colors, when I speak I spray my name up.").[51] The end of Grae's verse is the most intriguing, as Grae boasts, "from downtown swinging it, New York, [the] illest to rip it ever / flow like a river, fuck your girl like a nigga."[52] Grae exploits the language of mastery and her mastery of language to assert her dominance in lyricism, wordplay (freestyle association), her desirability to women, and her ability to sexually please/dominate a woman, just like "a nigga," affording herself the stereotypical prowess of Black masculinity. Grae demonstrates that she is lyrically superior to other (male) rappers and a threat to them musically as well as social-sexually. She can usurp and slip into the place heretofore occupied by a certain type of Black heterosexual masculinity. She is quite capable, because of her tremendous skill, of inserting herself into the position occupied for and by men, if she so desired. Grae's performance is a necessary critical intervention into the broad cultural and hip hop cultural depictions of Black femininity as passively complicit in misogynistic representations of female sexuality. Frankly, Grae is not interested in being a good girl, a sweet girl. In her music, she explores the bold frankness of Black female sexuality utilizing the linguistic and sonic structures of underground hip hop battle music to resignify the possible metaphorical, symbolic, and material positions a Black woman in hip hop performance and culture might occupy.

The Problem with Normal: Heteronormativity in Hip Hop Performance and Culture

Heteronormativity blocks the material experiences of Black people. Yet many Black people strive for a heteronormative persona even if it's not "reality."[53] In much of hip hop culture and performance there is an emphasis on maintaining the rigidity of categories, even if those categories fail to adequately speak to and manifest the material and psychic experiences of Black folks. Grae, through her performances, resists the bondage of heteronormativity. In this way, she allows one to "*see* the gendered and eroticized elements of racial formations as offering ruptural—i.e., critical—possibilities."[54] She shows Black heteronormativity as a performance and by exposing it as a show—a performative posture—allows the listener to engage with the critical possibilities of alternative or "queered" performances, and thus formations, to heteronormativity. These alternative performances to heteronormativity produce an anxiety at the site of their critique precisely because they expose the supposed naturalness of heteronormative expectations (rigid masculinity, acquiescent femininity, racial hegemony, nationalism, compulsory heterosexuality, etc.) as a learned set of behaviors. This is not to say Grae calls her work queer, even as her performances disrupt the audience's aural or visual expectations. Nonetheless, her performances and affect expose the holes in the seemingly natural, impenetrable world of Black heteronormative heterosexual relations. Grae's performances are "queer" in relation to heteronormativity and its effects; she offers an alternative, an invitation to question the ways that race, sexuality, desire, and violence play out through prescribed gender roles and circumscribed gender expression.

Jean Grae is a female hip hop performer in a male-dominated music industry and genre.[55] Her status as woman automatically marks her as a potentially lesser body in the masculine performance space of hip hop culture.[56] Grae, in line with the position of females in rap history, is in dialogue with the greater social arena, but also with her rap female and male counterparts. As Tricia Rose notes, "Dialogism . . . accommodates the tension between sympathetic racial bonds among black men and women as well as black women's frustration regarding sexual oppression at the hands of black men."[57] Grae goes beyond the dialogical dynamic of Black heterosexual relationships. She slides between the positions of male and female, as I have demonstrated with "The Illest," often creating a hybrid third. This hybridity disrupts the linearity of heteronormative dialogue and dialectic, introducing a new figure—an enigmatic voice in hip hop that does not equate sex with gender and does not limit deftness to males or masculinity. Jean Grae's place in the hip hop landscape occupies the liminal space of impossibility, insofar as she operates against what Peggy Phelan identifies as "mimetic correspondence."[58] Grae's purposeful impossibility (the hybrid third), irresolvability, and unattainability undo the "require[ment] that the writer/speaker employs pronouns, invents characters, records conversations, examines the words and images of others, so that the [listener] can secure a coherent belief in self-authority, assurance, presence."[59] Grae engages in the possibilities of a critical relationship to Black female sexuality that is neither reactionary nor acquiescent, nor particularly concerned with any overt agenda. Grae articulates a freedom of expression in relation to Black femaleness that critiques, inhabits, explores, loves, and questions all of the possibilities of being sexual, female, young, Black, and a performer, using her albums, lyricism, live performances, and other published materials to act as an agent of critical rupture in the world of hip hop music and American heteronormative values. Of particular interest to me is Grae's 2002 song "God's Gift," from her first full-length album, *Attack of the Attacking Things*. In this song, Grae performs from the perspective of a typical male "playa," explaining his philosophy of sex, gratification, and masculine desire. Grae consistently, relentlessly operates in the realm of the material in this song, not simply the metaphoric or metonymic. With complete candor, she confuses the boundaries between male and female, propriety and raunchiness, and breaches the expected topics of conversation for Black female performers. Her verses, with their easy mastery of language, image, and cadence, often appear as a hazy and misshapen bog that simultaneously invites the listener into her world and baffles the listener. Once the listener enters Grae's world, it is often quite challenging to discern just *where* one has been transported.

The interventions in this chapter are concerned with the relationship between race and sex(uality). Pornography does not explicitly address the ways that race, art, and sex are made perverse in the public eye and imagination, but is nevertheless a useful frame for thinking about the way Black female public and private persons are seen. The racialized Black body has a relationship to sex marked by its historical links to "freakdom," savagery, subordination, intimidation, and terrorization.[60] Extending Rebecca Schneider's argument to think about the ways that images of Black sexuality are encoded with historical and contemporary meaning, I ask, What are the challenges and anxieties around reifying, reinforcing, and rectifying the ways Black bodies are interpreted both interculturally and intraculturally?[61] The images of the Black whore and the Black stud are troubling, but they are familiar. Collective Black cultural response calls them racist and feels better at having "defeated" attempts to subject Black people to stereotypical representations. Black women and men each have vulnerable pitfalls in relation to heteronormativity; Black male performers studiously avoid vulnerability or imagined penetrability. Black men who betray their iconic virility, heterosexuality, and strength are often described in terms that feminize or dismiss their dialogical efforts to engage hegemonic Black male identity.[62] Black women operate in a slightly different economy in that they are always already in relation to their prescribed gender, sexuality, and race as they display their bodies or are displayed publicly. Black women's value is either bound up with sex or frantically denied sexual imperatives. Black women, as performers, are compelled to address their "image," meaning their level of sexual display. The Black female performing artist, especially in hip hop culture, is given two old tropes with which to play: the Afrocentric "Queen" and "righteous" woman, or the modernist, Eurocentric "whore." The Black artist who troubles the stereotypes with his or her own undefined and unspecific gender play is disruptive and anxiety-producing due to her stepping out of the approved modality of protest. She protests with uncertainty, irony, profanity, satire, and even grotesque sexuality. Black sexuality, like hip hop, has no moral center. There is no "right" way to be Black and sexually expressive. The point of sexuality is to be in dialogue with experience, desire, memory, sight, and fear. Jean Grae's irreverent and practical inhabitations of Black sexuality and gender expression terrorize and problematize the norms set out by heteronormativity.

There is a distinction between different methods of marking queer(ed) Black bodies. There are the bodies that are *marked*, that is to say, interpolated as queer (i.e., varying from the normative white body standard); bodies that nominate themselves queer (homosexual, pervert, invert, gender queer, transgender, bisexual, polyamorous, heteroflexible, metrosexual, odd, pierced, tattooed); and the bodies that repossess or "queer"—disrupt—their own images. It is important to articulate these distinctions in an attempt to make discrete the myriad frames in operation. These three frames in no way exhaust the possibilities of viewing

Black bodies in America, but do situate my arguments regarding the power of artists such as Jean Grae to produce a rupture in the fantasy of hegemonic whiteness and the fantasy of Black bodies attaining authentic heteronormativity.

Sounding (Off) Like a Boy: Jean Grae and Masculine Performance

The fact that her emcee moniker is Jean Grae alerts the listener to the possibilities of her shifting personalities, names, and abilities. Yet she remains a curious enigma who fits into none of rap music's assigned personae:

> Not a thug, not a drug seller, not a gun shooter / Not a stripper, sex symbol or anything you're used to / Marketing nightmare, I don't fit categories / just rap, make beats, and shit and sleep all these stories.[63]

Grae is not simply a *not*; she is, however, extremely difficult to categorize in hip hop's admittedly limited landscape. Grae shifts deftly between unrepentant naysayer of the mainstream and expressing desire for material success and recognition. She articulates a world where her female gender is viewed as a deterrent to authentic and innovative hip hop. In a review of one of her albums in the online magazine HipHopDX, the author strips her of her female identity in order to give her "props" as "one of the nicest emcees. Period. . . . [A]ll of [these women] possessed skills that made people classify them with *men* rather than with *women*"[64] (my emphasis). Grae, the unmarked woman, is hailed and marked by the (marked) man as being so excessively brilliant that she surpasses mere femininity and can be *re*marked as male. Her female identity is obscured (but not erased), because the multiplication of Grae's female status with her "mind-bending lyricis[m]"[65] is what creates the potential for her to be marked as male, as beyond female, as simply "one of the illest emcees gripping a mic today; male, female, animal, vegetable, whatever."⁶⁶ And, of course, there are no "animal[s], vegetable[s], [or] whatever[s]" occupying space in hip hop. Emcees with liminal identities are erased, dismissed, pathologized, and gossiped about viciously. Jean Grae is one of the few emcees disrupting hip hop's flat narrative regarding its relationship to blackness and alterity and the anxiety that such unfixed, transient formulations produce in its listenership. Grae slips and slides between hostile, repentant, suicidal, homicidal, "young and dumb," and wise and jaded all via performative disappearance. Phelan makes a case that "[p]erformance is the art form which most fully understands the generative possibilities of disappearance."⁶⁷ That is not to say that Grae is without her own anxieties concerning normative femininity, blackness or emcee identity; on the contrary, she actively pursues the dialectic to move in and through the spaces and places of disappearance she creates with her music, lyrics, and presentation.

Grae performs masculinity better than most male emcees recording music. "God's Gift," one of Grae's most dynamic and well-known songs, first caught my attention because I misheard it as one in which a male emcee was performing on her album—I wondered at Grae's choice to have someone else perform such an intensely brutal depiction of a composite male's estimation of women. When I realized that this was Grae's own performance, I became curious. In the song, women serve the protagonist's sexual purposes and he knows they know it. The song is slippery; it is hard to pin down whether Grae is playing a character or a caricature. The song is a gorgeous aural assault on the ears, starting with a piano playing in a descending minor key piano, sighing strings, and the sound of a scratchy old record as the character Grae plays lets the listener know, "It's aight [sic], you can get mad [laughter]. You knew the deal from the get go, know what I'm sayin'? If it's not you, it's another bitch (shit). It's all good. Whatever. Day to day. Bitch to bitch. That's how we roll. Playa: what?"⁶⁸ Immediately, I was intrigued by the role that Jean Grae was enacting. Here was a Black feminist experiment that was explicitly attempting to expose the misogynoir of everyday male-female interactions without announcing her performance or the critique as such. Grae had done better than call attention to misogynistic behavior, social order, and beliefs; she had embodied the disembodied voice of misogyny and patriarchy. Grae is both experimenting with a Black feminist project and performing gender—serious gender play, or gender play with weight and depth—in her performance in "God's Gift."

Grae uses her body—her voice and incredible skills as an emcee—to expose the masculine performance of misogynoir[69] and its affects. Grae's enactment of this particular masculine performance, one that is codified in the American social fabric and artistically rehearsed in hip hop, does in fact, to use Schneider's terms, "denaturalize gender" while simultaneously "historicizing the shadows, explicating or making explicit the haunting effects of naturalization."[70] The listener cannot escape the power and dissonance of Grae's voice saying these lyrics, in a dialectical relationship with the blunt, masterful "cutting" of deejay Mr. Len. A male voice[71] in the musical cut shouts, "Dumb bitch! Play your position!" The characters in the song are startling and unapologetic in their demand that the passive woman/women in this audio-world submit to the inevitability of masculine desire. Grae's character, speaking to (all) women, lets it be known, "I'm the reason ya'll breathe, reason ya'll been here from conception, reason ya'll believe in deception."[72] Grae explicitly performs the intrinsic or coded misogyny of other rappers masked as "praise" for (the parts of) women. When juxtaposed with rapper Biggie Smalls, aka the Notorious B.I.G., who speaks similarly of women's position in his life—"First things first, I Poppa, freaks all the honeys, dummies, Playboy bunnies, those be wanting money. Those the ones I like 'cuz they don't get nathin' but penetration unless it smell like sanitation"[73]—it is clear that Grae, the author and this character, is in a dialogical relationship with male desire and masculine performance within hip hop. Tricia Rose argues that the music and the voice in rap music "privileges flow, layering, and ruptures in [its] line[s]."[74] She further argues that hip hop:

create[s] and sustain[s] rhythmic motion, continuity, and circularity via flow; accumulate, reinforce, and embellish this continuity through layering; and manage threats to these narratives by building in ruptures that highlight continuity as it momentarily challenges it. These effects at the level of style and aesthetics suggest affirmative ways in which profound social dislocation and rupture can be managed and perhaps contested in the cultural arena.[75]

Grae is in a long line of female hip hop artists who comment on, respond to or investigate their reduced or problematic status as narrated by hip hop males. Salt-N-Pepa, MC Lyte, Yo-Yo, Queen Latifah, Lauryn Hill, Eve, Roxanne Shanté, Lil' Kim, Foxy Brown, Cardi B, Megan Thee Stallion, and many more address the interpellation of the female subject position in portions of their work. Salt-N-Pepa, with their song "Tramp" (1986), addressed double standards as they relate to sex relations when initiated by a man and what happens when a woman pursues sex. They play with role-reversal—the man in their song is called "tramp." Female emcees have addressed or demonstrated the idea of female def(t)ness on the mic in other songs such as Queen Latifah's "My Mic Sound Nice" (1986), Salt-N-Pepa's "Ladies First" (1990), and Lauryn Hill's "Lost Ones" (1998), but I know of no other female emcee who takes on a masculine voice and role to highlight the severity of gender violence and discrimination. Grae's ability to construct and perform a character whose lyrical flow is skillful (masculinized)—her character controls the mic and speaks with authority, authenticity, and conviction—her masterful layering of beats, her voice, the voice of the male chorus, and Masta Ace's production all build on the blocks of masculine performance. The song takes the phrase "dumb bitch" and, through its repetition via the DJ's cut interruption, constantly interrupts any comfortable aural pleasure the listener may experience. Even if one isn't bothered by the phrase "Dumb bitch! Play your position!" there is a way that Grae's delivery replaces the usual male speaker. This may give one pause: is it a man or woman speaking? Is this criticism or promotion of misogyny? The cuts dive in and out of the phrases "dumb bitch" and "play your position" to unsettle and disjoint the listener's experience of them. Those words are no longer simply in possession of the one who utters them; they resound as a part of Grae's response to their command. She refuses to "play [her] position" as a marginalized subject and supersedes the command to stay in her place by manipulating and rhetorically regurgitating the misogynistic imperative to stay ignorant, submissive, silent, and in her place.

I played this song for a group of young people from the Bronx, ages 13 to 19, during a portion of a community organizers' training I was conducting on language, vulnerable bodies, youth, and power. I purposefully gave the young people some of Grae's biographical information—age, gender, location, and recording history. I told them to think about what the performance and song were doing in relation to our earlier discussions about economics, race, and heterosexism in New York City. As the song played, they crept closer to the stereo trying to catch the words Grae spat in rapid succession. A deep, strong, disjointed bass drum and a driving bass guitar match the velocity of the words. The screech of the ascendant minor of the synthesizer creates a marvelous dissonant descant to contrast the track's bass-heavy feel. The song is hard to hear and difficult to listen to. I watched as the young people struggled to comprehend what was happening. They were confused by the words uttered by this female voice. I waited for their verdict. One girl stated, "That's either a boy or she's gay." Another girl agreed, "She's gay. That's all I'm saying." Another noted that the voice could not be a girl's, even though it sounded like a girl because of the content of the song, "But *she* said, at the end of the song, 'your best friend's on the way to my house.' So it has to be a *boy*." I asked the one boy in the institute what he thought. He replied that the tremendous lyrical skills of the emcee confused the gender for him, but when he listened, he realized it was a girl speaking from the male perspective; I smiled at and congratulated his insight. Then a superstar spoke up. One young girl who was about to enter Julliard in the fall said, "It seems to me that she's playing a character. Instead of talking about the stuff guys do—she *did* it." Others nodded their heads or looked at me for an answer (which I did not supply). I simply nodded at their efforts and asked them to think about why they assumed the rapper was gay based on a story she was telling or why they ignored ample evidence—her female-sounding voice, my biographical information—in order to fit this song into a heteronormative schema ("it's a boy") or dismiss the comment based on heteronormative ideas of heterosexuality ("she's gay"). Most of them were silent. Some said they liked the song and really wanted me to play it again. All of them looked a bit troubled about their gender assumptions and the "naturalness" of gender subject positions. I had made my point about the performativity of gender, so we took a break for lunch and talked about the ways in which music and performance, as one young person phrased it, can "really confuse [things]."

Jean Grae's power rests in her phenomenal insights, her immense vocabulary, and her ability to communicate ideas without preamble, apology, or contextualization. Rather than working from, or even against, the prescriptive roles laid out for young Black women, she deploys her voice, words, sound, content, presence, and affect as her weaponry against heteronormative gender expression, patriarchal imperatives, and hip hop hegemony. This of course, comes at a price: less mainstream success, criticism from certain circles of hip hop scholarship, dismissal from male hip hop purists, and a virtual blackout by feminist hip hop scholars. Yet Jean Grae continues, year after year, to offer thoughtful, mind-opening compositions that speak to the nuanced nature of human existence and Black female subjectivity in 21st-century America. Grae, to my mind, seems to have a wide agenda: being successful without resorting to hypersexualization, making fantastic music, speaking about love and vulnerability through hip hop performance, and continuing to critique her ongoing love affair with hip hop music and culture. How viable these career choices are depends on whether fans will continue to support (and it seems they will) this bold and commanding voice, which is often drowned out by the cacophonous power of heteronormative hip hop.

Spittin' 'Til They Shame You: Jean Grae and Abortion

So far, this chapter has rendered Jean Grae as a performer extraordinaire who imaginatively, symbolically, and representationally transgresses gender binaries in hip hop culture and performance. In hip hop culture, as in the rest of mainstream US popular and social culture, there is little reward for the kind of gender, race, and sexuality exploration, investigation, and play Grae demonstrates. Grae not only traverses the social and cultural ground of heterosexual relations within her life, she also explicitly invokes the realm of the mind as a space of potentiality, danger, confusion, and fantasy. Her name, Jean Grae, initiates this invocation. Grae's namesake, Jean Grey, the Marvel Comic's *Uncanny X-Men*[76] channels a power called Phoenix, who manifests, at one point, as a world-destroying force known as Dark Phoenix. Grey, the graphic-novel character, is a psychic time bomb. Although the most physically unassuming of all the X-Men (as opposed to the titanium-bodied Colossus; dashing, psychopathic, steel-clawed Wolverine; element-commanding Storm; or life-force-sucking Rogue), Grey turns out to be the most powerful and the most dangerous.[77] This name adoption is significant to the rapper Jean Grae, particularly as a symbolic shift from obscure or humorous references[78] to a more uncanny, potentially sinister alignment.

Freud's discussion of the uncanny assists this reading of Grae's video *Spittin' 'Til They Shame You* and her song on which it is based, "My Story."[79] I also delve into Jacques Lacan's "The Freudian Unconscious and Ours." Freud ends the second section of his musings on the uncanny in a disappointing but unsurprising place—the female genitalia is an uncanny site/sight for the neurotic man.[80] This, as mentioned earlier in the chapter, is for Freud, the ultimate unhomed: the familiar-yet-not abject site or imaginary place of the uncanny. How are we to approach the idea of the uncanny in relation to Black femininity, subjectivity, and body? She is wholly absent in Freud's schema, except for perhaps as a faint echo of "Mother Africa," the womb from which we all sprang. In terms of thinking of blackness and femaleness concurrently as multidimensional, not only bodily, we must construct her from her own representations of herself. The representations of Black femininity and the material presence of Black femininity are not an exact fit; of course, there is a gap. Rather than seeing this gap as only sinister or uncanny, perhaps we may think of it as the site of psychic potentiality. Lacan said, "the unconscious . . . show[s] us the gap through which neurosis recreates harmony with a real—a real that may not well be determined."[81] The function of the Freudian unconscious is to *show us the gap*, not to foreclose it. This gap, according to Lacan, is generative—"something happens" there. The neurosis arises to fill the gap, but it functions as a scar of the unconscious. The fear that causes the neurosis to attempt to stop the gap is what scars the unconscious. The neurosis fails, insofar as there is always another gap, and each subsequent gap leaves a scar. The scars themselves are a kind of narrative that changes over time. These psychic scars also function as another site of questioning, different than the gap, because the unconscious notices, returns to the scar, *reopening* the event, making something new, different, possible. This gap, the neurosis, and the scar it leaves, can all be thought of as moments of artistic impression. Psychoanalysis is sometimes used to theorize trauma, but so is art, and the two are infinitely compatible. If we can think through the various functions of the unconscious as creative processes in themselves, which generate more creative processes (as neurosis, symptoms, illness, dreams, memory, art), we might begin to make room for the unconscious as a more intersubjective place (as Lacan saw it), rather than as a site of personal, ego-based mental failings. Particularly if we approach the unconscious as a discourse, a useful simile, we can see it as interpersonal, cumulative, ongoing, contradictory, nonlinear, and confounding.

Jean Grae's song "My Story" and video *Spittin' Til They Shame You* relate the story of a young girl who's had two abortions and a miscarriage—this is her ode to her never-born children. The song and short film are stark, lovely, painful retellings of a teenage girl's decision to abort, the process of abortion itself, and the aftereffects of having an abortion and a miscarriage. This is no mere polemic about a woman's "right to choose" or a fetus's "right to life." Instead, the artwork lays bare the physical, mental, and emotional scars. I focus on the ten-and-a-half-minute *Spittin' 'Til They Shame You* (dir. Monihan Monihan, 2008), as it offers both visual and auditory material, giving us more with which to work. The film, inspired by "My Story," offers another view on her words—an additional representation of this potentially "autobiographical" story. The story, to whatever extent based on events that may have happened, is no longer Grae's; it becomes the product of an amalgam of Grae; her producer, 9th Wonder; the film's director, writer, and producer, Monihan Monihan; the co-writer (and Grae's then-boss at her then-record label), Talib Kweli; the actress who plays the Grae character, Lynette Astaire; and, of course, the listener-viewer.

The mise-en-scène of the film begins with the protagonist at an exhibition of her visual art in a gallery. She's speaking with a female friend who "wants the hook-up" for a painting of the protagonist. The friend relents, indicating she will purchase the painting for her new living room. The music begins, as the view switches to an industrial section of Brooklyn, with the Manhattan skyline on the distant horizon. Grae's character, alone on top of a building's roof, seems forlorn. The first lyrics, "If I could swim a thousand lakes to bring your life back,"[82] orient the audience toward the tragic nature of the song's content. The protagonist expresses her rage, sorrow, frustration, and pain relating to her abortions (and a later miscarriage) through the medium of painting. She scribbles, scratches, tosses paint on a canvas, carves black chalky questions ("If U [sic] care so much about LIFE then why do you support the WAR?")[83] on the white of the canvas before erasing them and attempting to paint another scene. Her process is solitary, complex, and messy. She is shown in desperate despair: contemplating suicide by gun, watching other women and men play/walk/be frustrated with their children, and reflecting on her own choices. Concurrently, she is giving birth to incredible and important art that arises from her choice to abort twice by the time she was 22. She is stalwart and heartbreaking, staring into the camera while a tear runs down her right cheek; she's facing the pain she's in. She's facing the viewer. The short film gives us vignettes of the protagonist in class sitting silently whilst her friends pass notes, but she's "doing a sad walk like Bill Bixby"[84] on Brooklyn streets, crying alone in her bedroom, cutting herself while her mother pleads for her to open the bathroom door, but also painting and creating. Grae's music and the film it inspired engage with the pathos of human experience and specifically represent the pain of girls and women who make or even face the decision to abort.

The way the uncanny functions in this song could be likened to a dream. Why? A song, much like a dream, is often a fantastical set of images (evoked by words) and symbols that may be narrativized but do not necessarily constitute a cohesive narrative. A song can be understood as an arena for collapsing, obscuring, interpreting, and complicating meaning. According to Freud in *The Interpretation of Dreams*, "dream-content . . . is presented in hieroglyphics, whose symbols must be translated, one by one, into the language of dream-thoughts."[85] Freud goes on to say that we should not "attempt to read these symbols according to their values as pictures, instead of in accordance with their meaning as symbols."[86] What, then, is the value of the protagonist's paintings being sold in a gallery? As the audience, we see the backstory that goes into the works: the protagonist holding hands with her friend at the abortion clinic; the insertion of right-to-life footage of aborted fetuses; the discontent, psychic breaks, and loneliness the protagonist experiences. This is what the first friend in the gallery is buying—the product of tremendous pain, transformed into a work of art. These works (we don't see the finished product) are beautiful, haunting, energetic, created from a place of deep sorrow, perhaps even torment. There are three endings in this film. The first is the end of the lyrics and music. As the song ends, Grae raps over 9th Wonder's jazzy woodwinds, "But it's never over / even if we had a child / they could had a brother or sister or both / I'm thinking about another life that almost got close / praying that in another time we could changes posts / If I could just reverse time, I would / I don't know what I would do, honestly, it's not good."[87] As the melancholic horns fade out and the haunting woodwinds die down, the literal sonic echo and echo memory is what remains. The film narrative ends on an ironic and somewhat *triste* note: the gallery friend did purchase the painting. She, her male partner, and their three children are moving into their new home. Here is an alternate future to what the protagonist could have had, had she not aborted. It is a happy conclusion, of sorts, which is a strange way to end. This ending is very heteronormative: "Look here, it was all a dream! You didn't really do that! Happy Black, normal family!" It's an anxious and trite ending to a deeply disturbing song. The artist-protagonist is nowhere in sight. Nearly a full three minutes are dedicated to showing us this Black domestic scene where mother, father, and children are all present and accounted for. Grae herself hated the video ending.[88] She said of it:

> What really hurts at this point is that [Warner Brothers] have now gone ahead and done the "My Story" video. I don't know if they're done or not. Initially, it was: I'm gonna get to read the treatment. And I said: "Thank you. I really appreciate you took the time out, especially for this song—it is, to me, the most important song on this album, the most important song I've ever done. But the treatment that you wrote, it really goes against the whole idea of the song: It's become, 'Everything's gonna be OK; it's a happy ending'—no."[89]

Indeed. Here, Grae delineates Black anxiety about a Black girl or woman having a complex response to her choice to abort: she is regretful, but also knows that she might make the exact same decision again. "My Story" is not a redemptive tale, but the video ends with an alternative to the protagonist's ambivalence by celebrating and naturalizing the nuclearized Black family. The artist's painting of a Black female hand, in a mudra, scattering seeds over a wilting flower, acquires a very different set of meanings and effects while the Black female child sits below it. Here's Grae idea of what the song was about:

> The whole idea of it was, no, I wanted to do a song that was this real about [having an abortion]. Taking you into the room. The anesthetic. You're going through the whole process, especially experiencing it as a teenager. And not having anyone to share that with. And I said: "Please don't do this." The next thing I heard, [Warner Brothers] were going ahead with it. Casting it. The most hurtful thing being that it's such an important song. The personal part of me baring my soul is fine. The political aspect of it—you couldn't have a more pro-choice song. So now, in essence, what you've done is taken the choice away for the video for the song called "My Story." I think it's the most disrespectful thing ever. It's really prompting me to have the kind of voice that I know I should have. I can't let it go. I can't let something like that go. And it's not fair.[90]

The video's blissful ending can't foreclose the energy of the song. It cannot, even with its overdetermined, all-is-well ending, erase the song's melancholia. The Grae of the sonic version does not marry (yet), have babies, and hang gorgeous, tortured works of art on the wall. And neither, it seems, does Tsidsi Ibrahim, the woman who morphs into Jean Grae to bring us the music that pain produces.

New York City and Brooklyn specifically figure largely in Grae's work and in this film, whether she's commenting on the way that Black people tend to stick too close to "their" block and the limitations one suffers when one doesn't attempt to travel ("Block Party");[91] or, on the cover of her album *This Week* (2004), sporting a New York Yankees jersey, sitting on the street corner, writing in her notebook; or name-dropping the legendary West Village hip hop store Fat Beats (now closed); or reinventing a song by New York icon Biggie Smalls (hidden track 4 on "Chapter One");[92] or, especially, when she's in dialogue with her favorite emcee, Jay-Z, on "Threats" and "Chapter One" ("still get high / analyze Jay-Z . . . my name Jean Grae / remake Jay-Z."). Her music and other writings obviously deal with a broad range of subject matter, but New York City is an important interlocutor for Grae. Murray Forman, discussing the relation of value, scale, and place in hip hop culture, points out how "place is produced according to rhythms of movement and patterns of use [and] 'sense of place' . . . is not based solely on a positive relation to known environment. . . . For the hip-hop culture, place may be significant for its familiarity, its nurturing factors, and its supportive infrastructures, but it may also harbor other, more menacing elements that are also centrally implicated in establishing criteria of significance."[93] In *Spittin' 'Til They Shame You*, director Monihan Monihan makes use of the New York cityscape, situating the protagonist sitting atop a Brooklyn rooftop, with the Brooklyn Bridge looming in the background. New York City becomes a supporting character in the video: the protagonist walking in the Brooklyn neighborhoods of Bed-Stuy,[94] Dyker Heights, and Flatbush; views of Department of Parks and Recreation playgrounds and basketball courts; the protagonist walking the streets alongside Brooklyn's Prospect Park—all underscore her use of the city as both landscape and confidant. She's seen with few people (her mother, gallery friend, friend accompanying her to the abortion clinic, schoolmates) and talks to no one, but she utilizes all of the city's surfaces.[95] The clinic where the protagonist obtains the abortion(s), Fountain Medical Group, is a real medical practice in Brooklyn's East New York neighborhood, which is challenged both economically and in the delivery of social services. The short film locates the protagonist as a traveler, one who explores the entire city, who wanders to think and see and experience the world as she struggles with being pregnant and with the physical and emotional aftermath of her pregnancy's termination. As Michel de Certeau made clear, "Walking affirms, suspects, tries out, transgresses, respects . . . the trajectories it 'speaks.'"[96] The use of the city's topography to create art (both in the world of the film and in Grae's own relationship to her work) signifies the centrality of New York City as a site in which to make art and a site that inspires art making.

   This chapter has examined the relationship of gender, race, and sexuality in hip hop culture and performance through Sigmund Freud's theory of the uncanny and W. E. B. Du Bois's theory of double consciousness. By situating Brooklyn-based emcee and producer Jean Grae in dialogue with Freud and Du Bois, this chapter, following the work of Black feminist scholars Hortense Spillers and Hazel Carby, has critiqued the manner in which Black femininity is erased, derided, or ignored in formulations of psychic, psychological, affective, and sociopolitical processes. Jean Grae serves as a template for thinking through the possibilities of Black female artistry in hip hop culture—and how that might speak to the wider ways in which Black femininity and psychic expression is constructed and performed. By exploring Grae's music in various stages of her career, this chapter has demonstrated the depth of her engagement with and critical thought concerning issues of gender, race, and sexuality, and their performative inhabitations that Grae makes central to her music and commentary.

4

Queer Hip Hop, Queer Dissonance

Why is the chapter on queer hip hop artists and queer hip hop production the last one in my book on queer hip hop aesthetics? In some ways, I wanted to save the "queer hip hop" chapter for last to foreground queer aesthetics as a practice, an embodiment, and a quality, in addition to its functioning as an identitarian social category, before deeply exploring a specific set of queer hip hop scenes that take place in New York and intersect with other scenes in the city. This expansive position on queer aesthetics is an attempt to locate how queerness in hip hop occurs in many places—some quite unexpected. Simultaneously, any project of mine on queerness will indeed include LGBTQ+ people; I'm not interested in a queerness without homosexuality or transsexuality. In this chapter, I turn toward queer historiography, queer archiving, and what Zenzele Isoke terms "black ethnography," which she formulates as "a response ... that goes beyond the empirical, beyond identity, and beyond the empty thrills of nostalgia."[1] Likewise, the queer archival, ethnographic, and historiographic methods I index here are in line with what Gayatri Gopinath names "queer curatorial practices" that "deliberately stage 'collisions and encounters' between aesthetic practices that may seem discontinuous or unrelated."[2] These queer methods are aesthetic practices that respond to the lacunae in traditional and/or disciplinary formations like anthropology, history, and philosophy. The capaciousness of my methods in this book—performance studies, Black studies, Black feminism, archival, music and sound, film and cinema, psychoanalytic, visual, historical, and now ethnographic—reflect both a need and a desire to be adaptable in order to tease out as much depth and breadth around queer hip hop aesthetics as possible.

This chapter extends previous work I've written on hip hop's queer historiography. In that work, I trace two threads of queer (LGBTQ+) hip hop formation: one through the first commercial rap song, "Rapper's Delight" (1979), in which one of the rappers, Big Bank Hank, sets up an imaginary queer foil (DC Comics superhero Superman) to shore up his own tentative masculinity.[3] In contrast to Hank's figuration of a "fairy-fied" Superman, I delve into the oeuvre of the first known gay hip hop group, the LA-based Age of Consent. In the second historical thread, I discuss the queer 1990s and 2000s, which both ushered in different yet related queer hip hop scenes.[4] Finally, I discuss the more recent trend of the last decade or so of more mainstream Black hip hop and R&B artists known and unknown—Frank Ocean, Syd the Kid, Lil Nas X, Mykki Blanco, Young M.A, Kehlani, Le1F/Mx Khalif, Zebra Katz, ROES/Angel Haze, Cakes da Killa, and others—commanding space as out queer artists. However, I focus on New York City rather than the triumvirate of the San Francisco Bay Area, Los Angeles, and New York City in relationship to queer hip hop history. As I stated in "Queer Hip Hop: A Brief Historiography," both LA and SF went on record *first* in having established out queer and trans hip hop artists and scenes. I attribute NYC's late and hesitant entry into queer hip hop to three major reasons: referring back to some of the issues I raised in the introduction, New York City hip hop, as well as hip hop from surrounding areas (Connecticut, New Jersey, Long Island, Philadelphia), has, in general, been concerned with various forms of authenticity. Though it's beyond the scope of this particular project, the foil figure in NYC hip hop has played a strong role in illuminating who is a "real hip hop head." That foil has alternately and concurrently been queers, faggots, "sucka niggas," women, bitches, "bitch-ass niggas," fake niggas, and so on. Depending on the era of NYC hip hop and the scenes one is discussing, any of the above formations could stand in for interlopers into the realness of NYC hip hop. That realness has always been fashioned by some masculine paradigm— whether that's real-life pimps, drug dealers, and gangsters (Bumpy Johnson), cinematic gangsters (the *Godfather* films), martial arts masculinity, comic book masculinity, or certain idealized aspects of rich white men. These particular forms of masculinity aren't inclusive of out/overt queerness, so queerness often ends up occluded in the formation of an "authentic" Black male rap figure.

A second contributing factor to New York City's late entry into a recognizable queer hip hop scene is the sheer variety of scenes and activism in New York City. Because of the gap—real and/or perceived—between hip hop communities and activism and LGBTQ communities and activism, queer and trans hip hop artists and fans often immersed themselves in Black hip hop communities or queer Black and Latinx spaces that welcomed hip hop culture. Many white-majority gay and lesbian clubs enacted racist and classist policies designed to exclude Black and Latinx queers from the 'hood by targeting certain forms of music, including hip hop. These policies continue to pop up, even during more "enlightened" times.[5] Part of this formation emerges from the whitewashing of contemporary queer and trans US history— organizing, in particular. That Pride marches and parades have become not only corporate-inspired bacchanalia (so not really bacchanalia) is a well-deserved critique. Less frequently observed, though increasingly so, is the fact that Black and Latinx trans women, lesbians, and gay men, as we all as a host of working-class queers across the racial, gender, and sexuality spectrum have been erased from the history of queer and trans organizing pre– and post–Stonewall Riots. In fact, *Stonewall* (dir. Roland Emmerich, 2015), one of the most egregious revisionist-history moves, attempts to make a white gay teenager from Indiana the hero of the Black and Latinx-trans-led Stonewall Riots. Marsha P. Johnson, Sylvia Rivera, and countless others are the background scenery for his "heroism." Fortunately, the film was panned as the formal, narrative, and historical disaster that it was.[6] Gay, lesbian, bisexual, transgender, queer, questioning, intersex, and asexual history is not white history, but the efforts to make it so has been so successful that gayness and queerness have been racialized as white. It is no surprise that a city proud of its many accomplishments, including being the birth of contemporary hip hop, would shun a dull, whitewashed gay identity. Couple that with disdain for "inauthenticity," and, well, the queer and trans hip hopper was often out of luck in finding hospitable hip hop spaces and queer spaces.

Even in their subterranean, DIY existence, queer and trans folks in hip hop made important contributions that were felt even if they were consumed in the overwhelming noise of the broader popular culture landscape. Two thousand and five marked a watershed for queer hip hop.[7] That year, two major LGBTQ hip hop festivals occurred: PeaceOUT World Homohop Festival,[8] the original queer and queer-ally hip hop festival in the Oakland/San Francisco area, and Peace Out East,[9] New York City's LGBTQ hip hop festival.[10] It was the year LGBTQ hip hop artists were codified in the documentary film *Pick Up the Mic* (dir. Alex Hinton, 2005), which premiered at the Toronto International Film Festival on September 11. The festivals and film, imperfect and hardly exhaustive of the panoply of LGBTQ hip hop artists who came before and after them, matter for the history of queer music, performance and culture; hip hop culture, performance, and music; and independent art-making. This chapter underscores the historical, ongoing, and evolving relationship of queer aesthetics to Black and hip hop aesthetics through the figures of the queer and trans hip hop artist.

As I've demonstrated over the course of this book, lesbian, gay, bisexual, transgender (LGBT) and queer, intersex, genderqueer, and gender-nonconforming (QIGGNC) bodies have been both integral to US hip hop cultural production and denied as integral to said production. Queer culture and hip hop culture have been arranged as antagonistic, both internally in each respective culture and externally by news outlets, thinkers, and pundits.[11] Yet many queer hip hop artists speak to the immense import of hip hop to their queer identities. Hanifah Walidah, a Brooklyn-and Massachusetts-based rapper, producer, singer, and filmmaker, noted that, when she was closeted, she "could see through [her] body language that [her] body was tight, that [she] was holding something in."[12] Queer hip hop pioneer Dutchboy reveals, "ironically, I didn't get back into hip hop until after my coming out process"; he continues, "I first became involved in performing hip hop . . . as an extension of my finding a place within . . . the queer or the LGBT community."[13] These artists underscore the relationality of their queerness and their hip hop identities. More fraught is the relationship to blackness and Black cultural production. The fact that many of the earliest known LGBTQ hip hop artists were white and non-Black reified perceptions related to the whiteness of queerness and the white queer as an unwelcome interloper into a Black (masculine) cultural production space.

Locating Queerness, Locating Hip Hop

Calling hip hop "queer" is certain to irritate or even enrage some hip hop artists and fans. The current hip hop moment is filled with strict (although ever-changing) sites of categorization of the authentic, the real, and the 'hood as metonyms for a particular kind of Black-popular-masculine affect—this presents a normative conundrum for a queer or queered project. It is a challenge for some to learn of hip hop's queerness—past, present, and future. This chapter indexes queer being (identity, subjectivity), doing (performance, performativity), and effects/affects. Queer is deployed here as a denaturalizing and destabilizing force—the coitus interruptus of hip hop heteronormativity, heteropatriarchy, and racial authenticity. As Annamarie Jagose claims, "queer opts for denautralisation as its primary strategy,"[14] and so I put it to use as a temporal, cognitive, and affective disruption to the apparent seamlessness of a unified hip hop presentation. Concurrently, I attend to the racialized and gendered dynamics and meanings associated with the terms "hip hop" and "queer" in order to tease out some of the axes on which they rotate. My thinking is informed by Cathy Cohen's insight into the limits of queer politics, in which she calls on queer theory to expand notions of queer to include straight or heterosexual bodies and performances that interrupt hegemonic heteronormativity, whether purposefully or not: "instead of destabilizing the assumed categories and binaries of sexual identity, queer politics has served to reinforce simple dichotomies between the heterosexual and everything 'queer.'"[15]

The work on queerness, Blackness, and hip hop arts and culture that has emerged since the early 2000s[16] is a rich and nuanced set of scholarly pursuits. In particular, Moya Bailey's theory of homolatency carefully explores the thorny terrain of Black male and masculine sexuality inside hip hop culture and performance. According to Bailey, "*homolatent* attempts . . . to encapsulate the ways in which masculinity and heterosexuality are signaled through tentative performative utterances."[17] Bailey explores and demonstrates through examples from Odd Future Wolf Gang Kill Them All, Jay-Z, Kanye West, Lil Wayne, and others how these performative utterances are based on pain, humiliation, and violence (against women, other men, other masculine folks) to solidify their bonds. And frankly, as she argues, though some of these performances and utterances temporarily disrupt, they ultimately serve to deepen and lengthen the lexicon of heterosexist logic, patriarchy, and misogyny.[18] The queer and/or trans hip hop performer must "challeng[e] what the standards of hip hop can be."[19] It's a tall order and is rarely, if ever, a seamless victory. However, some of the artists, performative moments, and movements I examine gesture toward and play in the realm of what I term "queer dissonance." "Dissonance" and its synonym "discord" are musical terms involving tones that are disharmonious, incongruous, harsh sounding, or lacking harmony *between* things. Adjoining queer to dissonance aims to aurally and visually expand and perhaps upend musical conventionality. The artists I discuss in this chapter embody some aspects of queer dissonance, while upholding other forms of the conventional musical, social, and structural.

Queer dissonance is explicitly, though not exclusively, about the music-making, music-listening, and artmaking practices of queer subjects. Queer dissonance speaks about, against, back to and with the forces that impact and inform it: postmodernity, racial, sex, and gender identity, queer cultures, hip hop cultures, capitalism, visual culture, region, religion, and more. It does not simply disavow or incorporate, or even mimic; it makes sonic room for what is said to be impossible. It is impossibility made aural and visual. It is shocking and bold, expanding the conventionality of music-making culture in hip hop, in this case. Here, queer dissonance points to the mechanism by which queer hip hop artists have irrecoverably joined these two supposedly disparate cultures for almost as long as hip hop culture has existed. Queer dissonance is sonic and visual expression against the irrationality of patriarchy, queer liberalism, white supremacy, heterosexism, and Black masculine authenticity.

Makers of queer dissonance—the queer hip hop artists—are also queer dissidents, in the primary sense of the word in that they differ from or disagree with what is established; they are variants. Dissidence resonates in relation to artists, scholars, and fans that actively challenge the notion of who is creating and historicizing hip hop culture. Hip hop and its historiography's standards around Black masculinity, authentic stories and histories, and preapproved displays of masculinity and femininity are made fraught by the reoccurring musical queer who simply will not shut up or go away. Not only are LGBTQ-identified people simply fans of hip hop or arbiters of "swag,"[20] queer folks seem to keep making hip hop music.[21] The queer dissident who produces queer dissonance is locatable sonically and visually on their, his, or her terms. She is not, in fact, readily apprehended by stereotypes of what queer or hip hop is or might be, even as she uses familiar queer or hip hop tropes, such as camp, drag, dialect and slang, rhyme battling, gestural affect, or hip hop stylized clothing.

Queer dissonance and dissidence is situated in the genealogy of Black feminism and queer of color critique. Specifically, queer dissonance follows the logic of Black feminist organizing and theory in "struggling against racial, sexual, heterosexual, and class oppression . . . [seeking to develop] integrated analysis and practice based upon the fact that the major systems of oppression are interlocking."[22] Similar to the Combahee River Collective Statement and the eight Black women who wrote it, a theory of queer dissonance arises from the artistic, material, and political visions of queer Black folks and other queer non-Black people. Queer dissonance is meant to function as a descriptor and a deployment in disrupting the lure of violent normative systems like white supremacy, patriarchy, and queer and trans antagonism. Both "queer" and "dissonance" operate as a tension or clash resulting from the combination of two disharmonious or unsuitable elements. For instance, joining queer and hip hop linguistically, musically, or materially still often elicits laughter, derision, bafflement, and other forms of disorientation from both orthodox hip hop heads and LGBTQ communities. Instead of viewing this as an impediment to "acceptance" or mainstreaming, queer dissenters can use queer dissonance to demarcate the spaces and places they inhabit and imagine. In this way, queer dissonance resonates strongly with queer of color critique, as well as being a queer aesthetic hip hop form. Queer of color critique is "a convergence with and departure from queer studies . . . [and] signal[s] the ways in which the dominant literary, philosophical, and aesthetic engagements with queer sexuality distanced themselves from the study of race and from politico-economic concerns."[23] Here, Rod Ferguson elucidates how queers of color, following Black and women of color feminists theory of the 1970s and 1980s, orient themselves toward a more holistic form of critique: one that includes embodiment, materiality, political economy, and historical and cultural context. Both queer and hip hop definitions suggest expansiveness, deconstruction, inclusivity, mixology, and creativity. A queer hip hop rendering attempts to illuminate the musical contributions of LGBTQ people and themes, showing how their creativity and musicality enrich hip hop and queer arts movements.

Queer Negation: Or, What Do We Mean When We Say "Black"?

Many scholars and artists have convincingly argued that rap music and, sometimes, hip hop more broadly is "black American music" and that its central characteristics are Black and/or African American.[24] Murray

Forman and Mark Anthony Neal note "hip-hop's undeniable African-American origins [and endeavor to] query[] the formation of distinct identities within hip-hop while simultaneously interrogating the definitions of authenticity that often dominate discussions pertaining to cultural hybridity and the risk of appropriation as hip-hop circulates ever further afield and is more deeply embraced in the social mainstream."[25] Forman and, separately, Imani Perry clarify some of the troubling ways hip hop's inherent cultural, aesthetic, historical, and material hybridity has been used to wrest hip hop cultural production and performance away from Black American and Black diasporic peoples, cultures, and traditions. While Forman gestures toward the pitfalls of authenticity as a response to the anxieties hybridity causes, he moves too quickly to the threats of appropriation by a larger social mainstream. Black authenticity and hip hop authenticity present unique problems for Black people and Black artists negotiating "non-authentic" Black subjectivities.

When blackness becomes a metonym for authenticity or an essential, authentic blackness, it is "linked to masculinity in its most patriarchal significations . . . this particular brand of masculinity epitomizes the imperialism of heterosexism, sexism and homophobia."[26] Yep and Elia offer the Logo series *Noah's Arc* as an example of a contra-authentic Black cultural product. The series, which ran from October 2005 to October 2006, centered on the lives of Black gay men living in Los Angeles. It "open[ed] up the discursive field to new horizons and possibilities for imagining, embodying, performing, renegotiating, and unfixing hegemonic blackness. . . . *Noah's Arc* is queering/quaring[27] authentic blackness."[28] While music and television are different media, and representation is a fraught project, images of Black men and women do have impact on viewers, listeners, and industries.[29] In the last two decades of hip hop music, the range of Black performance has continued to fluctuate, sometimes feeling overwhelming rote: for men/masculine people, the trope is the über-rich hip hop man as hustler/gangsta/pimp/heartbreaker, while women/feminine people are limited often to the vixen, female hustler, or thug, or sometimes a "positive" lady role. These conservative and restricted modalities of Black possibility are transmitted to and codified in the popular imaginary.[30] The Black performer who strays from the contemporary sanctioned roles of masculinity is often labeled with invectives imagined to be the most damaging: something related to being gay, a faggot, or possessing a "feminine" quality. In the following sections, I turn to different sites of queer hip hop production: first, I discuss Man Parrish, a NYC DJ who occupied space in hip hop and queer scenes and is still a well-regarded DJ. Next, I trace the golden age of queer hip hop—roughly the decade between 1995 and 2005—then turn to a pair of queer hip hop festival series I co-produced. This is not an exhaustive list, but an exemplary one that I intend to use to demonstrate the breadth and range of LGBTQIA+ hip hop performers, scenes, and performances. Admittedly, these examples do not encompass the "big name" queer performers like Big Freedia, Young M.A, Frank Ocean, Syd the Kid, Lil Nas X, or Tyler, the Creator. I wanted to focus on the longer history of NYC queer hip hop performance. Perhaps I'll revisit these performers and their impact in another decade from now.

Man Parrish: Hip Hop's First Queer DJ

In my essay "Queer Hip Hop: A Brief Historiography," I locate queer hip hop in two different rap groups: the Sugarhill Gang, the first rap group to record an album, and Age of Consent, the first out gay rap group. There is a history contained in and between those two divergent groups, and plenty that is left out. Here, I discuss Man Parrish, a foundational New York City DJ and producer. Manuel (Man) Joseph Parrish, a white man (variously [self-]described as Puerto Rican and/or Italian) is an openly gay man originally from Kansas City, Missouri, who made two immensely influential electro–hip hop records, "Hip Hop, Be Bop (Don't Stop)," first issued in 1982, and the equally period-defining "Boogie Down Bronx," issued in 1984.[31]

Man Parrish was briefly signed to Elektra Records after the extraordinary success of "Hip Hop, Be Bop (Don't Stop)," which sold two and a half million copies worldwide. Parrish emerged onto the New York City music scene from two parallel subcultures: the Studio 54/Andy Warhol/downtown art scene and the uptown/Bronx club/experimental DJ/hip hop scene. His big hits reflected this sonic and cultural mixture. Alongside artists like Kraftwerk, Jellybean Benitez, Afrika Bambaataa, and Art of Noise, Parrish was one of the originators of the post-disco, pre-house electro sound that paved the way for groups such as the hip hop and electro funk band Mantronix. "Hip Hop, Be Bop (Don't Stop)" is five minutes of funky electro-hip hop energy. Parrish created the analogue-synthesized sound using "only three pieces: Roland 808 drum machine, my PRO One, a small version of Prophet 5 for Polyphonic and special effects, and PROPHET 1 monophonic for the bass sound and some of the sequencers," according to an interview with the Brazilian magazine *Electronic Standards*.[32] It is an early electro/hip hop artifact that still sounds fresh, innovative, and engaging today. The song is mostly musical with a few haptic sounds and spoken-sung-rapped words such as "hip hop" repeated at intervals. It's a dance song and a groove song and a technical delight.

Parrish, a reclusive artist who still spins records at parties in New York City and beyond, had a quietly prolific career. Though he did not see much of the money from his "Hip Hop, Be Bop" sales, he remixed songs for an extraordinary range of acts from Michael Jackson to Gloria Gaynor to Boy George. Schooled at New York City's High School for the Performing Arts—the school on which the film *Fame* (1980) was based—Parrish had a flair for the theatrical. His DJ shows in the Bronx were said to be magnificent: filled with glitter, pyrotechnics, and dazzling light shows, bringing downtown Manhattan's dramatic sensibility to the avant-garde hip hop scene in the Bronx. Parrish notes in an interview with Harvard University's WHRB 95.3, that some of the praise for him was a bit hyperbolic, particularly the *New York Times* calling him the "Godfather of Hip Hop."[33] Parrish was in high demand for a period, so much so that he recalls when a young, unknown performer named Madonna was his opening act for a party at Studio 54. She sang her new, little-known song "Holiday." Man Parrish's work is starting to be "rediscovered" by US college radio, old school analog purists, and hip hop enthusiasts, as well as by many European and Australian music scholars and fans who consider his work foundational for its use of the Roland TR-808 drum machine and other progressive musical technologies.

It's no small fact that Man Parrish was an out gay man in and adjacent to hip hop cultural production in the 1980s. His presence as an active hip hop cultural producer revises the racist notion that Black folks and hip hop are inherently more homophobic than non-Black people and non–hip hop communities. Black people and Black people inside hip hop have language, cultural suspicions, religious influences, and awareness of white hegemony that all inform the ways they orient to sexuality and gender generally, and queer sexuality and gender in particular. And because hegemonic thinking interchanges Black individuals and Black people as a group when convenient, Black cultural and artistic expression is often reduced to personal beliefs, and those beliefs are then generalized to all Black people. Exemplary of this is a small but illuminating piece that Zimbabwean film, media, and music critic Charles Mudede wrote for the *Stranger* in 2005, in which he makes a connection between Man Parrish and gayness in early hip hop culture. I'll quote the entire blog entry at length as it's short and worth sharing in its entirety. Mudede gleefully proclaims:

> At the end of Mobb Deep's "Quiet Storm [remix]," which has a sick loop of "White Lines," [by Grandmaster Flash & The Furious Five, 1983] convict Lil Kim raps "It's the real/Hah, it's the real baby, hip-hop, hip-hop, hip-hop . . .". The way she chants "hip-hop, hip-hop" directly references Man Parrish's 1983 groundbreaking "Hip Hop Bee Bop (Don't Stop)." Man Parrish, one of the founding fathers of hiphop, is gay and white. He also produced in 1984 "Boogie Down Bronx," a solid street hit that featured a rapper named Cool Raul. Later, Man Parrish made a gay disco hit with Man 2 Man called "Male Stripper." What does it all mean? There is no such thing as a clear center, as a hard truth. Hiphop's birth was

wonderfully messy. Check out the video of "Hip Hop Bee Bop (Don't Stop)"; it challenges present notions of what is and what is not the soul of hiphop.[34]

Mudede is a wonderful writer, even if this excerpt is somewhat shallow. His writing on music and film is smart, deeply personal, and highly knowledgeable. This piece caught my attention for a number of reasons: he's a fan of Man Parrish's work! He understands the intertextual and citational references of hip hop! He uses Lil' Kim's "Quiet Storm (remix)" verse as exemplary! However, I was struck by the easy, seamless connections he makes between whiteness, maleness, and gayness without interrogating the ways he elides Lil' Kim in one of the best verses of her entire career. The critical move Mudede makes repeats a tendency to erase Black women as hip hop innovators, while "bigging up" white men. I'd like to spend some time thinking through this elision, Lil' Kim's own queer affect, and in the next section delve more deeply into the pass white men in hip hop often receive.

Mobb Deep's original "Quiet Storm," off of their 1999 powerhouse third album, *Murda Muzic*, features Prodigy and Havoc serving their signature laconic "dun(n) language," a dialect über-local to Queensbridge (a neighborhood in New York's borough of Queens) originated by their friend Bumpy, who had a speech impediment.[35] The remix of the song builds on the musically dark and foreboding interpolation of Grandmaster Flash and Melle Mel's "White Lines," by also sampling MC Lyte's "10% Dis." Emcees Prodigy and Havoc effortlessly glide in and out of the time signature, demonstrating they are masterful emcees, completely in the flow, as well as "serious" emcees, not just rappers. They talk that ill shit: murder, drugs, depression, and the general grime and grittiness of the wear and tear NYC life can have on Black men. And though Lil' Kim is a fellow Queens rapper, the "Queen B" is a somewhat unorthodox collaborative choice. However, as Greg Thomas reminds us, Lil' Kim is often rendered as an "unabashedly sexual rapper [who is] simply "unconscious" . . . . [I]sn't most or all Hip-Hop "mindless" and "meaningless," at best, today if not always; isn't the "rap" produced by this culture of the masses merely about titillation minus any mental stimulation? So goes the refrain of those who uphold the false divisions of Western bourgeois imperialism over Hip-Hop, consciously or unconsciously."[36] Thomas makes clear that the purity test of conscious versus commercial, or any other binaries, are Western forms of thinking that miss revolutionary potential in the many forms in which they appear. In his broader intervention, he persuades his readers to rethink Lil' Kim's lyricism as a "revolution within a revolution at the musical level of her lyricism" arguing her work is "about power, knowledge, and pleasure" and is "full-bodied and intellectually devastating."[37] In this recontextualized view, a Mobb Deep/Lil' Kim collab is hardly circumspect. For whatever criticisms of Lil' Kim—particularly that she didn't write her own rhymes—her delivery, lyrical dexterity, and performance presence are undeniable. In fact, her guest verse made the great original song an iconic remix. I take this long-routed response to Mudede's dismissiveness of Kim for two reasons: first, to highlight the ways Black women in hip hop are often de-cathected from the very performance culture they helped create, maintain, and continually innovate; second, to underscore the ways white and non-Black queer men and masculine folks are often afforded room in hip hop spaces because of their love for and skills in hip hop—without receiving the same feedback, backlash, suspicion, or criticism that Black women receive.

Whether or not Kim is directly quoting Man Parrish—it is just as likely she heard it from Keef Cowboy of the Furious Five, who is credited with coining the term "hip hop," or from Afrika Bambaataa and the Zulu Nation, who popularized the term to refer to the various art forms in the scene,[38] Mudede makes a slippage that erases Black women's creativity *and* Black men's originality. Man Parrish, who DJed in the Bronx as well as all over Manhattan, heard the term "hip hop" in those spaces and from records of Grandmaster Flash and the Furious Five, as well as from Bambaataa, whom he knew. If we are looking for hip hop's rhizomatic lineage tree, it is more intellectually and historically honest to think through these connections rather than pretend that Black people were not absolutely at the center of hip hop's invention. What is valuable to me about Mudede's claim is that Man Parrish was inside of early hip hop as a gay white man. He innovated, he created, and he collaborated alongside Black and brown folks, not as a white singularity.

When Parrish talks about this particular song, he elucidates the technical, historical, artistic, and cultural context of making an "ambient piece of music with a beat to it" in the early 1980s.[39] Parrish is careful to note that the music he was making would be considered freestyle or electro today, as the musical genres of hip hop and rap (think "Rapper's Delight") were not yet synonymous. Importantly, Parrish reminds audiences that he was a leader in the nascent hip hop (electro) scene, not that rap scene, though those worlds crossed over frequently and in short order hip hop described the various aesthetic art forms and cultural movements emerging from NYC youth cultures. In an episode of his YouTube show, Parrish talks about the challenges of making analog music at home, without the benefits of contemporary mixing tools and apparatus, as well as his inspiration for sounds and haptics that came from listening to and watching crowds at popular New York City clubs like the Fun House.[40] Parrish recalls how he and his music partner were inspired to add the dog barking sounds to "Hip Hop, Be Bop (Don't Stop)," because when the kids barked to a song in the club, it meant they liked it. He was sure to engineer the "sound" of a hit into his own music and replicate a stamp of approval from imaginary club kids (he and Raul made the vocal barks for the track). With a muted exuberance and a strikingly good memory, Parish describes the business of making a record: getting shorted by the record company and seeing no money from the millions of records sold, as well as getting a "form of payola" to get his record played on WKTU.[41]

Parrish's other foundational hip hop/electro hit, "Boogie Down Bronx," featuring rapper John "Ski" Carter of Freeze Force Crew, has an eclectic, fun, lo-fi sound that remains remarkably danceable today. Recorded in Parrish's childhood Brooklyn bedroom, Parrish recalls how this collaboration came from his own financial desperation (after signing a bad record deal) and the spark of creativity he saw from John Carter, who would rhyme on Parrish's doorstep every day. Parrish's long-term producer, Raul Rodriguez, suggested they collaborate with John and "Boogie Down Bronx" was born. At just 24 years old, Parrish had made two era-defining hits, but as he said, he was "poor, on welfare, and food stamps" because of his ignorance in dealing with predatory record companies.[42] Like other hip hop pioneers and practitioners in the early 1980s, he was young and inexperienced in the music business, but an extraordinarily talented music-maker. His lasting relevance to DJs, music tech nerds, clubs, music scholars, and other deep music fans, is a testament to his own impact and influence in his early 20s and in the contemporary moment.

Parrish's gayness wasn't an impediment to his success as a musical producer and collaborator. Parrish discloses his own short history as a teenage sex worker, as he had been living on the streets since he was 14 years old.[43] He is matter-of-fact about being gay, and his gayness did not seem to present any problems for ostensibly heterosexual collaborators and fans. Parrish's queer aesthetics, similar to Martin Wong's, were influenced by collaboration, experimentation, DIY expertise, and negotiating impoverishment, success, and the thin line between legal and illegal activities. In fact, "in those days," if I may use that phrase, you couldn't be a part of the NYC club scene, electro scene, or music and art scene without being among gay, lesbian, trans, and other sexual outlaws. Why would early hip hop culture be any different? Because early hip hop culture is conceived as Black, masculine, and improvised, it is also concurrently conceived as one-dimensional, unsophisticated, and antithetical to queer sexuality and gender. All the more so, queer sexuality and gender is conceptualized and imagined as white and middle-class, erasing Black, working-class, and poor men from queer possibilities and queer aesthetics. In the next section, I will think through the past two or more decades of coded Black queer sexuality and the Black queer hip hop subject.

The Golden Age of Queer Hip Hop

In 1997, the now-defunct Connecticut magazine *One Nut* published the infamous "Confessions of a Gay Rapper" article written by Jamal X.[44] The article was a supposed tell-all from a *Billboard* top-selling rap act. The anonymous rapper agreed to speak to Mr. X about his queerness. The magazine and article didn't get much traction until Wendy Williams, then a local New York City radio personality, read "Confessions" live on her top-rated show. Williams argued that it wasn't simply *a* rapper who was gay, but many: "Not rapper, *rappers!*"[45] This helped to usher in an era (that has yet to end) of visible and audible panic in hip hop (especially in rap and DJing cultures) around male homosexuality, queerness, or attraction to transgender women. The volatile mixture of hypermasculinity, gay panic, an explosion in hip hop record sales and popularity, and a much more visible US LGBTQ population created the perfect storm for repositioning authentic hip hop masculinity as antithetical to male homosexuality or bisexuality. Decades earlier, James Baldwin explicated the uncertainty and hostility that the queer person of color faced inside of the "queer world." Baldwin noted he was "black in that world, and . . . was used in that way, and by people who truly mean me no harm . . . they could *not* have meant me harm, because they did not see me."[46] There is harm done in going unseen or mis-seen. This not-seeing of the queer takes place in hip hop culture through dominant voices *speaking* for or about the queer. This shapes the queer as threatening to dominate Black masculinity and produces a discursive visual archetype of the gender variant queer that should be avoided by those adhering to authentic hip hop Black masculine ideals.

An encouraging situation that preceded and followed the "gay rapper" article was the public dialogue that people involved in the hip hop industry and fandom began to have about homosexuality, bisexuality, and gender. It wasn't always pretty, but it was occurring. In July 1997, Davey D, a respected DJ, hip hop historian, journalist, and community activist based in Oakland, California, wrote an editorial, "Gays, Lesbians and Hip Hop Culture," in recognition of Gay Pride Week. Though he hadn't yet written about the nascent San Francisco Bay Area LGBTQ hip hop scene (he would later), he wanted to talk about "the role gays and lesbians have played in hip hop culture," something he said "we've laughed about, smirked about and felt uncomfortable about, but have not resolved."[47] The same month the *One Nut* article was published, the *Source*, the longest-running hip hop magazine, published three articles about gay men and hip hop. Lesbians and queer women often weren't covered in-depth in hip hop magazines, although they were elsewhere. Though Queen Pen made a song, "Girlfriend," bragging about stealing a woman from her boyfriend,[48] gay men, "down-low" men, and bisexual men were the focus of hip hop's queer obsession. One of the *Source*'s three articles on gay men focused on Wendy Williams's reveal of "gay rappers." Another was by R. K. Byers, describing how he ventured to the legendary Black and Latino gay club the Warehouse, located in the South Bronx, to experience "hip hop's gay underground."[49] Byers encountered men of color who frequented the Warehouse, as well as the Octagon, a gay hip hop club in Manhattan. He was shocked to find gay men who looked like him or other straight Black and Latino men he knew. He rendered them as "crime-looking cats" that were partying at a club "straight outta *Love Jones*."[50] The final article was an open letter from gay writer and entrepreneur James Earl Hardy titled "Boys Will B-Boys: An Open Letter to All My Homie-Sexuals in Hip Hop." Hardy, author of the Afrocentric, same-gender-loving (SGL) hip hop *B-Boy Blues* series, offered this missive:

> You've been talked about, written about, gossiped about—especially in the late last year and a half, no doubt because of *that* article. But whatever nerves have been struck by *that* article, it hasn't forced most inside and outside hip-hop to truly acknowledge that homosexuals and rap artists can be, and are, one in the same.[51]

Hardy's words, directed solely at Black men who love, like, or have sex with other Black men, were important for the *Source*'s audience to read and gave further voice and imagery to the imagined/famous unknown gay or bisexual Black male rapper.

As this chapter has shown, there were already out LGBTQ hip hop performers, but none of them were famous. Some involved in hip hop are more interested in using gay as the anti–hip hop identity, rather than being curious about those who seamlessly embody gay or queer or trans and hip hop. Queer emcees started releasing albums and increasingly performing locally, regionally, and nationally in 1998. Perhaps all the "gay rapper" hype was helpful in attracting listening audiences curious about the work of gay, trans, and queer emcees. The rise of visible prominent LGBTQ entertainers and politicians, the consolidation of wealthy lesbian and gay individuals and organizations like Human Rights Campaign (HRC) into serious political forces, and the visibility of LGBTQ youth all helped queer hip hop to make sense as a phenomenon in the late 1990s. I'll now recount my own experience of "discovering" and encountering a queer hip hop scene in the early 2000s.

I first encountered members of DeepDickCollective, or D/DC, at the Homo Hop Massive festival in New York City in April 2002. I knew of Tim'm T. West through the usual queer channels: he and my then-girlfriend had gone to undergraduate together at Duke University and I was friends and work colleagues with one of Tim'm's ex-boyfriends. A number of us were scheduled to perform at the legendary dyke club Meow Mix located in Manhattan's Lower East Side. Over the course of the two-day festival, comedian-singer-poet and now filmmaker Robin Cloud, rapper/producer Dutchboy, emcees Tim'm T. West, Juba Kalamka, and G-Minus of D/DC, DJs Ross Hogg and Daryl Raymond, and I performed in the dark, dank, dyke nightclub. It was an exhilarating time. The packed crowd put Meow Mix at capacity; there were also standing room–only audiences at the related panel discussion at People of Color in Crisis, a social service center in Brooklyn catering to gay and bisexual men, men who have sex with men (MSM), and transgender women. The crowd at Meow Mix on that Saturday, April 27, was filled with hip hop heads, queer folks, and others who refused easy identification. It was breathtaking to see thug-looking men of all colors hanging side by side with shaved-headed Black, brown, and white lesbians. Everyone wanted to hear and see queer folks doing hip hop. Tim'm performed "Blingizm," which moved the crowd to dance while it critiqued the obsession in hip hop and American culture with "bling"—objects and evidence of material wealth.[52] Tim'm, a powerfully built, handsome, dark-skinned Black man from the US Southeast, looked like the archetypal hip hop artist: he was dressed all in blue—deep blue jeans, a sea-blue Triple Five Soul T-shirt, and a midnight- and sea-blue knit cap, his see-through "stunna" sunglasses gleaming under the small bar's lighting as he held the mic in one hand. His other arm, with musculature flexing, pulled us in with its gesticulations, compelling us to listen while we moved to his words:

> Bling, bling! How many times can you sing "Bling, bling"? How many lives lost in pursuit of the dream. . . . So shiny and metallic, metabolism stings the Sun. . . . FUBU will take your Benjamins, leaving you Washington. Boys look pretty in the city, what a pity they're cloaked in labels.[53]

That night I felt a part of something incredibly special. Like other queer hip hop artists and fans, I had experienced isolation in thinking I was the only one who lived and breathed hip hop. After the show, many of us vowed to stay in touch—these connections were how I heard of the PeaceOUT festival and secured an invitation to perform at the event in Oakland in September 2002.

The power of seeing queer Black men doing hip hop cannot be overstated. It's problematic, of course that so much emphasis is placed upon Black masculinity in hip hop, but it's understandable that the veneration of Black men happens in this space, one of the few where Black men reign supreme in the US. Many young and not-so-young Black people have deep emotional investments in hip hop and its legacy. Imani Perry has called hip hop (rap, in particular) a "masculine space" and indeed, it is a space that Black men have carved out as a site for creative articulation. At the same time, hip hop is an open space, ungendered and unfixed. There is value to the queer Black male hip hop performer as analog to his straight Black counterpart. In fact, he *is* needed to validate queer hip hop, so it will not be dismissed as an undertaking done by "them" (read: white queers) or only "femcees" (female rappers) or rappers of non-Black racialized groups. For better or for worse, these attitudes exist and D/DC is a powerful corrective to the notion that queer Black men couldn't be dope emcees. In fact, D/DC is one of the groups whose lyrics are included in the groundbreaking *Anthology of Rap* (2011), a volume intended to canonize "the best" of rap's lyrics and lyricism. Over their eight-year formal existence, D/DC's members were Kalamka, West, Goff, Ralowe Trinitrotulene Ampu (G-Minus), dancer Doug E., Dazié R. Grego, Jeree Brown (JBRap), Marcus René Van (Mr. ManMan), Leslie "Buttaflysoul" Taylor, Soul Nubian, Salas B. Lalgee, and Baraka Noel.

I Was a Gay Rapper: Queer Hip Hop in NYC's Early 2000 Era

My own hip hop stardom ambitions ended as I got deeply into my doctoral work in the mid- to late 2000s. By 2007, I had co-produced and recorded an EP, *B.Q.E.* (2003), and a full-length album, *The Digm and the Dutch* (2006), with my group B.Q.E.[54] B.Q.E. formed after Dutchboy (Jason "Judge" Muscat) and I met on February 20, 2001, at a community forum, Homie-Sexual Hip Hop, sponsored by GLAAD (the Gay & Lesbian Alliance Against Defamation). The forum was one of a slew held in the wake of the rise of white rapper Eminem and his penchant for homophobic lyrics. The NYC panel included author James Earl Hardy, hip hop artist Karter Louis, musician, music writer, and professor Jason King, hip hop DJ Star Perkins, and myself. GLAAD was savvy in choosing an all-Black panel: they protected themselves from accusations of racist targeting of hip hop as opposed to other forms of homophobic media arts, and they benefited from Black people speaking to and about hip hop. Fortunately, none of us was well-behaved and we discussed the nuances of Black art forms and white media response, many of us stating that Eminem was a way for white-dominated organizations and media to "safely" discuss homophobia and hip hop without accusations of racism from Black audiences. Judge and I met after that panel. In fact, a number of us walked and talked as we felt disgusted, upset, and frustrated with the ways mainstream LGBT organizations attempted to control and narrate our desires and passions related to hip hop cultural production and performers—even the problematic ones. On the corner of 27th Street and 6th Avenue, Dutchboy, Star, rapper Invincible, and I formed a hip hop cypher—an impromptu collaborative rap and beatbox performance—and let out our queer frustrations through rap, rhyme, and rhythm. Over the next six years, I would speak on innumerable panels, perform around the US and Canada, be asked to audition for an MTV reality show (I declined), almost get my music on HBO shows, appear in the documentary *Pick Up the Mic* (2005), and produce two LGBTQ music and education festivals with Dutchboy.

Dutchboy and I had a very fruitful collaboration. Besides the EP and full-length album that we co-produced and co-wrote, we conducted countless interviews, performed together in NYC and beyond, collaborated with multiple artists, and produced and curated two music festival series: the first was a small one- or two-night local showcase called Word/Life: Emcees and Poets in the Life. This showcase lasted from 2002 to 2003 and featured between 10 and 20 performances from artists like East Bay rapper Jen-Ro, poet and filmmaker Maurie Jamal, poet and lawyer Travis Montez, emcee and poet Tim'm T. West, and poet and author Yvonne Onakeme Etaghene. We held the showcases at local businesses like Bluestockings Feminist Bookstore in the Lower East Side of Manhattan and Halcyon Records (defunct due to the COVID-19 pandemic) in its original location in Brooklyn's DUMBO neighborhood. For many of the participating artists,

Word/Life: Emcees and Poets in the Life flyer, 2002. From author's personal collection.

this showcase was the first one in which the featured emcees, poets, singers, filmmakers, and dancers were mostly queer and trans. Just as importantly, this was an opportunity for Dutchboy and I to use our various connections and different social privileges to "put on" other artists—established and emergent—in the world of New York City hip hop performance. As hard as it may to be to imagine, even "liberal" and "queer" New York City was a fraught site for queer and trans performers, especially if they were Black or Latinx. The queer spaces didn't want us as they thought we wouldn't "fit" with their demographic (white, feminist, liberal) and the gay clubs dismissed us, though the lesbian clubs came through enthusiastically. The "straight" clubs and spaces often wanted exorbitant insurance coverage—above and beyond the usual million dollars' worth of insurance coverage for music venues in NYC. They both feared the violence associated by the media with (Black, 'hood) hip hop audiences, and could not imagine a queer hip hop audience worth their while. To that end, they would ask us for extremely high bar sale guarantees. These material difficulties generated unexpected effects: we became fluent in the languages of contract negation with clubs, spaces, nonprofits, bookstores, and other sites of commerce and community; we began to understand the capital entanglements and costs of categories, invisibility, and artistic production; we built upon, called on, and deepened community and professional relationships to provide space for queer and trans performers, calling in many markers. The most significant aspect of these worldbuilding activities for me involved the idea of restorative performances as indexed by Soyica Colbert, Douglas A. Jones Jr., and Shane Vogel: these incursive performances we constructed had "the capacity to warp or subvert the dominate through restorations—as repair or mending—of what has been forgotten overlooked, misremembered, suppressed, dormant, or denied."[55] This thematic of restorative performance is another way of delineating the possibility of queer hip hop aesthetics I've been discussing throughout *Hip Hop Heresies*. Following the praxis of both hip hop and queer art and activism, we *had* to make a way or there would be no space that was seen as appropriate to hold us. These efforts resulted in a takeover: fleeting, euphoric, delightful, convivial, painful, and thrilling. Colbert, Jones, and Vogel understand these "[r]estorative performances [as] disrupt[ive to] exploitative systems by making material repair or amends, however fleeting, to the exploited."[56] For many artists, including myself and Dutchboy, having the stamp of New York venue performances opened up many future opportunities. In fact, DJ Stephanie credited Word/Life's later incarnation, Peace Out East, with launching her career, as we vouched for her to spin at a then popular lesbian party, LoverGirlNYC.

After Dutchboy moved back to the San Francisco Bay Area, and I started my MA program at NYU in 2003, I solo produced Peace Out East in 2006 and 2007, after we had two successful years of putting on Peace Out East in 2004 and 2005. Those festivals, as well as Word/Life, cost us both thousands of dollars, hundreds of hours of labor and organizing, and countless days and weeks spent sending emails, making calls, creating marketing assets, and talking with the press. It was full-time work on part-time hours. We were fortunate that some of the work we did with Word/Life and Peace Out East was immortalized in *Pick Up the Mic*. I stopped producing Peace Out East for three reasons: money—it was costing upward of $15,000 a year to produce, and much of that came from my own strained accounts; I was a new graduate student in an intensive PhD program; and, finally, fatigue. After producing festivals of some kind for five years, I simply felt my bandwidth shrink to the point where I was not interested in continuing. I still remain immensely proud of the work we did to "queer" New York City hip hop in the early 2000s—it was no easy task, yet paradoxically appeared so seamless, sensible, and logical once the shows and festivals took off and gained attention. I will remain forever grateful to the artists, venues, producers, supporters, and others who believed in the vision of both Word/Life and Peace Out East, and without whom those indelible performances could have never happened.

Above and on facing page, Peace Out East flyers, 2004 and 2005. From author's personal collection.

PEACE OUT EAST

212.330.8399 ★ http://www.peaceouteast.com

Friday, July 15 at BOWERY POETRY CLUB
WORD/LIFE: emcees and poets in the life
Live music and spoken word featuring BARON
DEWAYNE DICKERSON ★ BUTTAFLYSOUL
TIM'M ★ YVIE E ★ DJ DARYL RAYMOND
308 Bowery @ Bleecker, Lower East Side
10pm ★ $10 ★ F to 2nd Avenue / 6 to Bleecker

Saturday, July 16 at INT'L ACTION CENTER
Video screening of "The Straight Black Folks'
Guide to Gay Black Folks" by Hanifah Walidah
39 West 14th Street #206, Union Square
1pm ★ $5 ★ L/N/Q/R/W/4/5/6 to Union Square

Saturday, July 16 at GALAPAGOS ART SPACE
Featuring SOCE THE ELEMENTAL WIZARD
EL-DON ★ DA LYRICAL ★ AGGRACYST
SHAYVONNA ★ PINO ★ DJ DUTCHBOY
70 N. 6th Street @ Wythe Avenue, Brooklyn
10pm ★ $10 ★ L to Bedford Avenue

Sunday, July 17 at NUYORICAN POETS CAFÉ
Featuring BQE ★ SHORTY ROC ★ KIN
RICOSHADE ★ GOD-DES featuring TINA G.
236 E. 3rd Street @ Ave B, Lower East Side
9pm ★ $10 ★ F to 2nd Avenue

SPONSORED BY

A Queer Hip Hop Future

In conclusion, I'd like to think about the sonic future of queer hip hop and queer artists making hip hop music. The years 2011 and 2012 saw out LGBTQ rappers from all US regions rising to prominence. None of them had significant ties to earlier homohop or queer hip hop movements. Azealia Banks, an out bisexual woman, blazed the way for queer commercial success when she became an internet star through her dynamic, house-influenced rap "212," released in September 2011. Banks helped secure industry success for Zebra Katz, creator of the infectious and dark "Ima Read." Mykki Blanco ("Waavy"), Angel Haze ("Coming Out My Closet"), and Le1f (now Mx Khalif) ("Wut"), as well as Frank Ocean, have garnered significant internet followings. The controversial social media rant-queen Banks's "212" had close to 202 million views on YouTube as of April 2021. Times have changed. Straight-identified rappers like Murs and Macklemore have made gay-positive songs. Murs made "Animal Style" to combat homophobia in and out of hip hop. His decision to play the role of the boyfriend in the video and kiss his video paramour promoted calls for him to "explain" his decision.[57] Macklemore made "Same Love" in part to honor his gay uncles and their love story; the song had just shy of 259 million views on YouTube as of April 2021.[58]

Hip hop has a future partly because the artists, fan base, music programmers, and others are able to more freely produce their music (and gain success) without initially being constrained by the profit-hungry record companies. The shift from the total power of major record labels to a more experimental and quirkier internet interface has made it possible for "weird" to become "cool" and profitable for the artist. Many queer hip hop artists, especially emerging mainstream ones, are refreshingly odd and countercultural, making songs about club drug culture (Blanco's "Waavy"), paying homage to Chicago and New York house music (Banks's "1991"), or making gloriously dark songs (Haze's "New York"). The wider access and proliferation of queer hip hop, queers making hip hop, and straights making hip hop celebrating queers marks a break in hegemonic hip hop authenticity and the insistence that hip hop has no queer interior. It's a bright, odd future, indeed.[59]

Conclusion

Queer Trans Black Aesthetic Futures

I do not think black and queer play well together. I think they often inhabit the same spaces, and even the same bodies, in uncomfortable ways, and I want to foreground their ongoing rubbing, leading, at times, to pleasure, and, at other times, to irritation, and even possibly to pain.
—Keguro Macharia[1]

The hip hop landscape has changed a great deal since I first started writing about queer hip hop as a grad student in the early 2000s. Southern trap and mumble rap have eclipsed New York City's signature boom-bap sound as the popular soundtrack of hip hop music; gender experimentation and gender trespass has gone mainstream: rapper Young Thug, rapper/singer/actor Jaden Smith, Kid Cudi, Young M.A, and others are at the forefront of pushing gender-neutral or gender-subversive fashion forward. Yet Black, queer, and hip hop, as the epigraph that opens this chapter reminds, still sit or play or stand in discomfort together. Even so, Lil Nas X, who became famous with his breakout country/hip hop hit "Old Town Road," featuring Billy Ray Cyrus (2019), has stunned the hip hop and mainstream world with his queer, conservative-trolling hit "Montero (Call Me by Your Name)," which premiered on streaming platforms such as YouTube, Spotify, and Tidal on March 26, 2021. The song itself is a love letter to 14-year-old Montero Lamar Hill (Lil Nas X's legal name), a letter of confident, defiant Black male femme queerness that can be spoken and shown to Montero by his 22-year-old self. Everything about the single announces itself as queer: from the queer intertextuality of the song's subtitle "Call Me by Your Name," taken from a 2007 gay romance novel of the same name,[2] to the single's cover art, which is a Black and queer(er) interpolation of Michelangelo's *The Creation of Adam* (1508–1512). In Lil Nas X's version,[3] he is both nude Adam and, unlike the original painting, nude God as well. He plays on the iconic religious imagery by including and implicating the viewer explicitly in the image's discourse: here God is looking at us, not Adam. Lil Nas's God holds a bow and arrow in which the arrowhead is a white glove, recalling both the god of love, Cupid, as well as communicating an innocent tentativeness or even protection (from touch, intimacy, disease). Lil Nas's twining performs a type of narcissistic imagining and perhaps is a critique of an old and enduring criticism of gay men as narcissistic and self-involved. The imagery is playful, sexy, and a giant departure from Lil Nas X's whimsical appearances associated with 2019's "Old Town Road."

Lil Nas's queer aesthetics are sonic as well as visual, with the song mixing hip hop beats, electropop, syncopated claps, and calypso influences, as well as dancehall and reggaetón. There is a promiscuity to the ways Lil Nas X and his producers infuse their musical influences and refuse to adhere to (bygone?) methods of Black male hip hop authenticity. But both the sonic version of the song and the provocative cover art were easily eclipsed by the music video for "Montero (Call Me by Your Name)," released on the same day as the single. The music video echoes the cover art as a contemplation on Christian religious themes and iconography, as well as Greco-Roman themes and motifs. In a March 29, 2021, interview with *Time*, Lil Nas reveals he wanted the video and its provocative imagery to "open up a dialogue about the continuing omnipresence of repression among LGBTQ youth, particularly within Christian spaces."[4] Lil Nas brings his personal encounters with Christian anti-gay and anti-femme messaging to the public sphere using queer hip hop aesthetics: overt sexuality, collage and experimentation, provocation, remix and intertextuality, drag, gender trespass, and a dismissiveness toward propriety. Additionally, as a member of Gen Z, he adroitly manipulates and deploys media—social, traditional, and new—to reify his message. He tells *Time*, "I grew up in a pretty religious kind of home—and for me, it was fear-based very much. Even as a little child, I was really scared of every single mistake I may or may not have made. I want kids growing up feeling these feelings, knowing they're a part of the LGBTQ community, to feel like they're O.K. and they don't have to hate themselves."[5] From *Time* to Twitter, Lil Nas X, a young, Black gay male rapper, has captured the global sensorium with his queer hip hop aesthetics. His ability to respond to anti-gay harassment with *extra* gay, sacrilegious, sexy, Christian-appropriative videos is part of his genius.

The video is cinematically trite, maybe even a bit sloppy. Yet in smartly manipulating Christian and Greco-Roman imagery, it perfectly performs as a zeitgeist incitement of the outrage-prone white Christian public, the sensitive Black Christian public, and the shockingly conservative hip hop gatekeepers—it's very easy to upset *all* of these constituencies. Lil Nas uses imagery as provocation: he feminizes himself throughout the video with long-haired wigs, makeup, and form-fitting stylized clothing; he positions himself in the feminine position—as the mythic Eve, before the Fall; as a stripper giving the Devil a lap dance; and, perhaps most astonishing and hilarious, pole-dancing his way to Hell after rejecting admission to Heaven. By manipulating the outrage machine, Lil Nas X and his directorial and production team drive up his viewership, listenership, and social media follows, and the conversation about him.[6] All of this is to illuminate the ways that queerness, blackness, and hip hop have moved from uncomfortable intimates to embodiment in one rebellious Gen Z nonconformist rapper. A queer hip hop aesthetic has the ability to usurp and dominate conversations in popular culture, media, social media, politics, and religion; it's been a long journey from white gay experimentation in LA or metaphorical illusions from New Jersey boy band rappers or even rumors of a "gay (Black male) rapper" or the beloved moments of independent LGBTQ rappers. Whether Lil Nas X has longevity as a performer and entertainer, he has changed the landscape of hip hop aesthetics forever.

In this final section, I'd like to bring it back to the New York City local through an example from the undergraduate Hip Hop Aesthetics course I teach at a private Catholic university in New York City. The example of pedagogical performance assists me in thinking about the future of queer Black hip hop aesthetics, specifically. The SARS-CoV-2 pandemic has been debilitating for students, faculty, staff, administrators, families, friends, and a host of relations. The pandemic has further exposed and exasperated fault lines of oppression and systemic violence, as well as pushed more and more people into and beyond precarity. Some days it's been difficult for any of us to show up to "Zoom University," and it certainly was tremendously difficult to finish this book. However, my courses and students have also generated discussions around vulnerability, anger, depression, cultural objects we love, and a vast well of dark humor. In one class in the spring 2021 semester, I asked students to break into groups to discuss different videos related to hip hop dance aesthetics. One group was assigned LA-based Tricia Miranda Dance School's choreography to August Alsina's song "I Luv This Shit."[7] I asked students to consider how hip hop aesthetics are expressed through various forms of hip hop dance and to use the readings to help them discuss the various dance forms. These undergrads are mostly juniors and seniors and mostly quite engaged and very knowledgeable about a range of hip hop cultural histories and aesthetics practices. Hip hop dance is often difficult for students to discuss because they lack dance and choreographic vocabulary and often feel shy about attempting to speak to that form. The students I teach are always game for attempting to close the lacuna between their knowledge, their know-how, and the things we learn in the course. Each group had a different dance referent: some watched videos by Black French twin brothers Les Twins, others watched various TikTok or Instagram dance challenges popular in the recent past such as the #bussit challenge, another group watched Black female dancer and choreographer Jalaiah S. Harmon, and yet another watched Bboy Skim from the world champion Korean b-boy crew, Jinjo Crew. All of the groups were engaged and asked intelligent questions, but the final group was strangely silent and disengaged. Students who usually had their cameras on turned them off and only one student spoke; they seemed to have had a lively discussion, yet I could sense a dis-ease coming from them that I could not quite name, and that they could not articulate.

Tricia Miranda's choreography to Alsina's "I Luv This Shit," is, like most of her work, intriguing, inventive, and fun—at least to this untrained eye. Miranda's studio back wall boasts a large sign declaring "Unity through Diversity," and often this "diversity" is embodied by various young white women featured prominently in some of the videos, even if they aren't the best dancers. But Miranda's studio welcomes all: fat dancers; little kids; effete men; Black, Asian, Latinx, white, Native, masculine women; and folks whose bodies don't fit the look of a hip hop dancer. Like many choreographers, she has signature moves that are sexed/gendered along a Western binary: man/woman or male/female. In this particular video, a Black female-bodied person performs a mixture of both the "male" and "female" parts, and as many of the YouTubers comment, she "kills it" and "gets them pregnant" with her moves.[8] Dominique Battiste, a professional dancer who has worked with Janet Jackson and Zendaya, uses her dancing body to disrupt, disassemble, and rearticulate gestures related to race, gender, and performance in her 90-second performance (the longest of any of the dancers').[9]

Battiste's part follows directly after the "women's" dance section. She is shot medium length at shoulder level, which conveys a sense of irregularity and innovation as most of the video has been shot wide at eye level. Battiste slowly swaggers for the camera, confidence oozing from her short, honey-brown body. She's dressed in what I call "dancer's attire"—some quirky combination of comfortable clothes you might see in a production of *Rent*. Battiste wears an orange-and-blue plaid shirt, buttoned only at the top few buttons. Underneath we see she wears a green sports bra and her softly muscled belly is exposed when she moves; she wears tapered black pants and black sneakers with white soles. Her natural 4C texture hair is cut in a "mohawk" hairstyle and dyed a bright blonde. She moves with poise, power, and fluidity; the other students are enamored and cheer her moves along.

There is a particular set of choreographed dance moves and improvisations that embodies Battiste's gendered disruption: when Alsina sings that he "stay on that Ciroc," Battiste mimics imbibing the alcoholic beverage. Next Alsina croons that he "stay taking shots," and Battiste enacts the double-entendre of the phrase by facing the camera and pointing her fingers like handgun barrels. These two gestures are done with precision and power—her moves are hard, her face is serious, her body looks strong. When Alsina warns us that "your girl be on my jock," Battiste twirls her middle, bounces on her tiptoes while bent at the knees, and then pops up to gesture defiantly toward her own jock. But here comes the twist: as Alsina tells us about what kind of nigga he is not—bitch, rich, or snitch—and that he is indeed a real nigga, Battiste uses this as an opportunity to interpret the choreography and lyrics in a way that visualizes these Alsinan negations. Battiste jerks her body, imitating a motor, and throws her arms across her body as she slides sideways effortlessly across the wood floor. She continues her interpretive dance by raising her right arm over her head, her index and middle fingers pointing out, and then bringing it down forcefully around chest level. This is a Black gestural haptic often associated with emphasis, especially when calling someone a "bitch nigga." That move flows seamlessly into another interpretation of "bitch nigga" wherein Battiste embodies a feminine nigga who cocks his hip, looks you up and down, and dismisses you as unworthy of his gaze, response, or presence. At this point, the studio dancers in the audience have lost their minds and are roaring with pleasure.[10] Battiste slips out of her improvisations and back into Miranda's choreography, but keeps us off-balance by continuing to mix different aspects of the "male" and "female" choreography with her own improvisations. At one point, when we (me) and the studio audience are sufficiently breathless, stunned, dancing along, and cheering, two Black male dancers, one who has thrown his snapback hat on the floor in surrender to Battiste's superiority, gather her off the floor and lead her off the stage à la James

Brown. The rest of us are left painting and wanting more, and maybe a little pregnant.

I understand my students' hesitation and lack of vocabulary. When I first watched this video in 2015, I too was stunned and surprised. Hip hop's queer aesthetics show up in the most unexpected places. Even though my students are savvy, many of them from New York City and its environs, there's also a naïve conservatism about them. By conservativism, I mean that they often see objects or performances or identities as fixed and not as constructed, fluid, and revisable. I dare say I am constantly shocking their sensibilities with my insistence on experimentation, exploration, and (de)construction. In my experience, students often approach hip hop as transactional and expendable—they want to get a hit of cool or new slang or a posture or a dance, but they don't tend to think of it as art and certainly not art that merits revisitation and examination. When an example of hip hop aesthetics disrupts the presumed heteronormativity of blackness, especially playfully, shamelessly, and publicly, we are often left without frame or words or explanation for how this fits into ideas of hip hop blackness. For me, this is ultimately one of the most useful and generative aspects of queer hip hop aesthetics: its ability to embody defiance, disrupt and reframe the terms of engagement with hip hop as a cultural production, and give us new models for sound, movement, and being.

Where do we go from here? Gender policing and gender rigidity are still present in hip hop and other forms of mass entertainment, but ruptures in gender and sexuality norms continue to occur in the form of rumors, coming out stories, regional and geographical clashes over masculinity and femininity, and the ongoing queering and transing of Gen X, millennials, and Gen Z. Hip hop cultural production may never own up to its inherent queerness, but hip hop is not the only way forward in considering how Black queer and trans aesthetics might continue to expand into the future. This book is concerned with hip hop's queer oeuvre: how the methods, spaces, and people in early and contemporary hip hop cultural production embody elements of Black, queer, and hip hop aesthetics. I argue that the tensions and fissures of these aesthetics generate incredible, provocative work, which eschews simple and boring hip hop products. Instead, the queer aesthetic elements reveal the complex ways blackness and hip hop hide their own queer artistic tendencies. In many ways, early hip hop pioneers—the technological geniuses, the corporeal magicians, the sonic wizards, and the visual masters—invited the future and its possibilities into spaces of material desolation and decay. Hip hop youths and young adults literally transformed the urban landscape and soundscape of New York City (and Philly, and LA, and Chicago), ushering in a yet-unfinished process of innovation, stagnation, and frustration that we call hip hop culture and production.

This ability to generate the future in the present through sight, sound, kinesthesia, and site-specific objects connects hip hop, Black, queer, and trans futures to the long history of speculative studies—and the even longer history of Black speculative studies in the Americas, which is an ongoing project of generating vital aesthetic materials to stave off anti-Black death forces. As hip hop music, especially, becomes more corporate, more white, and more insipid, Black avant-garde youth and young people continue to make language, images (memes, TikTok videos, Instagram stories), writing, music, and movements that are coded, experimental, and just a hair's breadth ahead of mass commodification. The future I see for Black people is one in which we center the politics of refusal: we refuse antiblackness, we refuse heteropatriarchy, we refuse white supremacy, we refuse plantation capitalism. Instead, we embrace our oddness, our queerness, our gender trespasses, our unique forms of communication in order to, again, make a viable Black future in the face of annihilation.

ACKNOWLEDGMENTS

As many people know, writing a book is an arduous process. Writing a book about subjects you love may be even more daunting. There is no way I could have written this book on hip hop, blackness, and queerness without the guidance, support, expertise, love, and confidence of many people.

I want to first thank my family who, though they sometimes looked at and listened to me with skepticism and bafflement, have always supported me, cheered me on, and let me know just how fucking bomb I am. To my older brother, Marcus, thank you for being a masterful hip hop scholar, theologian, incredible thinker, and one of my best friends. To my younger brother, Phillip, your laughter, love, warmth, and twinkling eyes are joys in my life—so glad we can see movies together again. To my sister-in-law, Ruthie, thank you for all of your fire, conviction, love, and honesty. To my niblings, Justo, Kaleb, and Phe—I love you all so much and look forward to you all taking over the world! And to my Mom-Mom, Marion, and my Mom, Gloria (RIP), thank you for coming to my invited talk at Norwalk Community College in 2011, just days before I defended my dissertation. You got to hear my words and cheer me on. Mommy, this one is for you.

I was fortunate to be a graduate student in NYU Performance Studies from 2005 to 2011 and an MA student at NYU's Gallatin School from 2003 to 2005, where I first took classes in the building next door in PS. I harassed a young, new assistant professor into being my advisor even though he demurred. Without Tavia Nyong'o's incredible and gracious guidance, this work would have evolved very differently. Not only did I get to be his first PhD student, I got to and get to be his friend! Thank you to the rest of my dissertation committee: Gayatri Gopinath, Ann

Pelligrini, Karen Shimakawa, and Jason Stanyek, who taught, read, listened, and laughed with grace and delight; to all of my professors at NYU: Jason King, Michael Dinwiddie, José Muñoz, Allen Weiss, Barbara Browning, BKG (Barbara Kirsenblatt-Gimblett), and Heather Lukes, who was a visiting professor at the time—you gave me the tools and skills I needed to make this work come to life.

I was at NYU at a time when so many brilliant others were there and I feel grateful to have spent time in the classroom, in cafés, at parties, in the library, at conferences, and in many other spaces with so many wonderful folks, including: andré carrington, Miles Grier, Jessica Pabón-Colón, Marc Arthur, Masi Asare, Ronak Kapadia, Branden Jacobs-Jenkins, Frank Leon Roberts, Yvonne Etaghene, Josh Chambers-Letson, Summer Kim Lee, Chris Tabrón, Sarah Kozin, Nomié Solomon, and many others!

Thank you to the amazing current and former PS admin and staff, especially Noel Rodriguez and Laura Elena Fortes.

I have been blessed to have the relative stability of full-time academic employment. I held an Andrew W. Mellon Postdoctoral Fellowship at Davidson College from 2011 to 2013, and I would like to thank all of my colleagues there in the Department of English and in the Writing Center, as well as faculty in other departments. You introduced me to the post-grad student world of academia. One extra wonderful thing that came out of that experience was a writing group with Laura Elder and Saeyong Park. Much of this book was read, revised, and commented upon by these two great scholars. Thank you!

To my colleagues and students in the American Studies Department at UNM, thank you so much for your warmth and welcoming enthusiasm. Even though I only spent one year with you (2013–2014), it was an incredible beginning to my career on the tenure track.

I'd like to thank all of my colleagues in the Department of English and the Critical Race and Ethnic Studies Institute at St. John's University. I'd like to especially name Dohra Ahmad, Steven Alvarez, Catina Bacote, Gabe Brownstein, Raj Chetty, Robert Fanuzzi, Anne Geller, Amy

King, LaToya Sawyer, Steve Sicari, Jen Travis, and Elda Tsou for their friendship, mentorship, and camaraderie. To the CRES team, Natalie Byfield, Jean-Pierre Ruiz, Manouchkathe Cassagnol, Bobby Rivera, Jeremy Cruz, Anthony Rodriguez, and Nada Llewellyn, thank you for helping me thrive and survive!

I want to send a shout-out to the Sexual Politics, Sexual Poetics Collective to which I had the pleasure of belonging. Your thinking sharpened my own: Amber Jamillah Musser, Ramzi Fawaz, Damon Young, Katie Brewer Ball, Uri McMillan, Kadji Amin, Jennifer Row, Jordan Alexander Stein, Zakiyyah Iman Jackson, and Roy Pérez. A special shout-out to Zakiyyah Iman Jackson, who has become one of the deepest and most important intellectual and friendship relationships of my lifetime. Thank you for the gift of you!

To my mentors and friends, Emily Bernard, Soyica Colbert, Andrea Hairston, and Francesca Royster, thank you for your boundless support, care, and letters of recommendation.

Thank you to the following friends, colleagues, dharma siblings, mentors, teachers, and relatives: Vanessa Agard-Jones, Laura Amodeo, Moya Bailey, Courtney Baker, Amanda Barrett, César Barros, Ian Bascetta, Sandy Bell, Tatiana Bertsch, Darius Bost, Martina Bouey, Regina Bradley, Lena Brinson, Sheena Brockington, Kinitra Brooks, Siobhan Brooks, Jayna Brown, Karen Brown, Kesha Bruce, Nsenga Burton, Chase Bauer Carlson, Derrais Carter, Sand Chang, Dasha Chapman, William H. Clark, Ebony Coletu, Brenda Collins, Collin Craig, Jax Cuevas, Debanuj Dasgupta, Lisa Davis, Thomas DeFrantz, Jennifer Denetdale, Adriana DiFazio, Ashley Dinges, Ángeles Donoso Macaya, Sameena Eidoo, Melissa Febos, Maria Felch, Gaylon Ferguson, Roderick Ferguson, Kwanda Ford, Samantha Francois, Caroline Fuchs, Malik Gaines, Racquel Gates, Anna Gennari, Liz Gil, Lyndon Gill, Claudelle Glasgow, Alyosha Goldstein, Antía Gómez Núñez, Joy Gutierrez, Karma Lödrö Gyendon, Aria Halliday, Lisa Harewood, Travis Harris, Arawana Hayashi, India Henriquez, Brian Herrera, Kenny Hillman, Alex Hinton, Mikela Bjork, Jen Houser, Trevor Houser, Tamara Issak, A. Naomi

Jackson, Jessica Marie Johnson, Javon Johnson, Kate Johnson, Axelle Karera, Kim Katzenberg, Maho Kawachi, Anne Kenan, Deborah Kimmey, Tiffany Lethabo King, Naoko Kojima, Aakhil Lakhani, Treva Lindsey, Jeff Lipstein, Adam Lobel, Alex Lubin, Hun Lye, Jahan Mantin, Jen Margulies, Tyson Marsh, Brandon Peter Masterman, Kyle T. Mays, Eileen McGauran, Danika Medak-Saltzman, Rita Meinzies, Steven Mentz, Ben Milam, Justin Miles, Koritha Mitchell, Alexandra Moffet-Bateau, Darnell L. Moore, Joan Morgan, Matthew Morrison, Ashoka Mukpo, Jason "Judge" Muscat, Mark Anthony Neal, Mimi Thi Nguyen, Ethan Nichtern, Sasha Nyary, Lama Dorje Odzer Justin von Budjoss, Lama Rod Owens, Imani Owens, Eric Darnell Pritchard, Susie Pak and Greg Pak, Maia Cruz Palileo, Terry Park, Ceci Parthner, Rhonda Patrick, Heather Pavlack-Smith, Robert E. Penn, Jr., Stephan Pennington, David Perrin, Will Pflaum, Jesse Philips-Fein, Ericka Tiffany Phillips, Therí Pickens, Joe Pierce, Khary Polk, Elliott Powell, Bryan Profitt, Matthew Pucciarelli, Stève Puig, Kevin Quashie, Ashanté Monique Reese, Sakyong Mipham Rinpoche, Bobby Rivera, Raquel Z. Rivera, Patrick Rivers, Candice Roberts, Yami Rodriguez, Tracey Rose, Gemma Roskam Baker, Jessica Rothkuo, Sandra Ruiz, Ellen Saltonstall, Mich Schreiber, Rebecca Schreiber, Evan Schwartz, Savanah Shange, Aishah Shahidah Simmons, Daesha Elliott, Jessica Stern, Jasmine Syellduah, Ben Tausig, Tchaiko Omawele, Hannah Thornton, Tony Tiongson, Myra Washington, Kyla Wazana Tompkins, Dennis Tyler, Lana V. Theresa Umali, Alex Van Gils, Sophia Wallace, Shelly Webb, Alex Weheliye, Mia Charlene White, Nia Witherspoon, and Cynthia Young. Thank you to all of my peers, colleagues, and co-conspirators at Black Performance Theory (BPT) and CLAGS at CUNY.

To the amazing graduate students I have had the pleasure to work with as committee members or closely in other ways: Sonia Adams, Nouf Arige, Michael Benjamin, Christine Capetola, Raquel Corona, Regina Duthely, Marthia M. Fuller, Meghan Gilbert-Hickey, Tina Iemma, Steven Ikeme, María Eugenia Lopez, Samantha McCalla, Erica McCrystal, Angela Mosley, Geziell Nash, Amity Nathaniel, Simone Smith, Anwar

Uhuru, Tejan Waszak, Kayla Wilson, Justine Wilson, and Timm Woods, thank you for sharing your ideas and amazing selves with me.

To my beloved pups, Tilopa Jones Smalls (2007–2018) and Drala Jones Smalls, your love buoyed me beyond measure.

I want to thank the Institute for Citizens & Scholars for awarding me the 2017–2018 Career Enhancement Junior Faculty Fellowship and the James Weldon Johnson Institute at Emory University for awarding me the 2019–2020 Postdoctoral Fellowship. Both of these postdoctoral fellowships made completing this book possible.

Thank you to everyone at NYU Press, especially to Eric Zinner for believing so strongly in this book and patiently waiting for me to finish it. Thank you to Dolma Ombadykow and Furqan Sayeed for answering endless questions and emails with delight and clarity. To my series editors, Karen Tongson and Henry Jenkins, thank you for believing in me.

To my developmental editor, Cathy Hannabach, you saw brilliance through the mess—thank you! To the anonymous readers of this manuscript, thank you for your care, thoughtfulness, labor, and excitement. You truly made this a better work!

Finally, to Martin Wong, Louis Venosta and *Berry Gordy's The Last Dragon*, Jean Grae, and all the queer, trans, and intersex hip hoppers, thank you for your vision and work.

To the ancestors, yidams, gurus, deities, dralas, and protectors, without you and your guidance, none of this was possible:

> Om Om Om
> Ki Ki Ki
> So So So
> Ashe Ashe Ashe!

An earlier, excerpted version of chapter 2 was published as "Eating Popcorn with Chopsticks: Revisionary Black Masculinity in *Berry Gordy's The Last Dragon*," *Criticism: A Quarterly for Literature and the Arts*, 58.2 (August 2017): 305–326.

An earlier, excerpted version of chapter 3 was published as "The Rain Comes Down: Jean Grae and Hip Hop Heteronormativity," in "Hip Hop Culture in a Global Context," special issue, *American Behavioral Scientist* 55.1 (January 2011): 86–95.

An earlier, excerpted version of chapter 4 was published as "Queer Hip Hop: A Brief Historiography," in *The Oxford Handbook of Music and Queerness*, ed. Fred Maus and Sheila Whitely (New York and Oxford: Oxford University Press, 2018).

NOTES

INTRODUCTION. HERETICAL DESIRE

1. New York City's subway system is consistently ranked by mathematicians and engineers as or as among the world's most complex. "World's Most Intricate Subway Networks," Geo Engineer, February 19, 2019, www.geoengineer.org.
2. For more on the historical relationship between the subway and graffiti culture, see Joe Austin, *Taking the Train: How Graffiti Art Became an Urban Crisis in New York City* (New York: Columbia University Press, 2002).
3. Azealia Banks, "1991," YouTube, September 2, 2012, www.youtube.com/watch?v=00M_9ca8hxE.
4. Tavia Nyong'o, "Queer Hip Hop and Its Dark Precursors," in "The Queerness of Hip Hop/The Hip Hop of Queerness," special issue, *Palimpsest: A Journal on Women, Gender, and the Black International* 2.2 (2013): 144.
5. Addison Gayle, Jr., "Introduction," in *The Black Aesthetic*, ed. Addison Gayle, Jr. (New York: Doubleday, 1972), xxii.
6. Ibid., xxi.
7. Hoyt W. Fuller, "Toward a Black Aesthetic," in *The Black Aesthetic*, ed. Gayle, 8.
8. Jeff Chang, *Total Chaos: The Art and Aesthetics of Hip-Hop* (New York: Civitas Books, 2007), x.
9. Kobena Mercer, *Travel & See: Black Diaspora Art Practices since the 1980s* (Durham, NC, and London: Duke University Press, 2016), 230–231.
10. In late summer 2020, rappers Cardi B and Megan Thee Stallion released a song and music video titled "W.A.P. (Wet Ass Pussy)." The ensuing collective hand-wringing and pearl-clutching from both right-wing racist misogynists and Black misogynists demonstrates the ongoing subversive power of hip hop aesthetics, especially when coupled with Black diasporic women unabashedly celebrating the economic, social, political, and sexual power of their pussies. For more on the song and ensuing controversies, see Gabriella Paiella, "Wait, What: The Week in 'WAP,'" *GQ*, August 14, 2020, www.gq.com.
11. For more on the relationship between performance and virtuosity or mastery, see Tavia Nyong'o's talk, "Metastases of Performance: Ubiquity, Marginality, Virtuosity," Humanities Futures series, Franklin Humanities Institute, Duke University, April 10, 2015, https://humanitiesfutures.org.
12. Chang, *Total Chaos*, x.

13 For various accounts of hip hop's origin story, see Murray Forman, *The 'Hood Comes First: Race, Space, and Place in Rap and Hip-Hop* (Middletown, CT: Wesleyan University Press, 2002); Tricia Rose, *Black Noise: Rap Music and Black Culture in Contemporary America* (Middletown, CT: Wesleyan University Press, 1994); Jeff Chang, *Can't Stop, Won't Stop: A History of the Hip-Hop Generation* (London: Picador, 2005) and *Total Chaos: The Art and Aesthetics of Hip-Hop* (New York: Civitas Books, 2006); Alan Light, ed., *The Vibe History of Hip Hop* (London: Plexus, 1999); and Will Hermes, *Love Goes to Buildings on Fire: Five Years That Changed Music Forever* (New York: Faber & Faber, 2011). For authenticity and emceeing in hip hop, see Peter Furia, *What Makes an Emcee Dope: The Art of Emceein' and Authenticity in Hip-Hop*, unpublished thesis (New Haven, CT: Yale University, 2005).

14 Nyong'o, "Queer Hip Hop," 24.

15 Nelson George, "Hip-Hop's Founding Fathers Speak the Truth," in *That's the Joint!: The Hip-Hop Studies Reader*, ed. Murray Forman and Mark Anthony Neal (New York and London: Routledge, 2004), 45–55.

16 Netflix, the subscription-based digital media streaming service, has an original ongoing series acquired from HBO, *Hip-Hop Evolution* (2017–), which looks in depth into early hip hop foundations. The series host interviews all three men I speak about here. There is no mention of Bambaataa's alleged sexual assaults.

17 George, "Hip-Hop's Founding Fathers," 46.

18 The *New York Daily News* broke the story of Ronald Savage, Bambaataa's first accuser, on April 9, 2016. The paper followed up with a story one week later that featured the testimony of three more men.

19 Universal Zulu Nation Open Letter to Survivors, Members, and Our Communities, https://docs.google.com/document/d/1yi72ns8pBWtcqKraH8GwX6wpEZVYIdAduYcl2d6J-3Y/edit.

20 Shawn Carter, *Jay-Z Decoded* (New York: Spiegel & Grau, 2010), 39.

21 Valerie Cunningham, "Introduction: The Necessity of Heresy," in *Figures of Heresy: Radical Theology in English and American Writing 1800–2000*, ed. Andrew Dix and Jonathan Taylor (Brighton: Sussex Academic Press, 2006), 1.

22 Ibid., 13.

23 Kara Keeling, *The Witch's Flight: The Cinematic, the Black Femme, and the Image of Common Sense* (Durham, NC, and London: Duke University Press, 2007), 2–3.

24 Imani Perry, *Prophets of the Hood: Politics and Poetics in Hip Hop* (Durham, NC, and London: Duke University Press, 2004), 10. See also Jeffrey O. G. Ogbar, *Hip-Hop Revolution: The Culture and Politics of Rap* (Lawrence: University Press of Kansas, 2007).

25 Perry, *Prophets of the Hood*.

26 This is explored in depth in the documentary *Founding Fathers: The Untold Story of Hip Hop*, YouTube, 2009, www.youtube.com/watch?v=1G13bRoB0-8.

27 Perry, *Prophets of the Hood*, 10–11.

28 This is not to erase the real contributions of Black and Latinx men. Like Tricia Rose, with her work on the economic, cultural, historical, and racial factors that contributed to hip hop, as well as her work on Black and Latinx women's roles in hip hop culture, I am attempting to widen the narrative to include the work of Asians, queer culture, and other overlooked factors in hip hop's formation and cultivation. This work focuses on pan-Asian influence and not, say, Latinx, as the literature on Latinx in hip hop is growing: see Juan Flores, *From Bomba to Hip-Hop: Puerto Rican Culture and Latino Identity* (New York: Columbia University Press, 2000), and Raquel Z. Rivera, *New York Ricans from the Hip Hop Zone* (New York: Palgrave McMillan, 2003). And my work on the Asian-Black American relationship in hip hop, by contrast, does not rely on the cultures having any origin in common. Much of the work on Latinos and Blacks in America focuses on their common African heritage; my work investigates what is bridged between race/cultures that seem so divergent.
29 Jean Grae, "God's Gift," written by Tsidsi Ibrahim, produced by Masta Ace, *Attack of the Attacking Things* (Third Earth Music, 2002).
30 Jay-Z and Foxy Brown, "Ain't No Nigga," written by Shawn Carter, Inga Marchand, Jonathan Burks, Dennis Lambert, Brian Potter, Tyrone Thomas, and August Moon, produced by Big Jaz, *Reasonable Doubt* (Roc-A-Fella Records/Priority Records, 1996).
31 Tricia Rose, *Black Noise: Rap Music and Black Culture in Contemporary America* (Middletown, CT: Wesleyan University Press, 1994), 3.
32 Paul Gilroy, *Against Race: Imagining Political Culture Beyond the Color Line* (Cambridge, MA: Harvard University Press, 2000), 266.

CHAPTER 1. WILD STYLIN'

1 Helen Heran Jun, *Race for Citizenship: Black Orientalism and Asian Uplift from Pre-emancipation to Neoliberal America* (New York: New York University Press, 2011), 4.
2 Mimi Thi Nguyen and Thuy Linh Nguyen Tu, eds., *Alien Encounters: Popular Culture in Asian America* (Durham, NC: Duke University Press, 2007), 9.
3 New York City was saved from declaring bankruptcy by a bailout from the federal government. See Elmer B. Staats, New York Seasonal Financing Act of 1975 Public Law 94–143, United States General Accounting Office, 1976.
4 Tricia Rose, "'All Aboard the Night Train': Flow, Layering, and Rupture in Postindustrial New York," in Rose, *Black Noise*, 21–34.
5 David Walkowitz, "New York: A Tale of Two Cities," in *Snowbelt Cities: Metropolitan Politics in the Northeast and Midwest since World War II*, ed. R. M. Bernard (Bloomington: Indiana University Press, 1990), 189–208.
6 For a thorough and fantastic read of the emergence of hip hop and other music scenes in early 1970s NYC, see music journalist Will Hermes's *Love Goes to Buildings on Fire*.

7 For more on the history of *Wild Style*, see https://wildstylethemovie.com.
8 As Jessica Nydia Pabón-Colón explains, hip hop graffiti art (aka aerosol art, spray-can art) is distinct from other forms of street art because it centers around the repetitive production of a tag name within a subculture grounded in Afro-Caribbean diasporic aesthetics: the construction of a vernacular different from the colonizer's language produced visually and linguistically (e.g., writers "bomb the system," sometimes in a "wild style" illegible to nonwriters). Jessica Nydia Pabón-Colón, *Graffiti Grrlz: Performing Feminism in the Hip Hop Diaspora* (New York: New York University Press, 2018), 1.
9 Diana Taylor, *The Archive and the Repertoire: Performing Cultural Memory in the Americas* (Durham, NC, and London: Duke University Press, 2003), 26.
10 Ibid., 28.
11 J. L. Austin famously claims, "to utter the sentence . . . is not to *describe* my doing . . . it is to do it. . . . I propose to call it a *performative sentence* or a performative utterance, or, for short, 'a performative.' The term 'performative' . . . indicates that the issuing of the utterance is the performing of an action—it is not normally thought of as just saying something." J. L. Austin, *How to Do Things with Words: The William James Lectures Delivered at Harvard University in 1955* (Oxford and New York: Oxford University Press, 1962), 6–7.
12 United Graffiti Artists, led by the legendary Rammellzee, showed their canvases at New York's Razor Gallery in 1972. The pieces were priced between $200 and $3,000. See Anthony Haden-Guest, *True Colors: The Real Life of the Art World* (New York: Atlantic Monthly Press, 1996), 122.
13 See Hazel M. McPherson, ed., *Blacks and Asians: Crossings, Conflict and Commonality* (Durham, NC: Carolina Academic Press, 2006), and Ian Condry, *Hip-Hop Japan: Rap and Paths of Cultural Globalization* (Durham, NC, and London: Duke University Press, 2006).
14 Wu Tang Clan is a hip hop group based in Staten Island, New York, that emerged in the early 1990s. Their first release, *Enter the 36 Chambers* (1993), was a watershed record for New York City hip hop, changing the landscape and soundscape of hip hop culture. At the time, LA-based Dr. Dre's funk sound was dominating the charts. Wu Tang Clan is made up of nine core members, some of whom take their performance names, ethos, and/or personas from Shaw Brothers *wu xia* martial arts films (e.g., Ghostface Killer and U-God, aka Golden Arms). They refer to Staten Island as Shaolin, which further layers the ongoing historical and mythical competition between the Wu Tang (or WuDan) and Shaolin schools of Chinese martial arts cultures. See their website (www.wutangcorp.com/forum) for more biographical information.
15 Roy Pérez, "The Glory That Was Wrong: El 'Chino Malo' Approximates Nuyorico," *Women & Performance: A Journal of Feminist Theory* 25.3 (2015): 280.

16 Ibid., 291.
17 Raquel Z. Rivera, *New York Ricans from the Hip Hop Zone* (New York: Palgrave McMillan, 2002), 136.
18 Ibid., 137.
19 Antonio Sergio Bessa, "Dropping Out: Martin Wong and the American Counterculture," in *Martin Wong: Human Instamatic*, ed. Antonio Sergio Bessa (London and New York: Black Dog Publishing, 2015), 18.
20 *Sweet 'Enuff* is part of the permanent collection at the Fine Arts Museums of San Francisco. See https://art.famsf.org/martin-wong/sweet-enuff-2007103a-b.
21 Bessa, "Dropping Out," 22.
22 Roland Barthes describes the punctum as "an element which arises from the scene, shoots out of it like an arrow, and pierces me." Roland Barthes, *Camera Lucida: Reflections on Photography*, trans. Richard Howard (New York: Hill & Wang, 1981), 26.
23 A crail grab is an air trick "where the skater grabs the toeside nose with the back hand." Skateboardhere, www.skateboardhere.com, accessed August 18, 2019.
24 Darius Bost, La Marr Bruce Jarrell, and Brandon J, Manning, "Introduction," in "Black Masculinities and the Matter of Vulnerability," special issue, *Black Scholar: Journal of Black Studies and Research* 49.2 (2019): 4.
25 Ibid., 4–5.
26 Jared Sexton, "Properties of Coalition: Blacks, Asians, and the Politics of Policing," *Critical Sociology* 36.1 (2010): 90.
27 As graffiti and visual artist (Aaron) Sharp said in a 2009 panel discussion, "There wasn't a hip hop scene, as such, it was various art and neighborhood subcultures [emerging around the same time]." Aaron Sharp, Dr. Yasmin Ramirez, Lady Pink, and Dr. Gayatri Gopinath, moderated by Arnaldo Cruz-Malavé, "Martin Wong: Explorations in Race and Masculinity in Graffiti Culture," panel discussion, Asian/Pacific/American Institute, New York University, October 28, 2009.
28 As Dan Cameron notes, "Although, ironically enough, most of Martin Wong's artistic successes took place in Soho, he represented an idealized composite portrait of the East Village artist." Dan Cameron, "Brick by Brick: New York According to Martin Wong," in *Sweet Oblivion: The Urban Landscape of Martin Wong*, ed. Amy Scholder (New York: New Museum Books, 1998), 2.
29 Ibid.
30 See Sean Corcoran and Carlo McCormick, eds., *City as Canvas: New York Graffiti/The Martin Wong Collection* (New York: Skira Rizzoli, 2013).
31 See "The Estate of Martin Wong," PPOW Gallery, www.ppowgallery.com.
32 Not to be confused with the Museum of Graffiti, established in 2019 and located in Miami. As of this writing, the MoG bills itself as the "world's first museum exclusively dedicated to the evolution of the graffiti art form." "About Us," Museum of Graffiti, April 13, 2020, https://museumofgraffiti.com.

33 "Doors Open at Graffiti Museum," *Art in America*, May 19, 1989, 31. Sourced from *Martin Wong Papers*; Series VIII: Albums; Fales Library and Special Collections, New York University Libraries.
34 Ibid.
35 For an insightful reading of the relationship between the virtuoso, freakdom, transgressive bodies, and punishment, see Tavia Nyong'o, "The Unforgivable Transgression of Being Caster Semenya," BullyBloggers, September 8, 2009, http://bullybloggers.wordpress.com.
36 Pabón-Colón, *Graffiti Grrlz*, 3.
37 For more on the history of graffiti art in New York City galleries and museums, see Haden-Guest, *True Colors*.
38 Three major artbooks have been published about Wong: Scholder, ed., *Sweet Oblivion*; Corcoran and McCormick, eds., *City as Canvas*; and Bessa, ed., *Martin Wong: Human Instamatic*.
39 Sean Corcoran, "Vision & Expression: Martin Wong and the New York Coty Writing Movement," in *City as Canvas*, ed. Corcoran and McCormick, 18–19.
40 Ibid., 15–19.
41 Ibid., 17.
42 Cameron, "Brick by Brick," 13.
43 *City as Canvas: Graffiti Art from the Martin Wong Collection*, Museum of the City of New York, February 4–September 21, 2014, www.mcny.org.
44 Felicia Lee, "A Medici to Spray Paint and Graffiti Artists," *New York Times*, January 28, 2014, 3.
45 Ibid.
46 For more on their current artwork, see Aaron Sharp Goodstone, www.artnet.com; Chris Daze Ellis, www.dazeworld.com; Lady Pink (Sandra Fabara), www.ladypinknyc.com.

Martin Wong's cadre of friends, associates, and acquaintances included many who were pioneers in various sectors of early hip hop culture, including Charlie Ahearn, the director/producer of the first hip hop film, *Wild Style* (1983). *Wild Style* is significant for a number of reasons: it was the first film to focus on the emergent graffiti, dance, turntable, and emcee culture in New York City; it centered mostly on graffiti and dance, rather than rapping and DJing; its actors, director, and producers were already a part of the hip hop scene and/or the downtown art scene, allowing for an intimacy with the culture. The cast includes graffiti artists Lee Quiñones and Sandra "Lady Pink" Fabrara as the leads. Graffiti artists Daze (Christopher Ellis), Zephyr (Andrew Witten), and Dondi (Donald White) worked on the art for the film. Fab 5 Freddy (Frederick Braithwaite) was both producer and acted in the film. Featured hip hop luminaries included DJs Grandmaster Flash and Grand Wizard Theodore and rappers Grand Mater Caz, the Cold Crush Brothers, and Double Trouble. Beats were made by Fab 5 Freddy and Blondie guitarist Chris

Stein. For more on the cast and crew, see www.wildstylethemovie.com, accessed February 14, 2011.

47 Joe Austin, *Taking the Train: How Graffiti Art Became an Urban Crisis in New York City* (New York: Columbia University Press, 2001), 4.
48 See Murray Forman and Mark Anthony Neal, eds., *That's the Joint!: The Hip-Hop Studies Reader* (New York and London: Routledge, 2004), especially the essays "Breaking: The History," "Hip-Hop's Founding Fathers Speak the Truth," and "The Politics of Graffiti."
49 This 18-minute segment contains some differently edited scenes that can be found in Ahearn's Wong-only video, *The Clones of Bruce Lee: The Art of Martin Wong* (New York: Pow Wow Productions, 1995).
50 Dan Cameron's essay on Wong's construction of New York City speaks to Wong's use of brick in his art. Cameron, "Brick by Brick," 1–16.
51 See Robin D. G. Kelley and Betsy Esch, "Black Like Mao: Red China and Black Revolution," *Souls: A Critical Journal of Black Politics, Culture, and Society* 1.4 (1999): 6–41.
52 Lee Quinones, "About," www.leequinones.com, accessed April 8, 2011.
53 Carlo McCormick, "Martin Wong: Artist & Collector," in *City as Canvas*, ed. Corcoran and McCormick, 31.
54 Founded in 1990, GAPIMNY offers support services for Asian and Pacific Islander queer and trans people. See "History," GAPIMNY, http://gapimny.org.
55 For more on the history of Saint Vincent's Hospital as the epicenter for HIV/AIDS care in NYC, see "NYC AIDS Memorial Park at St. Vincent's Triangle," NYC Parks, www.nycgovparks.org, and Michael J. O'Loughlin, "The Catholic Hospital That Pioneered AIDS Care," *America: The Jesuit Review*, January 24, 2020, www.americamagazine.org.
56 ABC No Rio, www.abcnorio.org.
57 This was *The Crime Show*, in which Wong showed two pieces and Piñero recited his work "Kill, Kill, Kill." See Yasmin Ramirez, "La Vida: The Life and Writings of Miguel Piñero in the Art of Martin Wong," in *Sweet Oblivion*, ed. Scholder, 33–51.
58 1982–1984, oil on canvas, 35½" x 48". Collection of the Metropolitan Museum of Art, New York, NY, Edith C. Blum Fund, 1984 (1984.110).
59 Rose, *Black Noise*, 9.
60 For more on the relationship between Basquiat's artwork and hip hop, see Liz Munsell and Greg Tate, eds., *Writing the Future: Basquiat and the Hip-Hop Generation* (Boston: MFA Publications, 2020).
61 For more on hip hop graffiti, see Craig Castleman, *Getting Up: Subway Graffiti in New York* (Cambridge, MA, and London: MIT Press, 1982); Jim Fricke and Charlie Ahearn, *Yes Yes Y'all: The Experience Music Project Oral History of Hip-Hop's First Decade* (Lebanon, IN: Da Capo Press, 2002); Norman Mailer and Jon Naar, *The Faith of Graffiti* (New York: Harper Collins, 2009 [1974]); Janice Rahn, *Painting without Permission: Hip-Hop Graffiti Subculture* (Westport, CT,

and London: Bergin & Garvey, 2002); and William Upski Wimsatt, *Bomb the Suburbs: Graffiti, Race, Freight-Hopping and the Search for Hip-Hop's Moral Center* (New York: Catapult Book, 2008).

62 "'Wildstyle' is a form of graffiti composed of complicated interlocking letters, arrows, and embellishment. . . . Dondi, from New York, has said that when he writes for other writers he uses wildstyle, and when he writes for the public he uses straight letters." Josephine Noah. "Street Math in Wildstyle Graffiti Art," Art Crimes, 1997, www.graffiti.org.

63 According to the online queer encyclopedia glbtq, "Wong was . . . substantially finished [with *Attorney Street*] when Piñero asked him to record the graffiti applied by one of his young followers to a playground wall. Subsequently, Wong added a lengthy transcription from one of Piñero's poems, as well as several of his own declarations, spelled out by hands in [American] Sign Language." Richard G. Mann, "Martin Wong," glbtq, 2007, www.glbtqarchive.com.

The poem in full: "I was born in a barrel of butcher knives. Raised between two 45s. On a Saturday night when the jungle was bright and the hustler [sic] were stalking their prey. Where the code was crime in neon lights and the weak are doomed to pay. Where addicts prowl with a tigers [sic] growl in search of their lethal blow. Where crime begun when daughter fought son and blood was shed for the sake of bread. Where even God was corrupt. And few go down crying as go down trying cause life in the ghetto is a bitter cup yea it seem I was a whore's dream I knew the slight [sic] of hand of a Murphy man. I could take a sailor poke with words a con man spoke. I knocked out lightning. Drowned a drop of water. Put handcuff on the wind lock thunder in jail. Slapped Jesus in the face and ran Satan out of hell."

64 Cameron, "Brick by Brick," 5.
65 See an image of the painting at the Metropolitan Museum's website: www.metmuseum.org/art/collection/search/483000.
66 See an image of the painting at the PPOW Gallery's website: www.ppowgallery.com/artist/the-estate-of-martin-wong/work/fullscreen#&panel1-1.
67 Sharp, "Martin Wong" panel.
68 Ibid.

CHAPTER 2. NIGGA FU

1 As Macarena Gómez-Barris and Licia Fiol-Matta state in their introduction to a special Latinx-themed issue of *American Quarterly*, "During the production of this volume, our dear colleague and friend José Esteban Muñoz passed. We dedicate the 'x' mark in Latinx to him. From his vision of a queer futurity, we understand that, while Las Américas might still grapple with violence, repetitions, and mnemonic returns, North and South, its future is open to contestations, reinventions, and even hope. The 'x' in Latinx marks that potentiality." "Introduction," in "Las Américas Quarterly," special issue, *American Quarterly*, 66.3 (September 2014): 504. They add, "Even if the authors in this volume do not

use the nomenclature 'Latinx,' we would like to, in this introduction to signal a route out of gender binaries and normativities we can no longer rehearse. From the South and in the borderlands, the 'x' turns away from the dichotomous, toward a void, an unknown, a wrestling with plurality, vectors of multi-intentionality, and the transitional meanings of what has yet to be seen." Ibid., n1.

2. I'd like to thank my sibling, Marcus J. Smalls, for the coming up with the term "Nigga Fu" during one of our many discussions about Black masculinity and popular culture.

3. There is much to say about the intermingling of Black aesthetics and Chinese martial arts. This chapter and book are not specifically about that but follow in the footsteps of film, television, and writing on the Black man, in particular, and Chinese (or sometimes Japanese and, in more recent years, Thai) martial arts. Well-known martial arts films from the Blaxploitation era of the 1970s like *Black Belt Jones* (1974) and *Black Samurai* (1977) to the neo-Blaxploitation film *The Man with the Iron Fists* (2012) and its sequel (2015) to neo-Blaxploitation satires like *Undercover Brother* (2002) and *Black Dynamite* (2009) explore iconic and often ironic tropes of US-based Black masculinity that mix fantasies of freedom, patriarchal violence, licentious sexuality, and the ability to violate racial restrictions, continuing to find audiences who enjoy this trope of the Black martial artist. For more on the connection between Black culture and Asian martial arts, see Robert Farris Thompson, "Black Martial Arts of the Caribbean," *Review: Literature and Arts of the Americas* 20.37 (2012); Daryl Joe Maedea, "Nomad of the Transpacific: Bruce Lee as Method," *American Quarterly* 69.4 (2017); and Myra Washington, "Asian American Masculinity: The Politics of Virility, Virality, and Visibility," in *The Intersectional Internet: Race, Sex, Class, and Culture Online*, ed. Safiya Umoja Noble and Brendesha M. Tynes (Lausanne: Peter Lang Group, 2016).

4. This tradition continues. See *The Man with the Iron Fists* (dir. RZA, 2012) and *The Man with the Iron Fists 2* (dir. Roel Reiné, 2015), which track the adventures of an escaped Black American enslaved male who ends up in Qing-era China.

5. For example, see W. E. B. Du Bois, *Dark Princess* (Jackson: University of Mississippi Press, 1995 [1928]).

6. M. T. Kato, *From Kung Fu to Hip Hop: Globalization, Revolution, and Popular Culture* (Albany: SUNY Press, 2007).

7. *Berry Gordy's The Last Dragon* was made for $10 million and grossed $25 million. Box Office Mojo, http://boxofficemojo.com.

8. For more on hip hop and film in the 1980s, see Kimberly Monteyne, *Hip Hop on Film: Performance Culture, Urban Space, and Genre Transformation in the 1980s* (Jackson: University of Mississippi Press, 2013).

9. Renette McCargo, "Book Review of *Hip Hop on Film: Performance Culture, Urban Space, and Genre Transformation in the 1980s*," *Journal of Hip Hop Studies* 2.1 (2015): 117.

10. Monteyne, *Hip Hop on Film*, 5.
11. Louis Venosta, in-person interview by Shanté Paradigm Smalls, New York City, July 29, 2013.
12. The US version opens with a montage featuring the arrival of a white male American martial arts competitor to Hong Kong, rather than the more traditional martial arts fight scene or demonstration.
13. Helen Heran Jun, *Race for Citizenship: Black Orientalism and Asian Uplift from Pre-Emancipation to Neoliberal America* (New York and London: New York University Press, 2011), 18.
14. Leilani Nishime, *Undercover Asian: Multiracial Asian Americans in Visual Culture* (Champaign: University of Illinois Press, 2014), preface.
15. Ibid., xv–xvi.
16. Ibid., xvi.
17. Sundiata Keita Cha-Jua, "Black Audiences, Blaxploitation and Kung Fu Films, and Challenges to White Celluloid Masculinity," in *China Forever: The Shaw Brothers and Diasporic Cinema*, ed. Poshek Fu (Urbana and Chicago: University of Illinois Press, 2008), 199–223.
18. David Desser, "The Kung Fu Craze: Hong Kong Cinema's First American Reception," in *The Cinema of Hong Kong: History, Arts, Identity*, ed. Poshek Fu and David Desser (Cambridge and New York: Cambridge University Press, 2000), 38.
19. Cha-Jua, "Black Audiences, Blaxploitation," 201.
20. Desser, "Kung Fu Craze," 25.
21. Victor Fan, "New York Chinatown Theatre under the Hong Kong Circuit System," *Film History: An International Journal* 22.1 (2010): 108–126, doi:10.1353/fih.0.0079.
22. Ed Guerrero, *Framing Blackness: The African American Image in Film* (Philadelphia: Temple University Press, 1993), 3.
23. Tamara Roberts, "Voicing Masculinity," in *Blacktino Queer Performance*, ed. E. Patrick Johnson and Ramón H. Rivera-Servera (London and Durham, NC: Duke University Press, 2016), 159.
24. Manthia Diawara, "Afro-Kitsch," in *Performing Hybridity*, ed. May Joseph and Jennifer Natalya Fink (Minneapolis: University of Minnesota Press, 1998), 178.
25. Ibid., 179, 181.
26. Tavia Nyong'o, phone interview with author, May 29, 2020.
27. Derek Conrad Murray, "Mickalene Thomas: Afro-Kitsch and the Queering of Blackness," *American Art* 28.1 (2014): 1.
28. Ibid., 3.
29. Mickalene Thomas, *Hotter than July*, 2005, acrylic, rhinestone, and enamel on wooden panel, Rubell Museum, https://rubellmuseum.org/30a-mickalene-thomas.
30. Murray, "Mickalene Thomas," 4.
31. Patricia Hill Collins, *Black Sexual Politics: African Americans, Gender, and the New Racism* (New York and London: Routledge, 2004), 188.

32 Mark Anthony Neal, *Looking for Leroy: Illegible Black Masculinities* (New York and London: New York University Press, 2013), 3.
33 Mimi Thi Nguyen, "Bruce Lee I Love You: Discourses of Race and Masculinity in the Queer Superstardom of JJ Chinois," in *Alien Encounters*, ed. Nguyen and Tu, 271–304.
34 Ibid., 273–274.
35 Stephen Teo, *Hong Kong: The Extra Dimensions* (London: British Film Institute, 1997), chap. 5, "The Romantic and the Cynical Mandarins."
36 Ibid., 76.
37 Jie Lu, "Body, Masculinity, and Representation in Chinese Martial Arts Films," in *Martial Arts as Embodied Knowledge: Asian Traditions in a Transnational World*, ed. D. S. Farrer and John Whalen-Bridge (Albany: SUNY Press, 2011), 101.
38 Ibid.
39 Ibid., 102.
40 Ibid., 101.
41 Collins, *Black Sexual Politics*, 190.
42 Jafari S. Allen, "Introduction: Black/Queer/Diaspora at the Current Conjuncture," *GLQ: A Journal of Lesbian and Gay Studies* 18.2–3 (2012): 214.
43 Ibid., 216.
44 Ibid.
45 Ibid., 217.
46 Fanon Che Wilkins, "Shaw Brothers and the Hip-Hop Imagination," in *China Forever*, ed. Fu, 226.
47 Ronald L. Jackson II, *Scripting the Black Masculine Body: Identity, Discourse, and Racial Politics in Popular Media* (Albany: SUNY Press, 2006), 49–50.
48 Cha-Jua, "Black Audiences, Blaxploitation," 216.
49 Judith Halberstam, *Female Masculinity* (Durham, NC, and London: Duke University Press, 1998), 29.
50 Ibid.
51 Lu, "Body, Masculinity," 107.
52 Ibid., 110.
53 Ibid., 113.
54 David Eng, *Racial Castration: Managing Masculinity in Asian America* (Durham, NC, and London: Duke University Press, 2001), 2.
55 A *kwoon* is a Chinese martial arts practice space, akin to the *dojo* in Japanese martial arts.
56 Most likely a sonic play on the Disney characters Huey, Dewey, and Louie, triplet nephews of Donald Duck.
57 Michael Schultz, *Berry Gordy's The Last Dragon* (Culver City, CA: TriStar Pictures, 1985), chap. 15.
58 For the position of the "coolie" in US-Caribbean labor, see Vijay Prashad, *Everybody Was Kung Fu Fighting: Afro-Asian Connections and the Myth of Racial*

Purity (Boston: Beacon Press, 2001), chap. 2, "Coolie Purana." For coolie labor and the discursive and biopolitical usages of Chinese and Indian coolie labor in Japan, see Mark Driscoll, *Absolute Erotic, Absolute Grotesque: The Living, Dead, and Undead in Japan's Imperialism, 1895–1945* (Durham, NC, and London: Duke University Press, 2010), chap. 1, "Cool(ie) Japan."

59 Neal, *Looking for Leroy*, 3.
60 Ibid., 4.
61 There are many definitions of fanfiction or fanfic. I'm deploying the term here with multiple resonances, referring to a piece of work that reworks and transforms other stories, as well as a work of speculation about a character or archetype. For more on fanfiction, see the introduction to *The Fanfiction Reader: Folk Tales for the Digital Age*, ed. Francesca Coppa (Ann Arbor: University of Michigan Press, 2017).
62 Judith Butler, *Excitable Speech: A Politics of the Performative* (New York and London: Routledge, 1997), 44.
63 Here "performative" is meant to invoke J. L. Austin's claim in *How to Do Things with Words* that to "say something is to do something." This doing is constantly shifting, has few loyalties, and is an open question, a declaration of exploration.
64 Butler, *Excitable Speech*, 51.
65 George Lipsitz, "'To Tell Truth and Not Get Trapped': Why Interethnic Antiracism Matters Now," in *Orientations: Mapping Studies in the Asian Diaspora*, ed. Kandice Chuh and Karen Shimakawa (Durham, NC, and London: Duke University Press, 2001), 300.
66 Amy Abugo Ongiri, "He Wanted to Be Just Like Bruce Lee: African Americans, Kung Fu Theatre and Cultural Exchange at the Margins," *Journal of Asian American Studies* 5,1 (February 2002): 31–40, doi:10.1353/jaas.2002.0009.
67 Ibid., 37.
68 In 1956, Richard Wright published a report of the Bandung Conference, a postcolonial gathering of 29 newly independent Asian and African nations. That report, *The Color Curtain: A Report on the Bandung Conference* (Cleveland and New York: World, 1956), stands as the inaugural 20th-century analysis of African-Asian relations. In the early 2000s, scholars theorized the subfield of Afro-Asian studies based on Bandung and many historical and cultural movements before and after that conference. For early 2000s Afro-Asian theorists, see Prashad, *Everybody Was Kung Fu Fighting*; Bill Mullen, *Afro-Orientalism* (Minneapolis: University of Minnesota Press, 2004); Fred Ho and Bill Mullen, eds., *Afro-Asia: Revolutionary Political and Cultural Connections between African Americans and Asian Americans* (London and Durham, NC: Duke University Press, 2008).
69 Karen Shimakawa, *National Abjection: The Asian American Body Onstage* (Durham, NC, and London: Duke University Press, 2002).
70 See Tricia Rose, *The Hip Hop Wars: What We Talk about When We Talk about Hip Hop—and Why It Matters* (New York: Hachette Books, 2008); Mark Anthony

Neal, *New Black Man* (New York and London: Routledge, 2005) and *Looking for Leroy: Illegible Black Masculinities* (New York: New York University Press, 2013); Collins, *Black Sexual Politics*.
71 Knittorious Sky, "Hiphop Archive Film Festival: Spring 2011," Hip Hop Archive, February 10, 2011, www.hiphoparchive.org.
72 "Bruce Leroy," Tumblr, www.tumblr.com/tagged/bruce-leroy.

CHAPTER 3. "CASEBASKETS"

1 Jean Grae and her husband, rapper Quelle Chris, moved to Baltimore, Maryland in 2020.
2 See Joan Morgan, *When Chickenheads Come Home to Roost: A Hip-Hop Feminist Breaks It Down* (New York: Simon & Schuster, 2000) and *She Begat This: 20 Years of the Miseducation of Lauryn Hill* (New York: Simon & Schuster, 2018); Gwendolyn D. Pough, ed., *Home Girls Make Some Noise: Hip Hop Feminism Anthology* (West Nyack, NY: Parker Publishing, 2007); Aisha Durman, *Home with Hip Hop Feminism: Performances in Communication and Culture* (New York: Peter Lang, 2014); Kyra Gaunt, *The Games That Black Girls Play: Learning the Ropes from Double-Dutch to Hip-Hop* (New York: New York University Press, 2006).
3 Uri McMillan, *Embodied Avatars: Genealogies of Black Feminist Art and Performance* (New York: New York University Press, 2015).
4 Bettina Love, *Hip Hop's Li'l Sistas Speak: Negotiating Hip Hop Identities and Politics in the New South* (New York: Peter Lang, 2012).
5 Tracy Sharpley-Whiting, *Pimps Up, Ho's Down: Young Black Women, Hip Hop and the New Gender Politics* (New York: New York University Press, 2007).
6 Sheldon Pearce, "Jean Grae/Quelle Chris: 'Everything Is Fine,'" Pitchfork, April 4, 2018, https://pitchfork.com.
7 Jean Grae, Bandcamp, https://jeangrae.bandcamp.com.
8 The Anomolies crew is a New York City–based hip hop collective featuring emcees, b-girls, graffiti artists, and DJs. Its core members are Big Tara, Helixx, Invincible, Pri the Honey Dark, and DJ Kuttin' Kandi. The crew made hip hop–oriented headlines in 2015 when they busted Hollywood actor Shia LaBeouf for stealing lines in a supposed original freestyle. For more on that controversy, see Mark Frauenfelder, "Who Is Shia LaBeouf Plagiarizing This Time: Rap Group Anomolies," Boing Boing, June 30, 2015, http://boingboing.net.
9 Invincible uses gender-neutral pronouns.
10 Grae is also a formidable critic, professing skepticism and sometimes bafflement at studies of her work, including something I wrote about her in 2010. While attempting to "clean up" her Wikipedia page, she encountered a passage quoting from my article "'The Rain Comes Down': Jean Grae and Hip Hop Heteronormativity," *American Behavioral Scientist* 55:1 (2010). She tweeted a screenshot of the passage, quoting my argument that Grae "rupture[s] the normative narratives of black sexuality." Her response: "Hello umm. What is this

in my Wikipedia and why and what?" Twitter, August 8, 2020, https://twitter.com/JeanGreasy/status/1291983131893956608?s=20.
11 For more on Black women performers and the avatar in the 20th century, see McMillan, *Embodied Avatars*.
12 Gwendolyn Pough, *Check It While I Wreck It: Black Womanhood, Hip-Hop Culture, and the Public Sphere* (Lebanon, NH: University Press of New England/Northeastern University Press, 2004); Sharpley-Whiting, *Pimps Up, Ho's Down*; Morgan, *When Chickenheads Come Home*; Collins, *Black Sexual Politics*; Durham, *Home with Hip Hop Feminism*; Brittney C. Cooper and Susana M. Morris, eds., *The Crunk Feminist Collection* (New York: Feminist Press at CUNY, 2017); Gwendolyn Pough, Elaine Richardson, and Aisha S. Durham, eds., *Home Girls Make Some Noise! Hip-Hop Feminism Anthology* (New York: Parker Publishing, 2007); Aria S. Halliday and Ashley N. Payne, eds., "Twenty-First Century B.I.T.C.H. Frameworks: Hip Hop Feminism Comes of Age," special issue, *Journal of Hip Hop Studies* 7.1 (2020).
13 Great books with which to start are Tricia Rose's foundational book on hip hop culture in New York City, *Black Noise*; Martha Cooper's work on female hip hop break dancers and pop-lockers, *We B* Girlz* (Brooklyn, NY: powerHouse Books, 2005); and Jessica Nydia Pabón-Colón's *Graffiti Grrlz*.
14 Claudia Tate, *Psychoanalysis and Black Novels: Desire and the Protocols of Race* (New York and Oxford: Oxford University Press, 1998), 12.
15 Geoff Klock, *How to Read Superhero Comics and Why* (London and New York: Continuum, 2002), offers a compelling literary and psychoanalytic analysis of the three major eras of superhero comics. Also see *X-Men and Philosophy: Astonishing Insight and Uncanny Argument in the Mutant X-Verse*, ed. William Irwin, Rebecca Housel, and J. Jeremy Wisnewski (New York and London: Wiley, 2009).
16 In terms of hip hop music, Prince Paul's studio album *Psychoanalysis: What Is It?* (1996) is perhaps the most glaring musical example. For writing on this album, see Nathan Fleshner, "Prince Paul's *Psychoanalysis: What Is It?*: The Rap Album as Psychoanalytic Self-Exploration," in *The Oxford Handbook of Hip Hop Music*, ed. Justin D. Burton and Jason Lee Oakes (London: Oxford University Press, 2018).
17 Klock, *How to Read Superhero Comics*, 4.
18 Mladen Dolar notes, "The English translation [of *unheimlich*], 'the uncanny,' largely retains the essential ambiguity of the German term, but French doesn't possess an equivalent, l'inquiétante étrangeté being the standard translation. So Lacan had to invent one, extimité." Mladen Dolar, "'I Shall Be with You on Your Wedding-Night': Lacan and the Uncanny," *October* 58 (1991): 5–6.
19 Hortense J. Spillers, *Black, White and in Color: Essays on American Literature and Culture* (Chicago and London: University of Chicago Press, 2003), 376.
20 Spillers is not arguing that there is no work that intersects blackness and psychoanalyses; rather, her assertion is that the broader field has yet to take up

psychoanalysis except in the rarified case of certain authors (see Frantz Fanon) or as part of trends (like that in the early 2000s when there was a renewed interest in Freud's essay "Mourning and Melancholia"). See *Loss: The Politics of Mourning*, ed. David Eng and David Kazanjian (Berkeley and Los Angeles: University of California Press, 2002).

21 See Judith Butler, *The Psychic Life of Power* (Stanford, CA: Stanford University Press, 1997).

22 Jean Grey (in some timelines) is married to fellow X-Men mutant Cyclops, aka Scott Summers.

23 Jean Grey's deaths and "deaths" are much too complex to go into here. Suffice to say Jean Grey, also known at various times in the X-Men universe (*Original X-Men* and *X-Factor*) as Marvel Girl, dies when she has to kill the alien force, Phoenix, that inhabits her body after a space radiation storm. Through various X-Men timelines and storylines, Grey is revived and revealed to have been cloned at least twice—once by evil mastermind Sinister, who has her clone, Madelyne Pryor, marry Scott Summers (Cyclops) in order to produce a mutant child; at another time, Grey is cloned as Phoenix/Dark Phoenix, who had been living as Jean Grey while the "original" Jean Grey was trapped at the bottom of the ocean. Phoenix/Dark Phoenix is reluctantly destroyed by the X-Men, who believe she is their Jean Grey gone bad. For the entire story, see *X-Men: The Dark Phoenix Saga* (1988 and 2006), originally published in *Uncanny X-Men* 129–137; also, *X-Men: Phoenix Rising* (1985 and 2001). For later Jean Grey iterations, including White Phoenix of the Crown and Hope, see *X-Men: Phoenix—Endsong* (2005), *X-Men: Messiah Complex* (2007), and *X-Men: Second Coming* (2010).

24 For one of Grae's most hilarious blog posts, see "The State of 'Eh,' Chapter 5: Big Crazy," January 1, 2010, http://jeangraesblog.blogspot.com.

25 The films *X-Men*, *X2* (dir. Bryan Singer, 2000, 2003), and *X-Men: The Last Stand* (dir. Brett Ratner, 2006) offer simplified introductions to the X-Men universe.

26 For a discussion of the significance of race and gender in relation to the X-Men character Storm, see andré m. carrington, *Speculative Fiction and Media Fandom through a Lens, Darkly* (PhD diss., New York University, 2009).

27 Sigmund Freud, *The Uncanny*, trans. David McLintock, intro. Hugh Haughton (New York and London: Penguin Books, 2003 [1919]), 132.

28 See andré m. carrington, *Speculative Blackness: The Future of Race in Science Fiction* (Minneapolis: University of Minnesota Press, 2016); Marleen S. Barr, *Afro-Future Females: Black Writers Chart Science Fiction's Newest New-Wave Trajectory* (Columbus: Ohio State Press, 2008); Michelle D. Commander, *Afro-Atlantic Flight: Speculative Returns and the Black Fantastic* (Durham, NC, and London: Duke University Press, 2017); and Sami Schalk, *Bodyminds Reimagined: (Dis)ability, Race, and Gender in Black Woman's Speculative Fiction* (Durham, NC, and London: Duke University Press, 2018).

29 Freud, *The Uncanny*, 141.

30 Hortense Spillers, "Black, White, and in Color, or Learning How to Paint: Toward an Intramural Protocol of Reading," in Spillers, *Black, White and in Color*, 284.
31 W. E. B. Du Bois, *The Conservation of Races*, ed. Jim Manis (Hazelton: Pennsylvania State University Electronic Classics Series, 2007), 12.
32 Paul Gilroy, *The Black Atlantic: Modernity and Double Consciousness* (Cambridge, MA: Harvard University Press, 1993), 127.
33 Ibid.
34 I use "her" to disrupt the overt and overwhelming masculinism of Du Bois, Freud, and Lacan.
35 Gilroy, *Black Atlantic*, 131.
36 Ibid., 133.
37 Hazel V. Carby, *Race Men* (Cambridge, MA, and London: Harvard University Press, 1998), 12–13.
38 See Sigmund Freud, "The Psychogenesis of a Case of Female Homosexuality," *International Journal of Psycho-Analysis* 1.2 (1920).
39 Ranjana Khanna's *Dark Continents: Psychoanalysis and Colonialism* (Durham, NC, and London: Duke University Press, 2003) investigates the relationship between Freudian psychoanalysis and colonialism.
40 Carby, *Race Men*, 10.
41 Ibid., 12.
42 Ibid., 16.
43 Du Bois's identification with Victorian ideals as noted by Cornel West: "The Victorian three-piece suit—with a clock and a chain in the vest . . . not only represented the age that shaped and molded him; it also dignified his sense of intellectual vocation, a senses of rendering service by means of a critical intelligence and moral action" (quoted in Carby, *Race Men*, 21). Carby goes on to compare West (self-declared intellectual heir to Du Bois) and Du Bois to highlight the way the latter "replaces and represses images of sexual desire" in the service of what is "irrevocably and conservatively masculine" (21).
44 Freud, *The Uncanny*, 143.
45 Tina Campt, *Listening to Images* (Durham, NC, and London: Duke University Press, 2017), 17.
46 Grae, "God's Gift."
47 Jean Grae is a trope on a character from *The Uncanny X-Men* named Jean Grey. This character is a young telepath who unleashes an alter ego, Phoenix, after she falls into a coma. Grey's alter ego has an evil side, Dark Phoenix and Grey often battles to keep Dark Phoenix suppressed and Phoenix in charge (controlled by Grey). Rapper Jean Grae, who was known as Whut Whut or What? What? depending on with whom one speaks, changed her name after her group Natural Resources disbanded: "I wanted to start all over and present myself again as a solo artist. Kind of a rebirth." Steven Samuels, "Jean Grae: Mental Illness," SOHH, August 12, 2005, http://sohh.com. Grae frequently alludes to and performs her

"craziness" in discussing her drinking, paranoia, suicidal and homicidal thoughts, and fantasies of an afterlife.
48 9th Wonder was part of the North Carolina–based group Little Brother. He produced Jean Grae's stellar album *Jeanius*. He's also produced for luminaries such as Jay-Z.
49 Immortal Technique, "The Illest," written by Immortal Technique, Jean Grae, and Pumpkinhead, produced by 44 Caliber Productions, *Revolutionary, Vol. 1* (Nature Sounds, 2004). It's unclear whether this is in dialogue with Mobb Deep's 2003 song also titled "The Illest." One would assume that there would be an awareness and implicit dialogical relationship between the two songs.
50 Grae in Immortal Technique, "The Illest."
51 *Wild Style* (1983) was one of the earliest films depicting the then-burgeoning hip hop culture. It focused on the life of a young Latino graffiti artist ("tagger" or "bomber") and graffiti culture as well as looking at elements of what would be called hip-hop culture—break-dancing and pop-locking, emcees (from the abbreviation for "microphone controllers," later known as "rappers"), fashion, and other forms of hip hop culture, including the uptown-downtown art scene exchange. Krylon is a brand of art spray paint used by many graffiti artists.
52 Grae in Immortal Technique, "The Illest."
53 Patricia Hill Collins speaks well about this relationship between blackness, gender, and heterosexism in *Black Sexual Politics*. She also discusses these specific dynamics relating to hip hop culture in *From Black Power to Hip Hop: Racism, Nationalism, and Feminism* (Philadelphia: Temple University Press, 2006). Mark Anthony Neal addresses the limits of heterosexist constructions of heterosexual masculinity in *New Black Man*.
54 Roderick A. Ferguson, *Aberrations in Black: Toward a Queer of Color Critique* (Minneapolis and London: University of Minnesota Press, 2004), 17. My emphasis.
55 The NPR show *The Record* hosted a great talk, "Hey Ladies: Being a Woman Musician Today," September 14, 2010, http://npr.org.
56 Although hip hop cultural production is almost 50 years old, the number of well-known female emcees, DJs, b-girls, personalities, designers, filmmakers, and executives is still nominal. The most famous of female emcees—Lauryn Hill, Missy Elliot, Lil' Kim, Eve, Foxy Brown, Nicki Minaj, Megan Thee Stallion, Cardi B, Rah Digga, Queen Latifah (who has not made a hip hop album in many years)—hardly speak to prolific numbers. Salt-N-Pepa, MC Lyte, Roxanne Shanté, the Real Roxanne, and other early female rappers are often glossed over in rap historiographies. It is outside of the scope of this paper, but it would be interesting to investigate the place of "old school" hip hop females in hip hop's cultural memory.
57 Rose, *Black Noise*, 148.
58 Peggy Phelan, *Unmarked: The Politics of Performance* (New York and London: Routledge, 1993), 5.

59   Ibid.
60   See Patricia Hill Collins's *Black Sexual Politics*. Of note is her chapter on freakishness in Black femininity, "Get Your Freak On: Sex, Babies, and Images of Black Femininity," and her chapter on the connection between Black masculinity and violence, "Booty Call: Sex, Violence, and Images of Black Masculinity." See Frantz Fanon's *Black Skin, White Masks* for discussions of Black (male) subjectivity, desire, and colonialism.
61   Rebecca Schneider, *The Explicit Body in Performance* (New York: Routledge, 1997).
62   There are multiple examples of this, but two interesting cases are the examples of André 3000 of Outkast and soul singer D'Angelo. Both of these men have explored various forms of "odd" Black masculinity. André has explored Afrofuturistic modes, southern "gangsta," an amalgam of those two modalities, and a Black neo-hippie aesthetic. Outkast has addressed rumors about André's performance of maleness, responding to questions of "What's up with André? Is he in a cult? Is he on drugs? Is he gay?" ("Return of the 'G,'" *Aquemini*, 1998). André calls these interpolations, "the wrong impression of expression." D'Angelo confronted heteronormative panic when he released his video for his song "How Does it Feel? (Untitled)" (*Voodoo*, 2000). The video was bare bones, with no set and D'Angelo's gorgeously naked Black male body being loved, wooed, and exposed by the camera. There was a great deal of response that D'Angelo had "sold out" in order to sell records, although the formula of getting naked to sell your product seems to only really work for women since women are constantly placed in the position of a-body-on-display-for-sale. D'Angelo's efforts at showing the unadorned Black male body (sans "tough" T-shirt or self-conscious display) were met with disgust from his previous male fans. Some online respondents called his video display "faggot shit" and refused to watch the video or listen to D'Angelo anymore.
63   Jean Grae, "blah blah," written by Tsidsi Ibrahim, *The Bootleg of the Bootleg* (Babygrande Records, 2003).
64   J-23, "Jean Grae—This Week," HipHopDX, October 18, 2004, http://hiphopdx.com.
65   Ibid.
66   Ibid.
67   Phelan, *Unmarked*, 27.
68   Grae, "God's Gift."
69   "Misogynoir" is a term coined and proliferated by Moya Bailey and Trudy. It "describes the anti-Black racist misogyny that Black women experience. Despite coining the term in 2008 and writing about the term online since 2010, we experience, to varying degrees, our contributions being erased, our writing not cited, or our words plagiarized by people who find the word compelling. It is not surprising that misogynoir would be enacted against the Black women who

brought the word to public acclaim but it is nonetheless troubling." Moya Bailey and Trudy, "On Misogynoir: Citation, Erasure, and Plagiarism," *Feminist Media Studies* 18.4 (2018): 762–768.
70 Schneider, *Explicit Body in Performance*, 23.
71 There has been some confusion about whose voice is in the sample. Some have asserted that is a member of the group Black Moon, but that remains undetermined.
72 Grae, "God's Gift."
73 The Notorious B.I.G., "One More Chance/Stay with Me," written by Mark DeBarge, Etterlen Jordan, and Christopher Wallace, produced by Sean Combs and Rashad Smith (Bad Boy Records, 1995).
74 Rose, *Black Noise*, 39.
75 Ibid.
76 The X-Men series has different titles demarcating various storylines, authors, and characters. *The Uncanny X-Men* is probably the most well-known title, but there are also *The Essential X-Men*, *X-Factor*, and *X-Men*.
77 For the complete Jean Grey/Phoenix/Dark Phoenix story, see *Essential X-Men*, Vol. 2 (1979, 2005), *The Dark Phoenix Saga* (2006), and *Phoenix Rising* (1985, 2001), all published by Marvel Publishing.
78 Grae was known as What? What? and, briefly, the Easter Bunny.
79 The short film is called *Spittin' 'Til They Shame You*, which is a line in the song it's based on, "My Story." On the bootleg version of the album *Jeanius*, the song is titled "The Rain Comes Down." YouTube, 2009, www.youtube.com/watch?v=5-_db3URjrk.
80 "[N]eurotic men state that to them there is something uncanny about the female genitals. But what they find uncanny ['unhomely'] is actually the entrance to man's old 'home,' the place where everyone once lived. A jocular saying has it that 'love is a longing for home,' and if someone dreams of a certain place or a certain landscape and, while dreaming, thinks to himself, 'I know this place, I've been here before,' this place can be interpreted as representing his mother's genitals or her womb." Freud, *The Uncanny*, 151.
81 Jacques Lacan, *The Four Fundamentals of Concepts of Psychoanalysis: The Seminar of Jacques Lacan Book XI*, ed. Jacques-Alain Miller, trans. Alan Sheridan (New York and London: W.W. Norton, 1979), 22. I'm using "unconscious" both in its noun form, as one of the "psychical systems . . . in [Freud's] theory of mental structure," and following Lacan's usage of it as discourse. See Dylan Evans, *An Introductory Dictionary of Lacanian Psychoanalysis* (London and New York: Routledge, 1996).
82 Jean Grae, "My Story," written by Tsidsi Ibrahim and Talib Kweli, produced by 9th Wonder, *Jeanius* (Blacksmith Records, 2008).
83 Ibid.
84 Ibid.

85 Sigmund Freud, *The Interpretation of Dreams*, 3rd ed., trans. Abraham A. Brill (Whitefish, MT: Kessinger, 2004 [1913]), 223.
86 Ibid.
87 Grae, "My Story."
88 To Harvilla's question about whether anything on "My Story" is embellished, Grae responds, "No. No. No. 'My Story' is a really important song. It took me about 10 years or so to do it." Rob Harvilla, "The Trials of Jean Grae: Why an NYC Rap Star Threatened Retirement, and Why She Hasn't Stopped Threatening Yet," *Village Voice*, July 9, 2008, www.villagevoice.com.
89 Ibid.
90 Ibid.
91 Jean Grae, "Block Party," written by Tsidsi Ibrahim, produced by Nasain Nahmeen, *Attack of the Attacking Things* (Third Earth Music, 2002).
92 Jean Grae, untitled track, written by Christopher Wallace, Sean Combs, Lou Donaldson, Marty and Bunny Debarge, Tsidsi Ibrahim, and Sean Carter, *The Bootleg of the Bootleg* (Babygrande Records, 2003). The intricate levels of sampling in this song are astounding. Grae is referencing Jay-Z's song "Excuse Me" (2002), which pays homage to the Notorious B.I.G.'s song "One More Chance/Stay with Me" (1995). Biggie's remix of his own "One More Chance" (1994) is built around a smart sampling of DeBarge, a popular 1970s and 80s R&B group from Detroit. The sample was revived when R&B singer/songwriter Ashanti incorporated elements of "One More Chance/Stay with Me" on her 2002 smash hit "Foolish."
93 Murray Forman. *The 'Hood Comes First: Race, Space, Place in Rap and Hip-Hop*. (Middletown, CT: Wesleyan University Press, 2002), 28–9.
94 Bed-Stuy is the nickname of the central Brooklyn neighborhood of Bedford Stuyvesant. Jean Grae sometimes lives in Bed-Stuy.
95 I say "surfaces" as there's no interaction with the subway.
96 Michel De Certeau, *The Practice of Everyday Life*, trans. Steven Randall (Berkeley, Los Angeles, and London: University of California Press, 1984), 99.

CHAPTER 4. QUEER HIP HOP, QUEER DISSONANCE
1 Zenzeke Isoke, "Black Ethnography, Black (Female) Aesthetics: Thinking/Writing/Saying/Sounding Black Political Life," *Theory & Event* 1.1 (2018): 149.
2 Gayatri Gopinath, *Unruly Visions: The Aesthetic Practices of Queer Diaspora* (Durham, NC, and London: Duke University Press, 2018), 4.
3 Shanté Paradigm Smalls, "Queer Hip Hop: A Brief Historiography," in *The Oxford Handbook of Music and Queerness*, ed. Fred Maus and Sheila Whiteley, 2018 (online pub.), 6, doi:10.1093/oxfordhb/9780199793525.013.103.
4 Ibid., 9–11, 12–18.
5 As recent as 2019, a gay male club located in the Boystown section of Chicago banned rap music and certain DJs from playing there. See "Gay Bar Reverses Its

Rap Ban and Its DJ Blacklist after Being Accused of Racism," Queerty, May 30, 2019, www.queerty.com.
6   See Stonewall Riot veteran Mark Segal's "I Was at the Stonewall Riots. The Movie 'Stonewall' Gets Everything Wrong," *PBS NewsHour*, 2015, www.pbs.org.
7   There is no unified term to refer to lesbian, gay, bisexual, transgender, and queer people (and their allies) who make rap music, b-boy/b-girl, make graffiti, or DJ. Some of the more popular terms in use: "queer hip hop," "gay hip hop," and "homohop." "Queer hip hop" is often, although not exclusively, used by artists to denote a critical intervention into both mainstream hip hop culture and mainstream gay culture, and both cultures' biases regarding the other. "Gay hip hop" (GHH) is often used by artists and media to describe LGBTQ people making hip hop. "Homohop" originated in the LGBTQ hip hop community, but is no longer widely used there. It has become a media designation, often used interchangeably with "gay hip hop."
8   "PeaceOUT World Homohop Festival," MySpace, www.myspace.com/peaceout-festival, accessed December 17, 2012.
9   "Peace Out East™," MySpace, www.myspace.com/peaceouteastfestival, accessed December 17, 2012.
10 Additionally, there were three spin-off festivals: Peace Out UK in London, Peace Out South in Atlanta, and Peace Out Northwest in Portland, Oregon, all held in 2005 alone.
11 For particularly relevant discussions of homophobia in hip hop, see Tricia Rose's *Hip Hop Wars*, especially pages 236–240; Terry Sawyer, "Queering the Mic," Alternet.com, March 18, 2004, www.alternet.org.
12 Touré, "Gay Rappers: Too Real for Hip-Hop?," *New York Times*, April 20, 2003, 2 (arts section).
13 Robert Penn, dir., *B.Q.E. Interview* (Robert Penn Productions, May 21, 2005).
14 Annamarie Jagose, *Queer Theory: An Introduction* (New York: New York University Press, 1996), 98.
15 Cohen Cohen, "Punks, Bulldaggers, and Welfare Queens: The Radical Potential of Queer Politics?," in *Black Queer Studies: A Critical Anthology*, ed. E. Patrick Johnson and Mae G. Henderson (Durham, NC, and London: Duke University Press, 2005), 22.
16 See Eric Darnell Pritchard and Maria I. Bibbs, "Sista' Outsider: Queer Women of Color and Hip Hop," in *Home Girls Make Some Noise: Hip Hop Feminism Anthology*, ed. Gwendolyn D. Pough, Elaine Richardson, Aisha Durham, and Rachel Raimist (Mira Loma, CA: Parker Publishing, 2007); Janell Hobson and Dianne Bartlow, "Introduction: Representin': Women, Hip-Hop, and Popular Music," and Adreana Clay, "'Like an Old Soul Record': Black Feminism, Queer Sexuality, and the Hip-Hop Generation," *Meridians: Feminism, Race, Transnationalism* 8.1 (2008); "The Queerness of Hip Hop/The Hip Hop of Queerness," symposium, Harvard University, September 21, 2012, https://

qohh-blog1.tumblr.com; Jessica N. Pabón and Shanté Paradigm Smalls, eds., "All Hail the Queenz," special issue, *Women & Performance: A Journal of Feminist Theory* 24.1 (2014).

17 Moya Bailey, "Homolatent Masculinity & Hip Hop Culture," in "The Queerness of Hip Hop," special issue, *Palimpsest: A Journal on Women, Gender, and the Black International* 2.2 (2013): 190.

18 Ibid., 191, 194–195.

19 Ibid., 196.

20 Carrie Battan, "We Invented Swag: NYC's Queer Rap," Pitchfork, March 21, 2012, https://pitchfork.com.

21 Danny Addice, "13 QPOC Rappers Dominating the Mic and Your Pride Playlist," Hornet, June 17, 2020, https://hornet.com.

22 Combahee River Collective, "Combahee River Collective Statement" (1977), History Is a Weapon, http://historyisaweapon.com.

23 Roderick A. Ferguson, "Queer of Color Critique," *Oxford Research Encyclopedias: Literature*, March 28, 2018, 1, doi:9780190201098.013.33.

24 Imani Perry, for instance, identifies the following four characteristics as determinants of hip hop music's status as Black American music: "(1) its primary language is African American Vernacular English (AAVE); (2) it has a political location in society distinctly ascribed to black people, music, and cultural forms; (3) it is derived from black American oral culture; and (4) it is derived from black American musical traditions." Imani Perry, *Prophets of the Hood: Politics and Poetics in Hip Hop* (Durham, NC, and London: Duke University Press, 2004), 10.

25 Forman and Neal, *That's the Joint!*, 3.

26 Guot A. Yep and John P. Elia, "Queering/Quaring Blackness in *Noah's Arc*," in *Queer Popular Culture: Literature, Media, Film, and Television*, ed. Thomas Peele (New York: Palgrave Macmillan, 2007), 31.

27 E. Patrick Johnson, "'Quare Studies' Studies, or (Almost) Everything I Know about Queer Studies I Learned from My Grandmother," in *Black Queer Studies*, ed. Johnson and Henderson, 126.

28 Yep and Elia, "Queering/Quaring Blackness," 31.

29 For more on Black representation and television, see Debra C. Smith, "Critiquing Reality-Based Televisual Black Fatherhood: A Critical Analysis of Run's House and Snoop Dogg's Father Hood," *Critical Studies in Media Communication* 25.4 (2008): 393–412, doi:10.1080/15295030802328020.

30 There is a tremendous amount of subversive possibility even inside these seemingly limited tropes of Black expression. For more on the subversive power of "negative" representation, see Raquel J. Gates, *Double Negative: The Black Image and Popular Culture* (Durham, NC: Duke University Press, 2018).

31 Eric Brightwell (blog), "Man Parrish," June 5, 2020, https://ericbrightwell.com.

32 Alain Patrick, "Excerpts from My Man Parrish Interview for Electronic Standards," review of "Man Parrish Featuring Freeze Force– Boogie Down (Bronx)," Discogs, August 8, 2015, www.discogs.com.
33 Man Parrish, live phone interview by music director, WHRB 95.3, 2003, www.manparrish.com/interview.
34 Charles Mudede, "The Gay Roots of Hip Hop," Stranger, July 7, 2005, https://slog.thestranger.com.
35 For more on the evolution of Dun(n) speech, see "Mobb Deep Explains Origins of Dun Language, Working with Q-Tip," HipHopDX, September 27, 2011, https://hiphopdx.com.
36 Greg Thomas, *Hip-Hop Revolution in the Flesh: Power, Knowledge, and Pleasure in Lil' Kim's Lyricism* (New York: Palgrave McMillan, 2009), 2.
37 Ibid.
38 Junior Francois, "'Hip-Hop' Was Coined by Keith 'Cowboy' Wiggins," Rap Dictionary, August 19, 2020, https://rapdictionary.com.
39 Man Parrish, "Hip Hop Be Bop—How a Classic Was Made," Man Parrish Stories, season 3, episode 9, YouTube, September 15, 2018.
40 The original Fun House was located at 526 West 26th Street in Manhattan's Chelsea neighborhood. For more, see the fan page: https://thefunhousenyc.com.
41 Payola is a form of bribery a record company pays to get a song or album in frequent enough radio rotation to make it a hit. Man Parrish, "Hip Hop Be Bop—How a Classic Was Made," season 4, episode 5, YouTube, September 22, 2018. Parrish often uploaded multiple videos in a single day, so some videos have the same date. As of September 2021, YouTube has removed over 40 of his videos chronicaling his life as a music producer in the early 1980s. Parrish wrote this in the comment section of his "Man Parrish Stories" channel teaser video: "Thanks Brian! Unfortunately I DONT have a backup, they are all gone. I BEGGED YouTube to let me have access to simply download them. They ignored me. I kept saying I need to back them up, and never got around to it. That was 40 days / 40 episodes of work gone, by some cancel couture pig @ YouTube. Shameful, I didn't use foul language and even tagged it 'inappropriate for children' using YouTube's own system. They didn't want me to speak about being sexually abused as a child or mentioning that I was a male prostitute for 6 months to survive being homeless. I hope this story goes viral to shame what they have done. Sad state of affairs they have made. Thanks for your kind words." YouTube, Man Parrish Music channel, September 2021, www.youtube.com/watch?v=bu7kya7odNo&lc=Ugz-35iLeXzovxdKv6Z4AaABAg.9RbMwEfWgMC9RcNjxp-EGt.
42 Man Parrish, "'Boogie Down Bronx'—How It Was Made," Man Parrish Stories, season 4, episode 6, YouTube, September 22, 2018.
43 Man Parrish, "I Was a Male Prostitute & Testified against the Mafia!," Man Parrish Stories, season 1, episode 3, YouTube, August 17, 2018.

44 Jamal X, "Confessions of a Gay Rapper," 1997, www.prismnet.com/~larrybob/gayrap.html.
45 Paula T. Renfroe, "She Got a Big Mouth: Hip-Hop Shock Jock Wendy Williams Tells All," *Source*, December 1997: 111.
46 James Baldwin, "Freaks and the American Ideal of Manhood," in *James Baldwin: Collected Essays*, ed. Toni Morrison (New York: Library of America, 1998), 824.
47 Davey D, "Gays, Lesbians and Hip Hop Culture," *Hip Hop Daily News*, July 27, 1997, www.daveyd.com.
48 Laura Jamison, "A Feisty Female Rapper Breaks a Hip-Hop Taboo," *New York Times*, January 18, 1998, www.prismnet.com/~larrybob/queenpen.html.
49 R. K. Byers, "A B-Boy Adventure into Hip-Hop's Gay Underground," *Source*, December 1997.
50 Ibid., 107.
51 James Earl Hardy, "Boys Will B-Boys: An Open Letter to All My Homie-Sexuals in Hip Hop," *Source*, December 1997.
52 For another read of "bling," see Krista Thompson, "Introduction: Of Shine, Bling, and Bixels," in *Shine: The Visual Economy of Light in African Diasporic Aesthetic Practice* (Durham, NC: Duke University Press, 2015).
53 Tim'm West, "Blingizm," written by Tim'm West, *Songs from Red Dirt* (Cellular Records, 2002).
54 B.Q.E. was a spoken word, rap, and neo-soul hip hop group that consisted of me, Paradigm, and Dutchboy (Jason Muscat).
55 Soyica Diggs Colbert, Douglas A. Jones Jr., and Shane Vogel, eds., *Race and Performance after Repetition* (Durham, NC, and London: Duke University Press, 2020), 8.
56 Ibid.
57 Jerry Portwood, "Murs Explains His Reasons for the Gay Kiss in 'Animal Style,'" *Out Magazine*, July 16, 2012, www.out.com.
58 I began writing the essay that would become this chapter in late December 2012. At the time, "212" had 39 million views and "Same Love" had 9 million. Macklemore and Ryan Lewis's song has soared in popularity, but has been criticized for his white cis-hetero privilege and his collapsing of homophobia with Black/hip hop culture. See Karen Tongson (and the vitriolic comments section), "'Same Love,' Same Old Shit?," From the Square, June 10, 2013, www.fromthesquare.org; Thaddeus Russell, "The Progressive Lineage of Mackelomore's and Lorde's Attacks on the Pleasures of the Poor," Reason.com, February 1, 2014, http://reason.com. Murs's "Animal Style" (www.youtube.com/watch?v=WwTSPcNSi4o) is provocative and *au courant* as it takes on the issue of gay male suicide, homicide, closetedness, interracial desire, and masculinity/masculine performance. Though the topics may seem somewhat conservative, in the realm of hip hop performance, this song and video is cutting-edge. See this interview with DJ Vlad for Murs's views on the video, his playing a queer male character, and some

of the reaction from other artists and fans: YouTube, September 25, 2012, www.youtube.com/watch?v=jBJyiW4XLrM. Incidentally, Murs's video had just over 700,000 views as of July 2021.

59 There's been a small but visible surge in queer hip hop scholarship, including the "Queerness of Hip Hop/Hip Hop of Queerness" symposium (http://qohh.tumblr.com/) organized by C. Riley Snorton and Scott Poulson-Bryant at Harvard University on September 21, 2012. And there have been at least two special issues of scholarly journals on queerness and hip hop: "The Queerness of Hip Hop/The Hip Hop of Queerness," ed. C. Riley Snorton, *Palimpsest* 2.2 (2013); and "All Hail the Queenz: A Queer Feminist Recalibration of Hip Hop Scholarship," ed. Jessica N. Pabón and Shanté Paradigm Smalls, *Women & Performance* 24.1 (2014).

CONCLUSION. QUEER TRANS BLACK AESTHETIC FUTURES

1 Keguro Macharia, *Frottage: Frictions of Intimacy across the Black Diaspora* (New York: New York University Press, 2019), 5.

2 André Aciman, *Call Me by Your Name* (New York: Farrar, Straus and Giroux), 2007. The novel was adapted for film and released in November 2017; it received an Oscar for Best Adapted Screenplay at the 90th Academy Awards.

3 The cover art was created by Croatian-Spanish conceptual performance artist Filip Ćustić Braut. For more on his work, see www.instagram.com/filipcustic1/?hl=en.

4 Andrew R. Chow, "Lil Nas X on 'Montero (Call Me by Your Name),' LGBT Repression, and the Influence of FKA Twigs," *Time*, March 29, 2020; updated March 31, 2021, https://time.com.

5 Ibid.

6 As of July 2021, the official video for "Montero (Call Me by Your Name)" has 292,159,921 million views on YouTube and Lil Nas X has 14.3 million subscribers on the platform. The song debuted at number one on the Billboard 100 and was still number one in the UK a month later, www.billboard.com. The rapper has 6.5 million followers on Twitter, 8.5 million on Instagram, and 17.6 million on TikTok with over 4 *billion* views of his content.

7 August Alsina, "I Luv This Sh*t," chor. Tricia Miranda, filmed by Tim Milgram, YouTube, March 9, 2015, https://www.youtube.com/watch?v=B9ypdIf85gI. The video had 14.7 million views and Tricia Miranda had 1.77 million YouTube subscribers as of April 2021.

8 See the YouTube comments section for Alsina, "I Luv This Sh*t," www.youtube.com/watch?v=B9ypdIf85gI.

9 The video is edited in such a way that Battiste and Denzel Chisolm, another stellar Black male dancer, bookend it. Chisolm's section is just a few seconds shorter than Battiste's.

10 This portion of the video appears at roughly 5:07–5:15.

INDEX

Page numbers in *italics* refer to figures

ABC No Rio: *Crime Show* exhibit, 46, 171n57
abortion, 88, 114–21
aesthetics (framework), 4–10, 24
African American Vernacular English, 14, 80–81
Afrika Bambaataa, 8, 10–12, 133, 136, 166n16, 166n18
AfriLatinx peoples, 3, 17, 34, 87
Afro-Asian people: aesthetics, 31–31, 46; and hip hop, 26, 87; and martial arts films, 3, 59, 73, 83; and masculinity, 58, 62, 73, 75
Afro-Caribbean diaspora, 168n8
Afrocentrism, 3, 107, 140
Afro-fabulation, 9–10
Afrokitsch, 63
Afro-latinidad people, 31, 33
Age of Consent, 124, 132
Ahearn, Charlie, 22, 26, 30, 50; *Artist Portrait Videos* (1988), 43, 44, 46; *Wild Style* (1983), 28–29, 44, 103, 170n46, 181n51
Ahearn, John, 22, 26, 43–44, 50
Allen, Harry, 8
Allen, Jafari S., 71
Alsina, August: "I Luv This Shit," 154–56
American Sign Language, 47, 172n63
Ampu, Ralow Trinitrotulene. *See* G-Minus
André 3000, 182n62
Anomalies, 88, 177n8
Anthology of Rap (2011), 143
Art in America, 38, 41

Artist Portrait Videos (1988). *See* Ahearn, Charlie
Art of Noise, 133
Ashanti, 184n92
Asian American people, 4, 26, 29, 41, 58, 67, 73, 83, 87
Asian masculinity, 58, 62, 68–70, 72–75, 78, 84
Asian people. *See* Afro-Asian people; Asian American people; Asian masculinity; Chinese American people
Astaire, Lynette, 116
Astor, Patti, 28, 50
Attica Prison riot, 6
Austin, J. L., 30, 81, 168n11, 176n63
Austin, Joe, 42
authenticity, 8–9, 16–17, 24, 124, 126, 131, 150

Bailey, Moya, 128, 182–183n69
Baldwin, James, 139
ball culture, 2–3
Bandcamp, 88
Banks, Azealia: "212" (2011), 150, 188n58; "1991" (2012), 2, 150
Banks, Billy, 55
Barbra 162, 40
Barthes, Roland, 169n22
Basquiat, Jean-Michel, 22, 26, 30, 37, 47
Battiste, Dominique, 155–56, 189n9
B-Boy Blues series, 140
Bboy Skim, 154
Benitez, Jellybean, 133

191

Benjamin, Sathima Bea, 91
Berry Gordy's The Last Dragon (1985): Black masculinity in, 22–23, 53–62, 65–67, 82–85; Leroy Green in, 54–62, 65–85, 87; and racial performance, 22–23, 75–82; Yi Brothers in, 55, 71, 75–83
Bessa, Antonia Sergia, 33–34
Big Bank Hank, 124
Big Freedia, 132
Big Tara, 177n8
Billboard, 139, 189n6
bisexuality, 32, 102, 139–41, 150
Black aesthetics (framework), 4–10, 24
Black Arts Movement, 6, 9
black ethnography (Isoke concept), 123
Black female psyche, 89, 92, 94, 97
Black feminism, 65, 87, 92, 110, 123, 129, 130; futurity, 100–101
Black masculinity: in Blaxploitation films, 61, 79, 83, 173n3; and Freud and Du Bois, 99–100; and Jean Grae, 23, 100–4, 108–13; in *The Last Dragon* (1985), 22–23, 53–62, 65–85, 173n3; and Martin Wong, 36; and queer hip hop, 129, 138–39, 142, 182n62
Black men: in film, 53, 55–58, 71–75, 78–79, 84; and heteronormativity, 84, 104–8; and hip hop, 3, 75, 167n28; queer, 140–43. *See also* Black masculinity
Black Moon, 183n71
blackness, definition of, 15–16
Black people. *See* Black men; Black women
Black Power Movement, 6, 65–66
Blacksmith Music, 88
Black Thought, 102
Black women: and Black men, 19–20, 95–96, 100; and the doppelgänger/double, 97–100; and heteronormativity, 104–8; in hip hop, 88–93, 111–12, 135–36, 165n10, 167n28, 181n56; and subjectivity, 113–14. *See also* Black female psyche; femininity; misogynoir
Blanco, Mykki, 124; "Waavy," 150
Blaxploitation films, 54–55, 59–61, 65, 79, 83, 173n3
Blondie, 170n46
Bluestockings Feminist Bookstore, 144
Bost, Darius, 36
Boy George, 133
B.Q.E., 143, 188n54
Braithwaite, Fred "Fab Five Freddy," 28, 170n46
Broda, Peter, 38
Bronx, 1, 8–9, 30, 37, 43–44, 78, 112, 133, 136; South Bronx, 4, 9, 11, 140
Bronx Museum of Art: *Martin Wong* exhibit, 50
Brooklyn, NY, 1, 4, 116–17, 119–20, 141, 144
Brown, Foxy, 18–19, 111
Brown, Jacqueline Nassy, 71–72
Brown, James, 156–57
Brown, Jeree (JBRap), 143
Butler, Judith, 81
Byers, R. K., 140

Cakes da Killa, 124
Camden, New Jersey riot, 6
Cameron, Dan, 48, 169n28
Campbell, Clive. *See* DJ Kool Herc
Campt, Tina, 101
Canibus, 102
Cannibal Ox, 101
Cantonese, 81
capitalism, 7, 10, 19, 49, 90, 128, 158
Carby, Hazel, 97–99, 121, 180n43
Cardi B, 88, 111, 181n56; "W.A.P. (Wet Ass Pussy)," 165n10
Caribbean DJ music, 9
Caribbean people, 3, 15
Carry, Julius J., III, 56, 62
Carter, John "Ski," 137–38
Cha-Jua, Sundiata Keita, 59

Chang, Jeff, 7–8
Chicago, 1, 150, 158
Chin, Michael G., 76
Chinatown, NY, 44, 76
Chinese American people: and Black aesthetics, 76–77; influence on hip hop, 16–17
Chinese Connection, The (1972), 80
Chisolm, Denzel, 189n9
Chow Yun-fat, 7
Chris, Quelle, 88
Christianity, 152–53
Civil Rights Movement, 6, 65
Cloud, Robin, 141
Cohen, Cathy, 127–28
Colbert, Soyica, 146–47
Cold Crush Brothers, 170n46
Collins, Patricia Hill, 66, 69, 181n53
Combahee River Collective Statement, 129
Consentiono, Donald John, 63
"coolies," 78, 84, 175–76n58
Cool Raul, 134
Corcoran, Sean, 41–42
Cortez, Diego, 50
Cosby, Bill, 12
COVID-19 pandemic, 144, 154
Crash, 22, 26, 37
Creation of Adam, The (Michelangelo), 152
Cunningham, Valentine, 13
Cyrus, Billy Ray, 151

dance, 154–157. *See also individual types*
D'Angelo, 182n62
Dark Phoenix. *See* Grey, Jean
Davey D, 139–40
David, Dwight, 58
Davis, Angela, 63
Daze, 22, 26, 28, 30, 37, 40–42, 50, 170n46
DC Comics, 124
Deadly Art of Survival, The (1978), 61

DeBarge, 184n92
de Certeau, Michel, 120
DeepDickCollective (D/DC), 141, 143
Desser, David, 59–60
de Young Museum (San Francisco), 27
dialogism, 105
Diawara, Manthia, 63–64
disco music, 1–2, 9, 59, 134
Divine, 33
DJ Khaled, 95
DJ Kool Herc, 10–11
DJ Kuttin' Kandi, 88, 177n8
DJ Noa D, 18
DJ Star Perkins, 143–44
DJ Stephanie, 147
Dolemite (1975), 65
Dondi, 28, 50, 170n46, 172n62
Donovan, Kevin. *See* Afrika Bambaataa
doppelgänger (Freud concept), 93–97, 99–100
double consciousness (Du Bois concept), 91, 93, 96–97, 99–100, 120
Double Trouble, 170n46
Doug E., 143
drag, 33, 63, 129, 152
Dr. Dre, 168n14
Du Bois, W. E. B., 91–93, 96–100, 120–21, 180n43. *See also* double consciousness
Dutchboy, 126–27, 141, 143–44, 146–47

East Village, NY, 33, 37, 50, 58
Elam, Michele, 59
Electronic Standards, 133
Elektra Records, 132
Elia, John P., 131
Ellis, Christopher. *See* Daze
emcees, 89, 103, 108–109, 111–12, 141, 143, 170n46
Eminem, 95, 143–44
Emmerich, Roland, 125
Eng, David, 74
Etaghene, Yvonne Onakeme, 144

Ethical Slut, The (2009), 20
Eurocentrism, 4, 72, 107
Eve, 111, 181n56
Exit Art (gallery), 27

Fabrara, Sandra. *See* Lady Pink
Fame (film and series), 133; Leroy Johnson in, 66–67, 78–79
fanfiction, 80, 176n61
femininity: Black, 17, 91, 98, 104, 114–15, 121; and Jean Grae, 100, 104–5, 108–9, 114–15, 121; and martial arts films, 57, 73–75; and queer hip hop, 129, 157
feminism, 17, 18, 99; hip hop, 88, 92, 113, 146. *See also* Black feminism
Ferguson, Rod, 130
Fiol-Matta, Licia, 172n1
Fists of Fury (1971), 60
Five Deadly Venoms (1978), 60
Forman, Murray, 119–20, 130–31
Fort Apache, The Bronx (1981), 27
Foxy Brown (film, 1974), 60
Foxy Brown (rapper), 18–19, 111, 181n56
Freeze Force Crew, 137
Freud, Sigmund, 91–100, 114–15, 117, 120–21, 183n81. *See also* doppelgänger; uncanny
Fuller, Hoyt W., 6
Fun House (club), 137, 187n40
Furious Five, 134, 136
Futura, 37

Game of Death (1978), 68
GAPIMNY, 45, 171n54
gay hip hop (GHH), 185n7
Gayle Jr., Addison, 5–6
Gay Men's Health Crisis (GMHC), 45
Gaynor, Gloria, 133
Gen X, 157
Gen Z, 64, 152–53, 157
George, Nelson, 10–11
Gilroy, Paul, 21, 96

GLAAD, 143
G-Minus, 141, 143
G-Minus (D/DC member), 141, 143
Goff, 143
Golden Harvest, 57
Gómez-Barris, Macarena, 172n1
Goodstone, Aaron. *See* Sharp
Gopinath, Gayatri, 123
Gordy, Berry, 62
Gordy, Kerry Ashby, 76
Grae, Jean: and abortion, 114–21; *Attack of the Attacking Things* (2002), 89, 106; and Black masculinity, 23, 100–104, 108–13; and Black womanhood, 87–93; "Block Party," 119; "Chapter One," 119; "Excuse Me," 184n92; "God's Gift," 17–18, 23, 89, 96, 100–101, 106, 109–110; and heteronormativity, 104–8, 177n10; and Jean Grey, 23, 93–96, 180–81n47; "My Story," 23, 114–19, 184n88; *Spittin' 'Til They Shame You* (2008), 23, 114–20; on "The Illest," 102–3, 105; *This Week* (2004), 119; "Threats," 119
graffiti, 11, 22, 25–31, 37–51, 87, 168n8, 170n46, 172n62, 181n51. *See also* Museum of American Graffiti; *individual artists*
Grandmaster Flash, 10–11, 135, 170n46; and the Furious Five, 134, 136
Grand Mater Caz, 170n46
Grand Wizard Theodore, 170n46
Grego, Dazié R., 143
Grey, Jean (superhero), 23, 89, 91, 93, 114, 179nn22, 23, 180n47
Guarriello, Taimak. *See* Taimak
Guerrero, Ed, 62

Haden-Guest, Anthony, 30
Halberstam, J. Jack, 73
Halcyon Records, 144
Hardy, James Earl, 140, 143
Haring, Keith, 37

Harlem, NY, 56–57, 67, 87
Harmon, Jalaiah S., 154
Harry, Debbie, 37
Harvilla, Tob, 184n88
Havoc, 135
Haze, Angel, 124, 150
HBO, 144, 166n16
Helixx, 177n8
Herbaliser, The, 101
heretics, definition of, 13–14
heteronormativity: Black, 18, 23, 65, 69–70, 79, 104–5; hegemonic, 61, 127; in hip hop, 13, 104–8, 127, 157, 182n62; and Jean Grae, 101, 113, 118; in *The Last Dragon* (1985), 53, 56
heterosexism, 11, 18, 112, 128–29, 131, 181n53
Hill, Lauryn, 88, 111, 181n56
Hill, Montero Lamar. *See* Lil Nas X
Hinton, Alex, 126
hip hop: aesthetics (framework), 4–10, 24; as Black American music, 14–15, 130–31, 186n24; commercialization of, 6–7, 124, 136; film, 22–23, 53–55, 61, 84–85, 170n46, 181n51; historiography of, 5, 12, 14, 25, 30, 32, 38, 41, 124, 129, 181n56; origins of, 8–11, 166n16, 169n27; studies of, 20–22. *See also* queer hip hop
HipHopDX, 108
Hip-Hop Evolution (2017–), 166n16
HIV/AIDS, 45–46
Hoffmann, E. T. A., 94, 99
Hogg, Ross, 141
homohop, 149, 185n7
Homo Hop Massive (festival), 141
homolatency (Bailey concept), 128
homophobia, 12, 14, 124, 131, 134, 139, 143–44, 150, 182n62, 188n58. *See also* heteronormativity; heterosexism
Hong Kong, 17, 55, 57, 60, 68, 174n12
house music, 1–3, 150

Hudson, Anne, 13
Human Rights Campaign (HRC), 141
hypermasculinity, 31, 84, 139

Ibrahim, Abdullah, 91
Ibrahim, Tsidsi. *See* Grae, Jean
Ikeda, Thomas, 56
Immortal Technique: "The Illest" (2001), 102–3, 105, 181n49
informed speculation, 45
Instagram, 88, 154, 158, 189n6
interracialism, 24, 29, 38, 188n58. *See also* multiracialism
Invincible, 88, 144, 177n8–9
Isoke, Zenzele, 123

Jackson, Janet, 155
Jackson, Michael, 77, 133
Jackson, Ronald L., II, 73
Jagose, Annamarie, 127
Jamal, Maurie, 144
Jamal X, 139
Jay-Z, 12, 102, 119, 128, 181n48; "Ain't No Nigga," 18–20; "Excuse Me" (2002), 184n92
Jaz-O (Big Jaz), 18
Jen-Ro, 144
Jinjo Crew, 154
Johnson, Marsha P., 125
Jones, Douglas A., Jr., 146–47
Jun, Helen Heran, 26, 58
Jungle Brothers, 2
Junglepussy, 88
Junior Wells and His All-Star Band, 63

Kalamka, Juba, 141, 143
Kansas City, MO, 132
Karate Kid, The (1984), 60
Kato, M. T., 54
Katz, Zebra, 124, 150
Keef Cowboy, 136
Keeling, Kara, 14

Kehlani, 124
Kelly, R., 12
Kid Cudi, 151
Kies, 40
King, Jason, 143
kitsch, 53, 63–65, 76, 80, 82
Klock, Geoff, 91
Koch, Ed, 27
Kraftwerk, 133
Kweli, Talib, 88, 101–2, 116

LA2, 37
Lacan, Jacques, 91, 114–15, 183n81
Lady Pink, 22, 26, 28, 30, 37, 42, 170n46. See
Lalgee, Salas B., 143
Last Dragon, The. See *Berry Gordy's The Last Dragon*
Latinx peoples: and blackness, 31–33; in hip hop, 3, 15, 17, 30–31, 167n28; and martial arts films, 53, 83; and masculinity, 16, 63; and queerness, 32, 63, 125, 140, 146; use of term, 172–73n1. See also AfriLatinx peoples; Afrolatinidad people
Lazar, 37
Le1f/Mx Khalif, 124, 150
Lee, Ang: *Crouching Tiger, Hidden Dragon* (2000), 74
Lee, Bruce, 31, 67–73, 75–76, 80, 84; *Enter the Dragon* (1973), 54–55, 57, 70
Lee, Lisa, 28
Lee, Spike: *Do the Right Thing* (1989), 63
lesbians, 102–3, 125, 140–42, 146–47
Les Twins, 154
Lewis, Ryan, 188n58
Lil' Kim, 88, 111, 136, 181n56; "Quiet Storm (remix)," 134–35
Lil Nas X, 124, 132; "Montero (Call Me by Your Name)" (2021), 151–53, 189n6; "Old Town Road" (2019), 151–52
Lil Wayne, 102, 128

Lipsitz, George, 82
Los Angeles, CA, 1, 3, 8, 36, 124, 131, 158
Louis, Karter, 143
Lower East Side, 58, 61, 141, 144; Martin Wong and, 31, 33–34, 44–50; Nuyorican enclave, 22, 26, 33
Lu, Jie, 68, 74
Luna, Teatro: *Machos,* 62–63

Ma, Remy, 88
Macchio, Ralph, 60
Macharia, Keguro, 151
Macklemore: "Same Love," 150, 188n58
Madonna, 77, 133–34
Malcolm X, 63
Man 2 Man, 134
Manhattan, NY. See East Village, NY; Harlem, NY; Lower East Side; Soho, NY
Mantronix, 133
Mao, Frederic, 76
Maoism, 44, 68
Marchand, Inga. See Foxy Brown
Marshall, Paul, 95
martial arts films: Black and Latinx audiences of, 53, 59–60, 82–83, 87; Black martial artists in, 22, 53–54, 173n3; Chinese, 17, 23, 53, 58–60, 62, 67–72, 168n14, 173n3; femininity in, 57, 73–75; masculinity in, 23, 53, 56, 62, 67–72, 75, 83–84, 124. See also *Berry Gordy's The Last Dragon*
Marvel Comics, 23, 40, 91, 93, 114
masculinity. See Asian masculinity; Black masculinity; hypermasculinity; player persona
Masta Ace, 101, 111
McCargo, Rennette, 54
MC Lyte, 88, 111, 181n56; "10% Dis," 135
Medina, Ashby, 76
Medina, Benny, 76
Megan Thee Stallion, 88, 111, 181n56; "W.A.P. (Wet Ass Pussy)," 165n10

Melle Mel: "White Lines," 135
Meow Mix (club), 141
Mercer, Kobena, 7
Metropolitan Museum of Art, 27, 46, 49
Metropolitan Transportation Authority, 39–40, 43
Mico, 37
millennials, 157
mimetic correspondence (Phelan concept), 105
Minaj, Nicki, 88, 181n56
Miranda, Tricia, 154–56
miscarriage, 115–16
misogynoir, 100, 109–10, 182–183n69
misogyny, 18–19, 64, 89–90, 92, 101, 104, 109–12, 128, 165n10. *See also* misogynoir
Missy Elliott, 88, 181n56
Mobb Deep: *Murda Muzic* (1999), 135; "Quiet Storm," 134–36; "The Illest," 181n49
Monihan Monihan, 116, 120
Monteyne, Kimberly, 54–55
Montez, Travis, 144
Motown, 56, 62, 77
Mr. Len, 101, 110
Mr. Lif, 101
MTV, 144
Mudede, Charles, 134–37
multiracialism, 5, 15, 26, 36, 58–59, 61, 70. *See also* interracialism
Muñoz, José Esteban, 172n1
Murney, Christopher, 56
Murray, Derek Conrad, 64–65
Murs: "Animal Style," 150, 188–89n58
Muscat, Jason "Judge." *See* Dutchboy
Museum of American Graffiti, 22, 25, 37–43
Museum of Graffiti, Miami, 169n32
Museum of the City of New York, 25, 28, 37, 41; *City as Canvas* exhibit, 42–43, 50–51

music. *See individual genres*
music videos: "Montero (Call Me By Your Name)," 152; "My Story," 115–19; "W.A.P. (Wet Ass Pussy)," 165n10
MySpace, 88

Neal, Mark Anthony, 66–67, 78, 131
Netflix, 166n16
neurosis, 114–15, 183n80
New Wave music, 9
New York City, NY: art scene in, 9, 17, 21–22, 26–27, 30, 37, 44–45, 87, 133; economic struggles in 1970s, 27; graffiti art in, 25, 28, 38, 42, 45, 170n46; hip hop education in, 154–57; and origins of hip hop, 8–9, 11–12; queer communities in, 33, 125–26, 146–47. *See also individual boroughs and neighborhoods*
New York Daily News, 166n18
New York Times, 133
New York University, 88, 147; *Downtown Crossing* exhibit (2009), 50; Martin Wong archives at, 25, 28, 50–51
Nguyen, Mimi Thi, 26, 67–68
9th Wonder, 102, 116–17, 181n48
Nishime, Leilani, 58–59
Noah's Arc (series), 131
Noel, Baraka, 143
NoName, 88
Notorious B.I.G. *See* Smalls, Biggie
Nuyorican people, 22, 26, 31–33
Nuyorican Poet Café, 30
Nyong'o, Tavia, 2, 9–10, 64

Oakland, CA, 126, 139, 142
Ocean, Frank, 124, 132, 150
Octagon (club), 140
Odd Future Wolf Gang Kill Them All, 128
Omi, Michael, 38
One Nut, 139–40
Ongiri, Amy Abugo, 82–84

Orientalism, 54, 56, 58, 61–62, 68, 70, 76, 78
Outkast, 182n62
Owens, Dana. *See* Queen Latifah

Pabón-Colón, Jessica Nydia, 39, 168n8
Pan-Africanism, 59, 60, 63
Parrish, Man, 23; "Boogie Down Bronx" (1984), 132, 134, 137–38; "Hip Hop, Be Bop (Don't Stop)" (1982), 132–35, 137, 187n41; "Male Stripper," 134
Patreon, 88
payola, 137, 187n41
Peace Out East, 23, 126, 147–49; spin-off festivals, 185n10
PeaceOUT World Homohop Festival, 126, 142
People of Color in Crisis, 141
Pérez, Roy, 31–32
Perry, Imani, 14–15, 131, 142, 186n24
Phase II, 40
Phelan, Peggy, 105, 109
Philadelphia, PA, 1, 3, 8, 124, 158
Phoenix. *See* Grey, Jean
Pick Up the Mic (2005), 126, 144, 147
Piñero, Miguel, 30–31, 46–49, 171n57, 172n63
Pino, 31
Pito (aka Little Ivan), 46–49
player persona, 17–19, 106
pornography, 103, 106
post-blackness, 64–65
Post Malone, 95
PPOW Gallery, 25, 27–28, 37, 51
Pri the Honey Dark, 177n8
Prodigy, 135
psychoanalysis, 87, 90–92, 98, 115, 123, 178–79n20. *See also* Freud, Sigmund; Lacan, Jacques
Puerto Rican people. *See* Nuyorican people
Pumpkinhead, 102

Queen Latifah, 88, 181n56; "Come into My House" (1989), 2–3; "My Mic Sound Nice" (1986), 111; "U.N.I.T.Y.," 17
Queen Pen, 140
Queens, NY, 4, 135
queer aesthetics (framework), 4–10, 24
queer dissonance, 24, 128–30
queer hip hop: Black masculinity in, 129, 138–39, 142, 182n62; early history of, 123–127, 132; femininity and, 129, 157; future of, 149–50, 157–58; golden age of, 124, 126, 139–43; scholarship, 128, 189n59; term, 127, 185n7
queer people and communities: Black, 140–43; in hip hop, 23–25, 123–24, 151–52; Latinx, 32, 63, 125, 140, 146; in New York City, 33, 125–26, 146–47; racism and classism in, 125–27, 138–39, 144, 146. *See also* lesbians; transgender people
Quiñones, Lee, 28, 30, 44, 170n46; *Howard the Duck* (1988), 40–41

racial affect, 76, 78–79, 82, 84
racism: in film, 53; and heterosexism, 74; and homophobia, 125, 134, 144; and kitsch, 64; systemic, 79. *See also* misogynoir
Rah Digga, 181n56
Rammellzee, 30, 168n12
rap music. *See individual performers*
Rapsody, 88, 101
Raw Dog: "Suki Yaki Hot Saki sue," 76–77
Ray, Gene Anthony, 66–67
Raymond, Daryl, 141
Razor Gallery, 168n12
R&B music, 2, 19, 63, 76, 101, 124
Real Roxanne, 181n56
Revolt, 28
Rivera, Raquel Z., 32
Rivera, Sylvia, 125
Roberts, Tamara, 62, 63

Rock Steady Crew, 28
Rodriguez, Raul, 137–38
Roland TR-808 drum machine, 133–34
Roots, The, 101–2
Rose, Tricia, 20–21, 27, 47, 105, 110–11, 167n28

Saddler, Joseph. *See* Grandmaster Flash
Saint Vincent's Hospital AIDS Ward, 45
Salt-N-Pepa, 88, 181n56; "Ladies First" (1990), 111; "Tramp" (1986), 17, 111
San Francisco, CA, 3, 27, 39, 124, 126, 140, 147
Savage, Ronald, 11, 166n18
Saweetie, 88
Schneider, Rebecca, 106, 110
Schultz, Michael: *Berry Gordy's The Last Dragon* (1985), 22, 53–54, 56, 60, 62, 75; *Cooley High*, 56
Seen, 37
Semaphore (gallery), 27
Set It Off (1996), 73
Sexton, Jared, 36
sexual violence, 11–12
sex workers, 88, 138
Shaft (1971), 65–66
Shanté, Roxanne, 111, 181n56
Sharp, 28, 37, 42, 50, 169n27
Shaw Brothers, 72, 168n14
Shaw Studios, 57
Smalls, Biggie, 110, 119, 184n92
Smalls, Shanté Paradigm: *B.Q.E.* (2003), 143; *Digm and the Dutch, The* (2006), 143; music career, 141, 143–148
Smith, Jaden, 151
Smith, Kiki, 30
Smith College, 18
Soho, NY, 37, 41, 50, 169n28
Soul Nubian, 143
Source magazine, 140
Spider, 40
Spillers, Hortense, 92, 95, 121, 178–179n20

Spotify, 151
Starski, Busy Bee, 28
Staten Island, NY, 168n14
Stein, Chris, 170–71n46
Stonewall (2015), 125
Stranger magazine, 134
Studio 54, 133
Style Wars (1983), 44
subways (in NYC), 1–2, 6, 28, 39–40, 42–43, 165n1
Sugarhill Gang, 132; "Rapper's Delight" (1979), 6, 124, 137
Superfly (1972), 60
superheroes, 68, 91, 124. *See also* Grey, Jean; Superman; X-Men
Superman (superhero), 124
Syd the Kid, 124, 132

Taimak, 55–56, 60–62
Tate, Claudia, 90
Taylor, Diana, 29
Taylor, Leslie "Buttaflysoul," 143
Teo, Stephen, 68
Thomas, Greg, 135–36
Thomas, Mickalene, 65–66
Tidal, 151
TikTok, 154, 158, 189n6
Time magazine, 152–53
Toronto International Film Festival, 126
Torres, Rigberto, 43–44
Tracy 168, 28
transgender people, 4–5, 125–26
trap music, 2, 151
Tricia Miranda Dance School, 154
Trudy, 182–83n69
Tu, Nguyen, 26
Tyler, the Creator, 132

uncanny (Freud concept), 23, 89, 91–95, 98–101, 114–15, 117, 120, 178n18, 183n80
Uncanny X-Men, The (1963–), 89, 91, 93–94, 114, 179n23, 180n47, 183n76

United Graffiti Artists, 168n12
Universal Zulu Nation, 11–12, 136

Van, Marcus René (Mr. ManMan), 143
Vanity, 55–56, 62
Van Peebles, Mario, 55
Venosta, Louis, 54–56, 62
Vogel, Shane, 146–47
vogue. *See* ball culture

Walidah, Hanifah, 126
Walkowitz, David, 27
Warehouse (club), 140
Warhol, Andy, 30, 133
Warner Brothers, 60, 118–19
Warriors, The (1979), 27
West, Cornel, 180n43
West, John, 76
West, Kanye, 128
West, Tim'm T., 141–44
What? What?. *See* Grae, Jean
White, Donald. *See* Dondi
Wicked Greg, 37
Wild Style (1983). *See* Ahearn, Charlie
Wild Style Crew, 28
Wilkins, Fanon Che, 72
Williams, Wendy, 139–40
Winant, Howard, 38
Witten, Andrew. *See* Zephyr
Wojnarowicz, David, 30
Wong, Martin: in *Artist Portrait Videos*, 43–44, 46; *Attorney Street* (1982–1984), 26, 31, 46–49, 172n63; and collaboration, 43–49, 170–71n46; and *Crime Show* exhibit, 171n57; *Divine* (1979), 33; and graffiti art, 25, 37–43, 44–46, 50–51, 51, 87; and hip hop, 25–26; *Mi Vida Loca* (1991), 33, 50; and New York City, 16, 25, 33, 49–51, 169n28; *Penitentiary Fox* (1988), 33; queer archive of, 27–33; queer painting of, 33–37; *Sharp and Dottie* (1984), 33; *Sweet 'Enuff* (1988), 26, 33–36, 169n20; and *Wild Style* (1983), 28–29. *See also* Museum of American Graffiti
Word/Life: Emcees and Poets in the Life (showcase), 144–45, 147. *See also* Peace Out East
Wright, Richard, 176n68
Wu Tang Clan, 31, 168n14

X-Men (superheroes), 89, 91, 93–94, 114, 179n23, 183n76. *See also* Grey, Jean; Uncanny X-Men

Yep, Gust A., 131
Young M.A, 124, 132, 151
Young Thug, 151
YouTube, 137, 150–51, 155, 187n41
Yo-Yo, 111
Yuk, Henry, 76

Zendaya, 155
Zephyr, 28, 37, 170n46
Zhang, Siyi, 74

ABOUT THE AUTHOR

SHANTÉ PARADIGM SMALLS (they/them) is Associate Professor of Black Studies and Faculty in the Critical Race and Ethnic Studies Institute at St. John's University. Smalls has held fellowships with the James Weldon Johnson Institute at Emory University, the Institute for Citizens & Scholars, and the Andrew W. Mellon Foundation. Smalls won the 2016 CLAGS Award for best LGBTQ manuscript.

www.ingramcontent.com/pod-product-compliance
Lightning Source LLC
Chambersburg PA
CBHW020408080526
44584CB00014B/1234